PRAISE FOR
Lives of American Women

"Finally! The majority of students—by which I mean women—will have the opportunity to read biographies of women from our nation's past. (Men can read them too, of course!) The Lives of American Women series features an eclectic collection of books, readily accessible to students who will be able to see the contributions of women in many fields over the course of our history. Long overdue, these books will be a valuable resource for teachers, students, and the public at large."

—**Cokie Roberts**, author of *Founding Mothers* and *Ladies of Liberty*

"Just what any professor wants: books that will intrigue, inform, and fascinate students! These short, readable biographies of American women—specifically designed for classroom use—give instructors an appealing new option to assign to their history students."

—**Mary Beth Norton, Mary Donlon Alger**
Professor of American History, Cornell University

"For educators keen to include women in the American story, but hampered by the lack of thoughtful, concise scholarship, here comes Lives of American Women, embracing Abigail Adams's counsel to John—'remember the ladies.' And high time, too!"

—**Lesley S. Herrmann, Executive Director,**
The Gilder Lehrman Institute of American History

"Students both in the general survey course and in specialized offerings like my course on U.S. women's history can get a great understanding of an era from a short biography. Learning a lot about a single but complex character really helps to deepen appreciation of what women's lives were like in the past."

—**Patricia Cline Cohen, University of California, Santa Barbara**

"Biographies are, indeed, back. Not only will students read them, biographies provide an easy way to demonstrate particularly important historical themes or ideas. . . . Undergraduate readers will be challenged to think more deeply about what it means to be a woman, citizen, and political actor. . . . I am eager to use this in my undergraduate survey and specialty course."

—Jennifer Thigpen, Washington State University, Pullman

"These books are, above all, fascinating stories that will engage and inspire readers. They offer a glimpse into the lives of key women in history who either defied tradition or who successfully maneuvered in a man's world to make an impact. The stories of these vital contributors to American history deliver just the right formula for instructors looking to provide a more complicated and nuanced view of history."

—Rosanne Lichatin, 2005 Gilder Lehrman Preserve
American History Teacher of the Year

"The Lives of American Women authors raise all of the big issues I want my classes to confront—and deftly fold their arguments into riveting narratives that maintain students' excitement."

—Woody Holton, author of *Abigail Adams*

Lives of American Women

Carol Berkin, Series Editor

Westview Press is pleased to launch Lives of American Women. Selected and edited by renowned women's historian Carol Berkin, these brief, affordably priced biographies are designed for use in undergraduate courses. Rather than a comprehensive approach, each biography focuses instead on a particular aspect of a woman's life that is emblematic of her time, or which made her a pivotal figure in the era. The emphasis is on a "good read," featuring accessible writing and compelling narratives, without sacrificing sound scholarship and academic integrity. Primary sources at the end of each biography reveal the subject's perspective in her own words. Study Questions and an Annotated Bibliography support the student reader.

Dolley Madison: The Problem of National Unity by Catherine Allgor

Lillian Gilbreth: Redefining Domesticity by Julie Des Jardins

Alice Paul: Perfecting Equality for Women by Christine Lunardini

Rebecca Dickinson: Independence for a New England Woman by Marla Miller

Sarah Livingston Jay: Model Republican Woman by Mary-Jo Kline

Betsy Mix Cowles: Bold Reformer by Stacey Robertson

Sally Hemings: Given Her Time by Jon Kukla

Shirley Chisholm: Catalyst for Change by Barbara Winslow

Margaret Sanger: Freedom, Controversy and the Birth Control Movement by Esther Katz

Barbara Egger Lennon: Teacher, Mother, Activist by Tina Brakebill

Anne Hutchinson: A Dissident Woman's Boston by Vivian Bruce Conger

Angela Davis: Radical Icon by Robyn Spencer

Catharine Beecher: The Complexity of Gender in 19th Century America by Cindy Lobel

Julia Lathrop: Social Service and Progressive Government by Miriam Cohen

Mary Pickford: Women, Film and Selling Girlhood by Kathy Feeley

Elizabeth Gurley Flynn: The Making of the Modern Woman by Lara Vapnek

Rebecca Dickinson

Independence for a
New England Woman

MARLA R. MILLER

University of Massachusetts Amherst

LIVES OF AMERICAN WOMEN
Carol Berkin, Series Editor

WESTVIEW
PRESS
A Member of the Perseus Books Group

Westview Press was founded in 1975 in Boulder, Colorado, by notable publisher and intellectual Fred Praeger. Westview Press continues to publish scholarly titles and high-quality undergraduate- and graduate-level textbooks in core social science disciplines. With books developed, written, and edited with the needs of serious nonfiction readers, professors, and students in mind, Westview Press honors its long history of publishing books that matter.

Published by Westview Press,
A Member of the Perseus Books Group

Find us on the World Wide Web at www.westviewpress.com.

Every effort has been made to secure required permissions for all text, images, maps, and other art reprinted in this volume.

Westview Press books are available at special discounts for bulk purchases in the United States by corporations, institutions, and other organizations. For more information, please contact the Special Markets Department at the Perseus Books Group, 2300 Chestnut Street, Suite 200, Philadelphia, PA 19103, or call (800) 810-4145, ext. 5000, or e-mail special.markets@perseusbooks.com.

Series design by Brent Wilcox

Library of Congress Cataloging-in-Publication Data

Miller, Marla R.
    Rebecca Dickinson : independence for a New England woman / Marla R. Miller, University of Massachusetts, Amherst.
        pages cm.
        —(Lives of American women) Includes bibliographical references and index.
    ISBN 978-0-8133-4765-3 (pbk.)—ISBN 978-0-8133-4766-0 (e-book)
    1. Dickinson, Rebecca, 1738–1815. 2. Women—Massachusetts—Hatfield—Social conditions—18th century. 3. Single women—Massachusetts— Hatfield—Social conditions—18th century. 4. Hatfield (Mass.)—Social conditions—18th century. 5. Hatfield (Mass.)—Biography. 6. United States—History—Revolution, 1775–1783—Social aspects. I. Title.
    HQ1439.H37M55 2013
    974.4'02092—dc23
                                                                            [B]
                                                                    2013005322

10   9   8   7   6   5   4   3   2   1

CONTENTS

Contents

SERIES EDITOR'S FOREWORD

Rebecca Dickinson, an eighteenth-century New England artisan, does not appear in the grand accounts of the movement for American independence. She did not rise in the Massachusetts assembly to demand the repeal of the Stamp Act; she did not command a regiment of soldiers at Valley Forge or Yorktown. Yet in her own life, she too waged a long struggle for independence and did battle with both the internalized and external pressures to marry and raise a family. Dickinson's experiences reveal much about the turbulent era in which our nation was born; her life serves as a window onto the role played by ordinary women and men in the political protests that led to a revolution, the importance of craft labor in a preindustrial world, the endurance of the spiritual in the age of Enlightenment and, perhaps most important, the complex legacy of a rhetoric of independence in the lives of Americans.

Dickinson was born in 1738 in the rural society of Massachusetts, where the arc of a woman's life carried her from youth to marriage and motherhood. But her path diverged from the expected; although she struggled with the centrifugal force of social expectations, she chose to remain single—and thus independent. Her needlework skills allowed her to support herself and to play a useful role in her community. This economic independence and the positive relationships she sustained with her clients shielded her against the negative associations her culture attached to the term "old maid."

Dickinson recognized both the perils and the rewards of her independence. Over the course of her long life she engaged in an internal dialogue with herself, captured in her diary, as she sought to understand how she came to choose an unmarried life and the mixture of satisfactions and regrets it entailed. If the men who signed the Declaration of Independence realized that their decision carried with it both opportunities and dangers, so too did Rebecca Dickinson recognize that a life of female independence was fraught with both risk and the promise of personal rewards. In her diary she confronted the reality of her decision bluntly: "Two is better than one," she wrote, "for if one fall the other can lift him up. But I must act my part alone."

Marla Miller's beautiful rendering of Dickinson's life paints a portrait of the early struggles of women to make a place for themselves outside the established boundaries of marriage and family. The Dickinson that Miller portrays for us was not, by nature, a rebel; she did not carry on an open war against the norms of her society. Rather, in her piety, her loyalty to friends and extended family, and her pride in meaningful work, she adhered to the traditional values of her New England roots. In her own quiet way, however, Rebecca Dickinson was forging a new path for women, one that the next generation would follow all the way to Seneca Falls.

In examining and narrating the lives of women both famous and obscure, Westview's Lives of American Women series populates our national past more fully and richly. Each story told is not simply the story of an individual, but of the era in which she lived, the events in which she participated, and the experiences she shared with her contemporaries. Some of these women will be familiar to the reader; others may not appear at all in the history books that focus on the powerful, the brilliant, or the privileged. But each of these women is worth knowing. In their personal odysseys, American history comes alive.

Carol Berkin

AUTHOR'S PREFACE

Reading an Eighteenth-Century Diary

Rebecca Dickinson's is a powerful voice. Recollections of her personality that survive in local memory tell us that in her day—that is, the last half of the eighteenth century and early years of the nineteenth—Dickinson was a lively, opinionated, and smart woman, as well as a shrewd social observer. It is easy to imagine her as the sort of person whose remarks about others made people gasp and laugh at the same time. Sometimes her tongue ran away with her so that even she was taken aback by the things she had said to her neighbors between church services. She could also be kind, and even sentimental. But that is not the picture of her that survives in the crowded lines of her diary. Instead, the five hundred entries preserved in her journal are drenched in sadness, even self-pity. Page after page records hours of doubt, fear, melancholy, and despair. That gap—between the actual woman who lived and the record she left behind—is significant. Unlike the vast majority of women in early New England, Rebecca Dickinson (also sometimes spelled "Rebekah" and "Rebeca") never married, and that one fact became the central subject of her weekly musings. Small hints scattered throughout that text suggest that Dickinson truly cherished her life alone, unencumbered as it was by many of the challenges of family life. That she found it so much more difficult to give voice to her joy than her pain is part of the lesson her diary holds for us.[1]

In 1892, when a local historian named Margaret Miller submitted excerpts from Dickinson's manuscript to the *New England Magazine*, editors rejected the text as "too dolefully dolesome, too awfully theological and metaphysical" for their pages.[2] But it is precisely the dolefully dole-some, the ceaselessly searching, sorrowful quality of this text, that makes it so compelling. At first meeting Rebecca Dickinson is a sour com-panion. A "bullock unaccustomed to the yoke" of singlehood, she used her diary as a place to record feelings of shame, vulnerability, and frus-tration, even thoughts of suicide. She would refer, now and then, to a "bitter stroke" that "mowed down" her "earthly hopes," hinting that it was some romantic catastrophe that had caused her single state. But more often she worried that it was the result of her weak faith, God working to save her soul by depriving her of earthly distractions like a husband or children. Whatever the causes of her singlehood (and as we will see, they were multiple and complex), Dickinson feared she had been "cast out from the people" for her "odd ways." But if Dickinson's singlehood dismayed some of her neighbors (as it may or may not have—though she believed so, no letters or diaries survive to confirm it), others recalled her with affection long past her death. "To old people who remember her," Margaret Miller wrote, "or knew her by hearsay she was a 'Saint on Earth,' a 'marvel of piety.'" Others described her as the "most industrious woman that ever lived." Samuel Partridge, a life-long resident of Hatfield, knew Dickinson from his boyhood as a "very intelligent woman" whose "sayings were frequently repeated, she being regarded as a sort of oracle." One resident referred to her as "Aunt Bek, it being the habit in those days to call single women who were loved by that community title, and Aunt Bek was well-liked by all."[3]

The disconnect between Dickinson's sorrow-filled account of her own life and that offered by others, between her private and public iden-tities, is at least in part an artifact of the source itself. A diary can seem like the best, truest document a historian could wish for—the closest thing to the mind of our subject. But diaries can be misleading: few of us would want to be remembered only for the things we wrote down in our most private moments, whether they were hours of worry, despair, or joy. Even hundreds of pages of a person's most intimate confessions to herself cannot tell us the whole story of her life or her character; on the contrary, they can trick us into mistaking a fraction for the whole. The challenge of this remarkable source is to read past the gloom that overtakes some of her pages, to see the larger life behind them.

Rebecca Dickinson first began keeping her own diary during the event-filled years of the American Revolution. Decades later she would write that she began writing for her "own amusement" after she reached age thirty (that is, about 1768), in the "happy days" of her "young years" when her "mind was stored with poetry" (August 2, 1789). Was it the growing political tension that prompted those early writings, or some romantic drama? Whatever the cause, they undoubtedly contained a rich portrait of life in a prosperous eighteenth-century farming village. Given Dickinson's connections with prominent families both in support of and opposed to the revolution, her diary surely offered insight into the struggle for political independence as it played out on New England's western frontier. Among other things, in those pages she recorded an account of Reverend Joseph Lyman's "first coming," including the Patriot minister's initial sermons, entries that would surely illuminate the town's drift toward rebellion.

But we can never know what those entries captured, because in her forties Rebecca Dickinson began destroying them. Casting off the temporal for the eternal, she resolved to bring new purpose to her journals: "They were but poorly written and I would be glad to look them over if I were to live in the world [that is, if she cared about such petty, earthly things]. But they are gone and I wish that the others were more correct and less of this world with them—for what profit is there in the thoughts of many scenes that are passed and gone? It served to amuse the mind, but nothing like the affairs of eternity" (February 10, 1788). She would muse that in those lively years, her "mind . . . wrote too freely on some of the objects of time" (June [21?], 1789; August 2, 1789)—objects almost surely concerning Hatfield's response to the revolution and the actions of its Tories and Patriots, topics that would very much interest readers today. We can only speculate about our loss.

By the time she put pen to the paper that now survives, the purpose of the exercise had changed. Dickinson's diary had become a source of companionship, a place to confide her innermost thoughts and to focus on her faith. Spiritual journals like Dickinson's were quite common; religious tradition in New England had long urged the faithful to record their spiritual journeys. Diary keeping was a secular tradition as well, as women used this narrative form to keep track of any number of domestic concerns. Across the river from Dickinson, in the town of Hadley, Massachusetts, her client and friend Elizabeth Porter Phelps called her own private record her "memorandum book"; though it noted the biblical text from which the minister's weekly sermons were drawn, it was principally a log of work done on her farm, visits made and received, and the general routines of life in her large, prosperous family. But for Dickinson, as a devotional exercise the journal offered an opportunity to monitor the state of her soul, to record "God's special mercies." Because she wrote the majority of her entries before, between, and after services at Hatfield's Congregational church, it is not surprising to discover that her diary sometimes reads like a sermon. Consciously and unconsciously, she borrowed so liberally from religious texts of all kinds that it sometimes becomes nearly impossible to tell where quotation and paraphrase leave off and her own words begin. Long passages from Watts's *Psalms of David* weave throughout the text, still floating through her mind from the day's services or carefully copied from her own edition of the small, leather-bound book. Days when she could not balance the demands of work and home and her desire to write in her journal caused real disappointment: "This little family who are but three [herself, her mother, and her nephew] . . . has hindered me from writing. . . . [T]here is some work which takes up my mind from my beloved pen" (August 1, 1790). Indeed, the very existence of her journal Dickinson attributed to the absence of home and family that might have interfered with her ability to write. "My solitary life, my lonely life," she wrote, was a "great advantage to my pen which has written some thoughts which I could never recollect" (August 2, 1789).

Some spiritual journals were meant in part for the edification of others—children who would benefit from their parents' reflections, or community members who might emulate a neighbor's piety. But there is no evidence that Dickinson had this aim in mind. In fact, she kept her diary under lock and key (although she wasn't always alone when writing; sometimes she wrote in her journal while talking to others, though the distraction could produce "nonsense"; November 23, 1787). Dickinson's age in the year that she abandoned her secular diary and committed to this spiritual account—having probably passed beyond menopause—suggests that neither daughters nor sons were her imagined audience. Perhaps she already had a sense that her nephews and nieces would inherit whatever legacy she would someday have to bequeath, but the journal makes no reference to any expectations of that kind, or indeed of any other. So far as we know today, Dickinson penned her entries for herself and herself alone.

But that is not to say she couldn't envision herself as an author with something to contribute to readers. Once, after suffering through four weeks of illness, Dickinson tried to raise her "drooping spirits" by reminding herself (in a reference to Matthew 6:34a) to "take no thought for the morrow[:] let the morrow take thought for the things of itself. [S]ufficient for the day is the [evil] thereof." "I wish to see a book written on the subject," she mused, "but the time is too short for me to write my many thoughts" (April 8, 1790). Time, not ability or merit, was the obstacle that Dickinson believed prevented her from sharing her considerable expertise on living with uncertainty.

In her diary Dickinson could confide her darkest thoughts without fear of criticism. It became, in essence, a best friend willing to listen at any hour and to the same complaints no matter how often made. As students of journal keeping have explained, the cathartic function of personal writing skews our picture of any diarist, because only some aspects of the writer's character get preserved in the text. Journals almost by definition represent a certain division of self, a simultaneity of author and audience, as the diarist is both the writer and the reader. Dickinson herself seems to have recognized that paradox. She "awaked lonesome" one Sunday morning to the disquieting realization that perhaps loneliness itself was "all the relation that I had." Her solitude loomed so large that it seemed to exist independently and yet, strangely, was her closest companion. "The soul and the body are closely joined," she continued, "and are the nearest relatives of any two in this life" (July 13, 1787). In writing, then, Dickinson found an intimacy life had denied her. Her journal in many ways records a conversation, or correspondence, from body to soul, from soul to body.

But if journals can be read as a sort of interior communication, we as readers can nevertheless know only part of the exchange. Dickinson's journal, because she turned to it largely in hours of despair, offers us one perspective on her life. Patient reading, however, yields glimpses of

another. Though the majority of passages capture her most painful moments, as she herself observed, "those dark hours don't come every day"
(August 20, 1787). Brighter hours are captured, too. Murmurs of choice
and satisfaction thread through the melancholy of the text, hinting that
the diarist found attractions in her life alone—attractions she could
barely admit as she struggled to reconcile the competing depictions of
singlehood provided by her religion, her community, popular culture,
and her own observations and experience.

Dickinson's diary is preserved today partly because it was appreciated by Margaret Miller. But other local historians took notice, too,
not just of Rebecca Dickinson, but of her sisters as well, providing hints
not only about the eighteenth-century past, but about how events and
interests in the intervening centuries have shaped the ways we encounter
that world today. In the second quarter of the nineteenth century Hatfield resident Lucretia Partridge remembered Rebecca Dickinson as a
"woman of unusual force and originality of character."[4] Partridge had
also known Rebecca's sister Irene, the recollection of whom prompted
her to note that "all three" Dickinson girls—Rebecca, Miriam, and Irene
(Lucretia had forgotten the other sisters, Martha and Anne, perhaps because they had moved out of town)—"had marked traits of character."[5]
Miriam Billings, in particular, was a "picturesque figure." Partridge described her walking to church in winter, "wrapped in a long crimson
broadcloth cloak trimmed with ermine, carrying a footstove, and moving at a pace which most people would find it hard to keep step with;
energy and determination written all over her tall thin form." Billings
was remembered as a hardworking mother and wife who knew how to
card and spin (though she hired someone to do her household's weaving), and who went every year to the family's dairy farm to oversee the
making of the cheese. Yet she was also an avid reader; Partridge reported
that few women of that day had "so full and intelligent knowledge of
history as she possessed." Even late in life, when Miriam was confined
to her bed, she would be found "sitting and talking with great emphasis, knitting all the time with such energy that one could hear the click-
ing of her needles all over the room." Plainly Rebecca Dickinson was
one among a family of strong and memorable women, and, as we shall
see, her sisters' stories weave constantly through her own.

Indeed, looking in on Rebecca's sisters helps flesh out not only her story, but also that of women in eighteenth-century New England more generally, because they conformed to social norms in ways that Rebecca did not. Miriam in the family tavern; Martha at the northern edge of empire; Anne as she struggled with an absentee husband; and Irene, who died too young: these and the other Hatfield women help place Dickinson's experience in context. Other sources help fill in her tale as well. Oral history written down in the nineteenth century fills in part of the picture, as do artifacts made and preserved in the town. In addition to the passages from her diary, newspapers, church records, court records, and sermons convey the tone of the times, while suggesting the many ways different kinds of sources contribute to historical understanding.

"I am apt to be greatly puzzled to find myself here alone," Dickinson wrote, "but I know the matter is a secret to me" (June [?], 1789). Unraveling that secret consumed the better part of her journals through these tumultuous years. "My story," wrote Dickinson, "frightens half the women of the town" (June 21, 1789). As such, it reveals the public and private consequences of an act one woman in eighteenth-century New England failed to commit. As Dickinson was well aware, her life threw into bold relief the anxieties and apprehensions of her female neighbors. Her departure from the norms of her day, as a woman who never married and never raised a family, who relied only on her own skill for her livelihood, reveals the contours of life for women across revolutionary New England. As they watched and wondered at her single existence, they confronted the significance of marriage in their own lives. Her journal thus provides a window onto two worlds: that of women like Rebecca Dickinson and of other women frightened by them.

How, one might ask, does an everyday person from early America come to the attention of historians and their readers? Rebecca Dickinson would now be entirely forgotten, along with thousands of everyday men and women who lived through the revolution, if it were not for the fact that she kept a diary, and that diary survived. Rebecca Dickinson's journals—227 pages containing around five hundred entries written between 1787 and 1802—preserve the difficult "journey of life" of a woman struggling to "act her part alone" in an era of tremendous social, political, and cultural upheaval. Discovered nearly eighty years after her death, tucked in the garret of the western Massachusetts home in which she died, this extraordinary document affords a rare glimpse into the rhythms of daily life in early America, the common concerns shared by women across New England and beyond, from medical beliefs and practices ("The corpse of the wife of Joshua Dickinson was taken up in order for the cure of her granddaughter after she had lain in her grave three years"; August 3, 1788), to the composition of the New England family (four "being the number so many pitch upon as being a proper number"; March 17, 1788), to some of the rarer delights that graced early American life ("There are two foreigners here . . . from Italy with shows and music—an organ—which was so charming it drew tears from my eyes"; April [26], 1795).

My effort to understand the world of Rebecca Dickinson began more than twenty years ago, just after I completed my junior year in college. I was a student at the University of Wisconsin–Madison, a history major with a particular interest—encouraged by two extraordinary professors, Charles Lloyd Cohen and Sargent Bush Jr.—in early American history and culture. To pursue those interests, in the summer of 1987 I jumped in my Pontiac Sunbird and headed off to spend ten glorious weeks attending the Summer Fellowship Program at Historic Deerfield, a museum of early American history and art in western Massachusetts.

The program aims to introduce undergraduates to the world of museums and historic sites and helps them contemplate graduate school. A requirement was (and remains) the completion of a research paper, and I chose to write about the special roles and responsibilities of ministers' wives. Among the many sources I consulted that summer was the diary—or, rather, photocopies of the diary—of Rebecca Dickinson, which I examined in search of insight into the lives of Hatfield, Massachusetts, Reverend Joseph Lyman and his wife, Hannah Huntington Lyman. At the end of that summer, then Director of Academic Programs Kevin M. Sweeney (more recently professor of history at Amherst College, and another historian whose deep knowledge of and respect for the past inspired me then, and continues to inspire me now) asked me whether I thought the diary, which at that time was still in family hands, could support a larger study. I barely knew what was in it, but the opportunity to be the first person to really study any eighteenth-century diary was thrilling, and certainly irresistible. I jumped at the chance.

And so, upon my return home, eager to learn Dickinson's story, I began work on a senior thesis under Professor Cohen. I became deeply immersed in the diary, absorbing Dickinson's language and voice as I transcribed her words. I spent countless hours identifying the people and events mentioned and explored the diary's main themes in a long introduction that contemplated Dickinson's faith and her response to singlehood. The experience was challenging, but also exhilarating, like finding a portal to the past. Today I still advise undergraduates not to think of a topic and then go in search of documents, but rather to find a fascinating primary source and write about whatever it has to tell them.

After graduation I headed south to pursue graduate training at the University of North Carolina at Chapel Hill, thinking a change of scenery might lead me toward southern women's history, but I couldn't shake the pull of the New England landscape or the draw of Dickinson's compelling voice. I completed a thesis on Dickinson's singlehood en route to a master's degree in history. As I worked to understand her emotional and intellectual responses to her life alone, I also had to come to grips with more mundane matters, including how she earned her living. Those questions led me to study her work in the clothing trades and to pose a series of questions about gender and artisanry in early America, research that found fruition in a doctoral dissertation, several articles, and eventually a book, *The Needle's Eye: Women and Work in the Age of Revolution*.

Years later, when I returned to Dickinson's diary with the aim of developing this biography, I had just completed work on a book about another early American craftswoman—Betsy Ross, the legendary maker of the nation's first flag—a figure far more famous today than Rebecca Dickinson, but about whom in many ways we know far less. Ross, like Dickinson, was an artisan (an upholsterer) who had to navigate much of the drama of the revolution without the help of a husband (though in Ross's case it was as a young widow, then the wife of a privateer who was captured at sea, and again as a widow); that project helped put Dickinson's experience in a new light. This retelling of Dickinson's story continues to emphasize her experience as a never-married woman in early New England, but in the larger context of revolutionary America. The independence referred to in the book's title is meant to cue both Dickinson's experience as a woman who witnessed the dissolving of her colony's imperial bonds and emergence within an independent nation, and the ways in which Dickinson both created and experienced a place in the world as a woman independent of—and also bereft of, as she herself sometimes felt—the ties of a husband and children.

Revisiting Rebecca Dickinson now, twenty-five years after I first encountered her, reminds me of those first moments when I began to see how the voices of women long gone can continue to resonate today. To my present readers, I hope these pages teach you something about the American past. And I also hope you find subjects that engage your own curiosity, passions, and affections for as long and as keenly as these have engaged mine.

ACKNOWLEDGMENTS

This project has been something of a homecoming, a return to my first interests as a budding scholar, and I remain grateful to all of the mentors, colleagues, and friends who have supported this work over these many years.

It has been with great pleasure that I return once more to narrate Dickinson's story, drawing on the 1998 article and 2006 book, but also including both old material never before published and new research into the years preceding the September 1787 afternoon that she began the surviving portion of her journal—research that I had not yet had any opportunity to undertake, but had long wished to. I am grateful first to Carol Berkin for giving me this chance to return to Dickinson's fascinating world, and also to Priscilla McGeehon, Annie Lenth, and Sharon Langworthy for their thoughtful work shepherding the book through the editorial process.

And it is with much delight, too, that I thank here the same people acknowledged in those earlier works. For their thoughtful comments, careful criticism, and ongoing interest in Rebecca Dickinson over the several years during which I was immersed in her life and diary while a graduate student in North Carolina, I wish to thank Judith M. Bennett, Charles L. Cohen, R. Donald Higginbotham, Jacquelyn Dowd Hall, Anne Digan Lanning, Laura Jane Moore, John K. Nelson, Kevin M. Sweeney, Laurel Thatcher Ulrich, and Harry Watson. An essay on Dickinson's sense of herself as a woman alone drawn from those projects won the Walter Muir Whitehill prize in colonial history and was published in the *New England Quarterly* in 1998; some of the prose that follows here appeared first in that journal's hospitable pages. The editor of the *New England Quarterly*, Linda Smith Rhoads, helped tremendously with the preparation of that essay, and I thank her here once more for her early interest and enthusiasm as well as permission to draw on that prose for the book now at hand. (Those acknowledgments also note that research for the project was funded by two Elizabeth Fuller Fellowships from Historic Deerfield, Inc., an Esther Butt research grant from the University of Wisconsin at Madison, and several grants from the History Department and the Graduate School of the University of North Carolina at Chapel Hill, support that I am pleased to recognize once again here.) By the same token, I thank Clark Dougan of the University of Massachusetts Press for granting permission to use passages from my *The Needle's Eye*.

New thanks are now due to others who have helped me amplify my understanding of Dickinson's world. Most important, Kathie Gow at the Hatfield Historical Society became a great ally in the hunt for Dickinson, and Huddie and Cory Bardwell answered numerous questions about Hatfield history and sources. George Ashley of the Hatfield Historical Commission fielded questions about the built environment, and Eric Weber and Ralmon Black kindly helped sort out my queries in Williamsburg. Hatfield Town Clerk Louise Sylsz allowed me to spend hours poring over the town's eighteenth-century records. Josh Lane, Lynne Basset, Suzanne Flynt, Linda Eaton, Christie Jackson, and others helped me untangle puzzles concerning Dickinson's extant needlework. David Bosse at Deerfield's Memorial Libraries always responds quickly and kindly to my various requests. The historians who reviewed all or part of the current text as it was revised for publication, including Ann Marie Plane, Woody Holton, and Alice Nash, were wonderfully supportive; their astute questions and comments greatly improved the contents. Kevin Sweeney is to be thanked again, and doubly so, for his close and helpful reading of this revised manuscript as it neared completion, and especially for sharing his own interpretation of the coming of the revolution in western Massachusetts, a point of view reflected in key passages herein. And last but hardly least, Cheryl Harned and Jessie MacLeod provided valuable editorial and research assistance and general collegiality. I am grateful to all.

INTRODUCTION

The Independence
of Rebecca Dickinson

"Two are better than one, for if one falls the other can lift him up. But I must act my part alone." When Rebecca Dickinson penned these words in the pages of her journal in the summer of 1789, she wrote from years of experience. Fifty years old and still single, she well knew how hard life could be for women who, unlike the vast majority of adults in early America, had never married. An evening at her brother's home had put her in a contemplative mood. Visiting there was Henry Dodge, a bachelor who had courted her sister Irene more than fifteen years earlier. Irene had long since married; Henry had not. "He appeared to sit by her and I believe he has never forgotten her," Dickinson mused. Dodge's plight was only too familiar to Dickinson. She returned home to her weather-beaten, red saltbox house just across from the Congregational meetinghouse in Hatfield, Massachusetts, got out her pen, and wrote, "How great the loss is to lose the partner of our life, for in the beginning they were made male and female." "There is great need of the help of each other through the journey of life," she continued, "but I must act my part alone . . . in a world where they go two and two, male and female" (June [], 1789).

Rebecca Dickinson was a skilled craftswoman in her thirties when she first started keeping a diary, but by the time she wrote these lines she was an "old maid," to use the term popular in her day. A "fish out of water," a "cat on a roof," a "sparrow alone on a rooftop"; Dickinson's life had unfolded differently from those of most other women she knew, and she believed that made her the subject of suspicion, and even scorn.

In this way, her era seems not so very different from our own. "Even today," as one historian has observed, "when children play the card game 'Old Maid,' in which they match as many pairs as possible while avoiding the card with no mate, they are being socialized to believe that married couples are winners and singlewomen (but not men) are losers. The 'old maid' is something to be avoided at all costs." "Where did those ideas come from," one rightly wonders, "and when did the figure of the 'old maid' originate?"[1] The stereotypical "old maid" is so familiar to us today that it is difficult to imagine a time before this particular caricature came into being; however, both the term and the set of images it triggers emerged in the early eighteenth century, not long before Rebecca Dickinson was born, and came into full flower just as she reached middle age and late adulthood. Dickinson, then, was part of one of the first generations of women to feel this particular stereotype's sting. Over the course of her life she watched as popular culture increasingly ridiculed and even demonized women who never married. She herself cherished aspects of her life alone, but few around her saw anything enviable in her situation.

As Dickinson grappled with the meanings of independence, so did her nation. By the time she wrote these words, the men and women of British North America had been debating, and then dissolving, their colonial ties to the mother country for some twenty years. Having now fought and won a war to free itself from British rule, the new United States had just held its first presidential election. That same spring George Washington began the first of his two terms as president, Massachusetts's own John Adams becoming vice president. In March the U.S. Constitution (ratified a year before in Massachusetts) was declared to be in effect. As an artisan who earned her living making apparel,

Dickinson surely read with interest that, on the day of his April 1789 inauguration, Washington wore a suit of dark brown broadcloth made of fabric produced in nearby Hartford, Connecticut, a gesture toward American manufacturing independence.

Rebecca Dickinson's experience offers a chance to consider the ways political independence and marital independence were entwined for eighteenth-century craftswomen. Women who never married were unusual in that era in America, though they were not the rarity Dickinson implies. At least that is when considering white women: across colonial America, many African and African American women—the vast majority of whom were enslaved—could not legally marry, so whether or not they were able to preserve stable unions with men (and many did, though unions between enslaved laborers were always at risk and required the consent of owners), they were by and large excluded from the advantages of legal marriage. Among Dickinson's European counterparts, varying by place and time, roughly 10 percent of adult women remained single. Most estimates suggest that in colonial Massachusetts, roughly 8 to 10 percent of adult women would never marry, a demographic imbalance in the second half of the eighteenth century producing a slight rise in the numbers of unmarried women.

Dickinson's sense of being a shocking aberration for having remained single therefore is not quite correct; indeed, records document other never-married women in Hatfield, and her own diary refers to several of them. Perhaps part of her feeling that she was an outlier, at least later in her life, came from the fact that she (at her own choosing) lived part of each year alone. Society and culture in early Massachusetts was deeply rooted in the household. Families were large, and most homes contained more distant relatives as well as servants, apprentices, and others. It was a crowded world in which people shared rooms, even beds, and privacy as it is understood today was inconceivable. No comparable statistic is available for Massachusetts, but in the bordering colonies of New York and Rhode Island, not even 1 percent of people lived alone.[2] "How often they have hissed and wagged their heads at me," Dickinson wrote, "by reason of my solitary life" (September 16, 1787). Perhaps here her sense of her own peculiarity and the community's skepticism, if not disapproval, was more accurate.

Understanding the lives of women like Dickinson—women who tested the boundaries of social convention—helps us better understand those conventions. Since the flowering of women's history as a field of scholarly inquiry, a tremendous literature has emerged that tracks the changing shape of American women's lives between the beginning of European settlement and the first decades of the republic. Historians have sketched out a general trajectory in which New England's Puritan goodwives in time were succeeded by Republican Mothers (white, middle- and upper-class, married women whose principal role in the newly formed United States of America was to raise good citizens). These women were themselves followed by activists whose interest in social reform (justified in part by the obligations of motherhood) ultimately launched the quest for women's suffrage. Born in 1738, Rebecca was a child of the Great Awakening, a religious revival that transformed communities along the eastern seaboard of British North America. She lived to see the new social, cultural, intellectual, and political forms and ideas associated with the era now termed the "Enlightenment" take hold, but her own mind was shaped by an earlier time. She was a thirty-five-year-old gownmaker in 1773, when Massachusetts men dumped tea into Boston's harbor and helped ignite a revolution. She was almost fifty in 1787 when delegates met in Philadelphia to consider a new constitution. But motherhood (republican or otherwise) would not shape her relationship to the emerging nation. In Dickinson's final years, as the War of 1812 erupted and then drew to a close, the lives of white women like herself, from comfortable families who were neither affluent nor poor, had increasingly come to reflect new interests in education and voluntary associations—and at the same time tended to involve less in the way of artisanal skill. Some historians have observed a "Cult of Single Blessedness" emerging in the decades following the American Revolution, in which increasing numbers of women, inspired by the era's rhetoric of independence, consciously chose to remain single. But Rebecca Dickinson (who reached maturity in the 1760s, well before those cultural transformations occurred) was not a member of that generation. Some of the themes that run through the broad outlines of "single blessedness" would have sounded familiar to her; others not at all.

In eighteenth-century rural New England, Dickinson may have been principally defined by her gender and (eventually) her marital status, but she had other identities as well: Christian—and more specifically a follower of the Calvinist variety of the Protestant faith—and craftswoman. When most Americans think about working people in the eighteenth century, they imagine men. Burly blacksmiths sweat over hot forges; artful cabinetmakers and wood-carvers with chisels and mallets produce the beautiful chairs that today command fortunes on the antiques market. One can easily picture the ambitious young printer Benjamin Franklin pushing his wheelbarrow through colonial Philadelphia, or the elegant Paul Revere, teapot in hand, gazing out from the canvas of John Singleton Copley's iconic portrait of the successful silversmith. Early America's craftswomen may be harder to conjure in the mind's eye, but Rebecca Dickinson was every bit an artisan as Revere or Franklin. She, like they, completed a period of training recognized as her apprenticeship and tutored other aspiring craftspersons in the distinct mental and physical abilities that gownmaking demanded. She was an expert, to whom her community turned when they needed garments both attractive and functional. Viewing artisanal skill from the point of view of laborers like Dickinson reminds us to enlarge our view of women, and of work, and remember that these craftswomen worried about politics and the economy just as much as their fathers and brothers did.

As relations between Parliament and England's North American colonies soured, the major tool of political resistance to emerge was the boycott of imported goods, a strategy that created a crisis for the rural gownmaker just as it did for male importers and urban craftsmen who both used these items and sold goods that competed with them. How Dickinson handled the trauma that was the American Revolution reminds us that the independence movement was far more complicated than a contest between tax-resisting colonists and a tyrannical Crown. As artisans watched the political volley between imperial administrators and leaders of the American protest movement, they calculated and recalculated their position from whatever vantage point they occupied given their particular trade, clientele, and location. In this, Rebecca

Dickinson was no different from thousands of other artisans throughout the rebelling colonies.

But her work in the clothing trades put Dickinson in a particular position vis-à-vis the series of ruptures that led to the revolution. As the leaders of the protest movement increasingly emphasized political action grounded in consumer behavior—that is, the nonimportation, nonexportation, and nonconsumption agreements that constituted the first mass boycotts in American history—craftswomen like Dickinson, at the peak of her career during the years of revolt, found themselves at the center of the crisis. For Dickinson, marital and political independence went hand in hand. Without access to a husband's support, what would she do, should her community shun the imported textiles that formed the basis of her livelihood? Did she greet these movements with enthusiasm, apprehension, or both? And how would she navigate their aftermath, the new political, economic, social, and cultural orders that emerged in their wake? Rebecca Dickinson's life helps us see with fresh eyes the era of independence writ large as it was experienced by one craftswoman in rural New England. To be sure, other women associated with this time and place are more famous. Rebecca Dickinson was neither as influential, nor as articulate, as Abigail Adams, the wife of the patriot and later president John Adams. She was not as cerebral as Mercy Otis Warren, the gentlewoman whose plays and essays helped shape public opinion in these tumultuous years. And she was not as adventurous as Deborah Sampson, a young woman who dressed as a man to serve in the Continental Army. But she was more typical than any of these figures, because like most everyday people, as a working woman in the small town of Hatfield, Massachusetts, she watched the historical events of her age from the margin, not the center.

Dickinson's Hatfield helps us better understand the nature of that rebellion as it unfolded in communities well beyond the urban hotspots congenial to fomenting revolution. Boston, Massachusetts, as the site of the "Boston Massacre," "Tea Party," and other important events—and the home of Samuel Adams, Paul Revere, and other icons of the age—looms large in our revolutionary vision, but in the 1770s the vast majority of Massachusetts residents lived outside that city, in the countryside. Popular historical imagination paints a picture of New England's minutemen striding off to battle, quick to object to the Crown's infringements on their rights as Englishmen. But Hatfield, like many rural places, warmed only slowly to the cause, and when it did, the emotions that moved the townspeople were as much local as global, as much practical as principled. Long governed by the preferences of a small handful of powerful elite families known as the "River Gods," Hatfield tended to be conservative. In other words, as Israel Williams, the "Monarch of Hampshire County," went, so went the town—and Williams had no reason to support any change to the status quo. But the leadership of Williams and his peers came into question as the political crisis unfolded. After Reverend Timothy Woodbridge left the pulpit of the Congregational church and the Reverend Joseph Lyman (a passionate advocate of protest) filled his place, public opinion began increasingly to embrace the emerging rebellion.

If Joseph Lyman brought new notions to Hatfield, he nurtured old ones as well. Lyman was as "good a Calvinist" as Dickinson "could wish." Calvinism—the Protestant sect founded by Swiss theologian John Calvin—held sway over much of New England in the eighteenth century, and faith and politics were no less entwined then than they are today. Women and men both found their roles in the coming of the American Revolution mediated through the church. Dickinson's faith was central to her life, and her diary sheds light on the Congregational church as it evolved from its Puritan underpinnings. Whatever else it has to tell us about her life and times, Dickinson's diary was primarily a spiritual journal, a place to contemplate the meaning of God's choices for her life. Rebecca Dickinson believed in an active God whose intense concern for her soul shaped every aspect of her existence and whose judgment shaped the course of public life as well. Anything and everything could be read as signs of his regard.

While Dickinson's life presents a view of eighteenth-century gender expectations, the experiences of craftswomen, and the nature of Calvinism in rural New England, her struggle to sustain an independent life and to find a larger meaning for it parallels her colony's and her country's struggle to achieve political and economic independence. Both demanded sacrifices, and both produced anxieties. Both unfolded not in an instant, in any one act, decision, or moment, but instead gradually, as a series of choices and events that moved incrementally, over a period of years, toward independence. She cherished the ability to determine something about the course of her own life, apart from the ups and downs that so often came with husbands and children. This was the promise held out by independence: that for all its hardships, Dickinson was able to preserve some degree of control unavailable to women who accepted the many uncertainties associated with marriage and motherhood. But for Dickinson independence meant vulnerability as well as autonomy. For the nation independence conferred self-determination, but independence was also a gamble, and once achieved came with its own strains and perils. A "sparrow alone on a rooftop," for Rebecca Dickinson singlehood was without doubt a source of unending pain; at the same time, it was a source of opportunity as well—even independence.

1

Origins and Awakenings

Rebecca Dickinson was born in July 1738, the oldest daughter of farmer and dairyman Moses Dickinson and Anna Smith Dickinson. Following tradition, her proud parents named her after her grandmother, Rebecca Barrett Wright Dickinson. The town where Rebecca was born—Hatfield, Massachusetts—had been thriving since the 1660s on rich farmlands fed by the Connecticut River. Hatfield began as a tiny outpost on the western edge of England's North American colonies. By the time Rebecca was a small girl playing with her sisters in her family's farmyard, it was a prosperous farming village called home by some of the most powerful men in New England.

The world that Rebecca Dickinson knew in childhood was framed by two great concerns: security in this life and in the life to come. On the one hand, colonists on the far margins of England's expanding empire lived in a constant state of tension with both the Native peoples (whom they eagerly displaced) and their powerful European allies (the French, who settled just to the north in Canada). On the other hand, English families had become acutely worried about their prospects of getting into heaven. They feared that their Puritan forebears' efforts to create a godly community had in fact gone wrong. Hatfield had been forged by more than a half century of political, military, and religious upheaval. Although its location on some maps of the day may have made it appear to be on the periphery of the Crown's global concerns, that very position put it at the heart of the imperial maelstrom. By the time she reached her twelfth birthday, Rebecca Dickinson surely understood her town's volatile eighty-year history and her place in it.

Though Hatfield would become home to some of Massachusetts's most influential citizens, it was never especially large and remained about the same size throughout Dickinson's lifetime. The population in the year of her birth is not documented, but in 1765, when Rebecca was twenty-seven, residents of Hatfield (which then included the villages of Whately and Williamsburg) numbered 803; by the time Massachusetts declared its independence eleven years later, Whately and Williamsburg had broken away as separate towns, leaving just 582 people in Hatfield proper. In 1790, when Dickinson was fifty-two, the first U.S. census recorded 703 people inhabiting 103 houses; ten years later, only about 100 residents and 20 more houses had been added.

A description of Hatfield written a few years after Dickinson's death gives us a glimpse of the character and reputation of the town. Timothy Dwight, a Yale-educated clergyman, traveled around New England, observing the towns and villages of the early republic. "Hatfield," he wrote, "is built chiefly on two streets: the principal running north and south near a mile, the other about as far east and west. The houses are generally decent, and a small number in a better style."[1] Dwight noticed something else about the village: "The inhabitants have for a long period been conspicuous for uniformity of character. They have less intercourse with their neighbors than those of most other places. An air of silence and retirement appears everywhere. Except travelers, few persons are seen abroad besides those who are employed about their daily business. This seclusion probably renders them less agreeable to strangers, but certainly contributes to their prosperity. Accordingly, few farming towns are equally distinguished either for their property or their thrift."

In 1738 Moses Dickinson had distinguished himself for neither property nor thrift. Tax and probate records suggest that he was a man of average means who farmed, keeping dairy cows and raising mostly grains on about fifteen and a half acres of land. But what he lacked in prosperity he made up for in pedigree. As Rebecca Dickinson was growing up, she was safe in the knowledge that she belonged: her ancestors, both the Dickinsons and the Waites, had been among the very first to settle along what eventually became Hatfield's main street.

Hatfield owed its existence to the larger Protestant Reformation that had transformed Europe, and the whole of the Atlantic world, in the sixteenth and seventeenth centuries. Beginning in the 1560s a movement eventually known as Puritanism rocked England. These reformers hoped to "purify" the Church of England, an institution they felt had become hopelessly corrupt, tainted by unnecessary rituals and fraudulent beliefs. Their back-to-basics movement hoped to restore the integrity of the faith. The Bible, they asserted, and not priests, should be the ultimate source of spiritual authority. Followers of the radical reformer John Calvin (including New England Calvinists like Rebecca Dickinson, two centuries later) came to embrace five core beliefs: the "total depravity," or inherent sinfulness, of humankind; one's inability to affect in any way whether or not one was among the "elect" whom God had already chosen for eternal life; the limited nature of Christ's atonement, which was a sacrifice made only for the predetermined elect, not for everyone; the irresistible nature of grace (meaning that just as people cannot achieve status among the elect if not predestined for it, neither can they deny it if they are); and the "perseverance of the saints"—that is, the idea that once a person has been saved, nothing can happen to change that.

For some Puritans the opportunity presented by England's colonization in North America was too good to pass up: Why try to repair the flaws of England, when a blank slate awaited in the New World? They could begin again, and this time they would get it right.

The men and women whose passionate commitment to their faith led them in the 1630s to the shores of New England believed that the eyes of the world were upon them. They would be a "city on a hill," a great experiment that would model the true religion for their European counterparts. Because so much was at stake, the families and religious leaders who came to New England were alert to any threat to their project. Disputes over theological issues—seemingly minute and inscrutable conflicts to us today, but with implications for all of heaven and earth at the time—split old communities and gave birth to new ones, driving settlement in early New England. In the series of events that led to the founding of Hatfield, followers of Reverend Thomas Hooker left Cambridge, in the Massachusetts Bay Colony, and in 1636 settled at Hartford in Connecticut. Two decades later another group, guided in part by the Reverend John Russell, leader of a congregation in Wethersfield, also departed for new, fresh ground. Russell's followers were spurred by several controversies surrounding baptism and church membership, debates that would soon come to be associated with the "Half-way Covenant," which allowed children whose parents were not full members of the church—that is, not yet proven to be among the "elect"—to be baptized nevertheless. In 1659 a number of families followed Russell to a new settlement to the north, a place straddling the Connecticut River in the Nolwottog (also known as Norwottock and Nonotuck; Nolwottog is used in this book) homeland. The English had purchased the land from the Nolwottog, but did not immediately displace them. Umpanchala, Chickwallop, and Quonquont, the sachems or leaders who negotiated this transaction, reserved for their own people the right to plant, harvest, hunt, and fish there. (A century later Rebecca Dickinson may have purchased baskets or herbal medicine from Indians who remained in their homeland long after these deeds were signed.) The English named the new place Hadley, after Hadleigh in Suffolk County, England.

Although Hadley was created at least in part through vigorous theological debate, the founding of Hatfield was less dramatic. Several of the families who had joined the Hadley migration in 1659 had settled on lands on the west side of the Connecticut River. In time residents on that side of the river found it troublesome to attend meetings in the town center, so they petitioned for permission to form their own, independent community. Hadley's leadership tried to resist their neighbors' effort to break away, but geography and demography weighed against them, and Hatfield was established as a separate town in 1670, taking its own name from a place in England's Hertfordshire County.

Like many towns on the western fringe of Britain's empire, Hatfield quickly found itself involved in warfare. The newly established town enjoyed only a few years of peace before the conflict known as King Philip's War began in southern New England and spread quickly up the Connecticut River. The valley's Nolwottog and their neighbors had a common history of trade and alliance with other Native peoples in New

England, including the Mohegan and Pequot to the south, the Nipmuc and Wampanoag to the east, and the Abenakis to the north. All of these groups experienced the growing pressure of losing land, but for the most part they had been able to live peacefully alongside the English for more than fifty years. Those who chose to remain on lands acquired by the English had to conform to English laws and convert to Christianity, which produced other kinds of social and cultural stress. These pressures erupted into violence in 1675 after the murder of John Sassamon, a Christian Indian who served as a translator and intermediary between the English and the Wampanoag. The English arrested, convicted, and executed three Wampanoag men for the crime. The Wampanoag protested that this usurped their right to pursue justice according to their own laws. A Wampanoag attack on the town of Taunton, Massachusetts, led to a loose intertribal alliance, with Narragansett, Nipmuc, Pequot, Abenaki, and other tribes taking a stand to drive out the encroaching English. King Philip's (or Metacom's) War, its name reflecting the Wampanoag sachem's leadership, became the first in a series of Anglo-Abenaki wars to erupt between the late seventeenth and the mid-eighteenth century.

In September 1675 there were attacks on several towns in the Connecticut River Valley, including Hadley and Deerfield, by raiding parties of Nipmucs from central Massachusetts (and perhaps local Pocumtucks and Nolwottogs as well). In mid-October 1675 the fighting came to Hatfield. War continued over the winter and into the spring. In the summer a series of decisive victories turned the tide in favor of the colonists. In August 1676 a band of Englishmen and their Native allies found and killed Metacom, cutting off his head and displaying it in Plymouth for some twenty years thereafter.

However, in northern New England, from the Hatfield area up to Vermont and stretching east to New Hampshire, Maine, Nova Scotia, and New Brunswick, other groups with little or no connection to Metacom attempted to drive the English from their respective homelands. A series of raids continued for about two years after Metacom's death. In September 1677 Hatfield was attacked by a force of Pocumtucks and Nolwottogs who had taken refuge in Canada, and several English settlers were killed. The Natives took several colonists prisoner and transported them back north. Among seventeen colonists walking to Canada that fall was a woman named Martha Waite, along with her three small daughters, Mary, age five; Martha, age four; and Sarah, age two.

Pregnant at the time of her capture, Martha Waite delivered her child while still a hostage. She named her daughter Canada "as a living memorial of this captivity."[2] (Another mother who gave birth during this time christened her child "Captivity," ensuring that neither the child nor her community would ever forget the dramatic events that surrounded her entrance onto the world stage.) After about eight months English negotiators working with the Native forces' French allies secured the captives' release. The surviving prisoners returned to Hatfield. Canada Waite eventually married and became mother and later grandmother to a number of children, including Rebecca Dickinson.

These conflicts in Hatfield and its environs were not merely local; in fact, they were not even regional. The violence that began with King Philip's War became inextricably entangled with other disputes in what was nothing less than a global struggle for dominance over the North American mainland and Caribbean islands, a vast area today considered part of the "Atlantic world." Both England and France had long been working to establish control of the northern section (Spain having claimed the vast territory to the south, up to and around what is today the Gulf Coast and the western United States) of the so-called New World. In addition to several islands in the Caribbean Sea, England claimed a vast area stretching along the eastern seaboard of the North American mainland, from what are now the Carolinas through much of what is today Maine and into the interior to the various mountain ranges that hindered further settlement. Meanwhile "New France" flourished along and north of the St. Lawrence River, in lands around the Great Lakes, down the Mississippi and along the Gulf coast, while France and Britain competed for Newfoundland and Hudson Bay. Alliances with Native nations were an essential element of that international chess match. As the two European empires fought to maintain supremacy, the peoples who had already long occupied the territory faced impossible choices. What course was the surest path to survival? Alliance—with whom? Warfare—with whom? As France and England vied for control, wars between the European superpowers erupted in New England and drew in Native allies. For communities like Hatfield, these wars were also in part religious wars, because the "papist" French were the longtime rivals of Protestant England. Narratives of warfare and captivity written by former captives like Mary Rowlendson and in jeremiads from ministers like Increase Mather only strengthened their view of themselves as a chosen people, tested by God.

Dickinson's grandmother did not need her unusual name to remember her community's vulnerable position in that world. Hatfield continued to experience violence in these decades. Just six years after Canada Waite's 1696 wedding to Joseph Smith, the Third Anglo-Abenaki War, or Queen Anne's War, began. The English monarch declared war on France, and fighting spread to New England the following year. When Deerfield was attacked by French and Native forces in February 1704, Smith, with other men from the town, rushed to defend it, but they were unable to save Canada's father. England and France made peace through the Treaty of Utrecht in 1713, but the French did not inform their Abenaki allies that as part of the deal they had given England lands claimed by the Abenaki. This led to another Anglo-Abenaki War, in the 1720s, in which the Abenaki had to fight without the help of their erstwhile French allies. This war was really a series of conflicts better known by their local names, such as Grey Lock's War in western Massachusetts (named for an Abenaki chief) and Father Rasle's War in Maine (named for the Jesuit priest who was killed at Norridgewock in 1724 during an English attack).

Rebecca Dickinson, then, arrived in a world that between the 1677 raid on Hatfield and her birth in 1738 had been punctuated by warfare. In the fall of 1737 Anna Smith, the seventh child of Joseph Smith and Canada Waite, married Moses Dickinson. The Dickinsons, like the Waites and the Smiths, were among Hatfield's earliest settlers. Moses Dickinson was twenty-six years old, and Anna was twenty-five, when they wed. Rebecca arrived in a timely fashion, nine months later. In 1738, when baby Rebecca—named for the grandmother with whom Moses and Anna were probably living at the time she was born—took her first infant breaths, Hatfield was enjoying a welcome period of calm. Following the close of this fourth Anglo-Abenaki War, the town had enjoyed several years of development and expansion. (Fighting among the British, the French, and their Native allies erupted again in 1744 and continued throughout much of the 1740s, affecting Deerfield in 1746, but this conflict had relatively little impact in and around Hatfield.) When Rebecca was eleven Canada Waite Smith died, taking part of her community's memory of the events surrounding her captivity with her. The age of settlement was giving way to real establishment and stability, a time of relative peace that would set the stage for the town's midcentury prosperity.

During these years a group of local leaders emerged who came to be called River Gods: a handful of influential, intermarried families (including the Williams and Partridge families in Hatfield) from towns along the Connecticut River who held the most important political, military, and ecclesiastical positions in the valley. But while the Williamses and Patridges were feathering their well-appointed nests, so were newly-weds Moses and Anna Dickinson, although theirs was a smaller and more modest one in a red house just a stone's throw from the Congregational meetinghouse. With two broad stories facing the street and a single-story lean-to addition in the rear, houses in this style reminded people of the slanted wall-mounted boxes used to preserve salt, and "saltbox" is the term still used today for such dwellings. The home was crowded. Moses acquired the house, in which he had been raised, in 1742, when his seventy-three-year-old father Samuel, in consideration of the love and affection he held for his children Moses and Benoni, transferred ownership of the family homestead to his sons, providing that they agree to comfortably support and care for him and his wife for the remainder of their lives. Moses and Anna would raise their own young family while caring for Moses's parents as they aged.

After Rebecca's birth, five more children followed: Samuel, Martha, Miriam, Anna, and Irene. Rebecca was the oldest child in a family of six, the first to enter school, the first to embark on an apprenticeship, the first to mark all of the milestones that accompanied childhood and youth in eighteenth-century New England.

It appears that the fairly crowded Dickinson household included another person as well. A series of entries in town records suggests that Moses and Anna were routinely credited for "keeping" Dorothy Allis, an older woman who was apparently unable to support herself. In colonial Massachusetts towns provided relief to indigent neighbors by placing them in the care of a local family and then reimbursing that family from public funds for the expense of the additional room and board. Dorothy Allis was one of a small number of women living on town support in the early years of Rebecca's life. It appears that she remained a member of the Dickinson household until at least 1750, when Rebecca turned twelve, and so was a fixture throughout her childhood. Unlike other women on public support in those years, Allis was able to earn her keep. Moses Dickinson's debits to the town for Allis's care were offset by credits for her labor. Many years later, when Rebecca began to worry about her own ability to support herself, the specter of women like Dorothy Allis would weigh heavily on her mind.

If Moses Dickinson was the head of Rebecca's temporal family, his household received its spiritual guidance from the Reverend Timothy Woodbridge. A Connecticut native and Yale College graduate, Woodbridge was installed at the Hatfield Congregational Church in 1739, just after Rebecca was born. He first served as an associate minister, appointed to help the aging Reverend William Williams for a few years. After Williams died, Woodbridge assumed control of the pulpit. Despite Rebecca's observation that Reverend Woodbridge was "never gifted in the ministerial way," she would later refer to him as her "spiritual father," whose piety was like a "burning and shining light" to her and her community (March 8, 1789).

Ministerial gifts became the subject of serious scrutiny during the early years of Rebecca's life, when events now called the Great Awakening swept over New England. It is impossible to overestimate the importance of religion in Dickinson's world. The First Congregational Church in Hatfield (only the fourth established in western Massachusetts) was, and would long remain, the only church in town. But in the 1730s and 1740s it confronted both the joys and the challenges presented by widespread religious enthusiasm.

The men and women of Northampton, Massachusetts, a comparatively large community bordering Hatfield to the south, witnessed in the mid-1730s an eruption of spiritual emotion, which the Reverend Jonathan Edwards fueled from his pulpit. As the decade progressed, the spiritual "awakening" spread to other towns nearby. In 1735 Hatfield's Rev. William Williams reported that a "general concern" about godly living was transforming the countryside, that "vain and idle company is left; and an air of seriousness to be observed; careful attention to the word preached; and abundance came to us with that important question, *what must we do to be saved?*"[3] Across Hatfield, anxious people sought out their ministers from sunrise to sunset. Conversation abandoned the earthly and embraced the divine as attention turned to the state of one's soul.

A pamphlet describing these events attracted the attention of a charismatic English evangelical preacher by the name of George Whitefield, who had already launched a transatlantic effort to revive and reform the faithful. When a tour across Britain's North American colonies brought Whitefield to western Massachusetts, he particularly hoped to visit Northampton, and Edwards eagerly welcomed him. On the morning of October 17, 1740, Whitefield, en route west from Boston, preached to an enthusiastic crowd in Hadley. He would describe it as a place where "a great work"—that is, a spiritual revival—had been carried out "some years ago"; his sermon "was like putting fire to a tinder," and caused many there to "weep sorely." He then crossed the river to Edwards's church in Northampton (where he had much the same effect). But a visit to Hatfield the following day left Whitefield uninspired. "Found myself not much strengthened," he wrote, suggesting perhaps a general lack of interest in the evangelist's theatrical style among the cool people of Hatfield.[4]

Hatfield's Rev. William Williams, the uncle of Jonathan Edwards and a member of the prominent Williams family, was a seasoned, Harvard-educated clergyman in his seventies with a half century of service in Hatfield under his belt by the time revival erupted. His wife was Christian Stoddard Williams, the daughter of the influential Reverend Solomon Stoddard, which placed their household near the epicenter of spiritual authority in the valley. Williams's son Elisha had in 1726 become president of Yale College, and two other boys had also become ministers. Another son, Israel, then in his early thirties, would acquire so much political and military power that he would come to be called the "Monarch of Hampshire County." The family's response to almost any event dictated how that event would unfold elsewhere, and Reverend Williams embraced the religious fervor.

But Williams would not live to see the millennium begin or to see his nephew Jonathan become increasingly unsettled by the emotion sweeping the community. He died in August 1741, his funeral sermon delivered by Jonathan Edwards. As much as the clergy welcomed the flowering of interest in matters eternal, growing numbers became concerned about the revival's other consequences. The weeping, the convulsions, and other displays were difficult to assess. Did they really signal true conversion, or were people just getting carried away with themselves? Some of those converted became so certain, even arrogant, about their piety that their conversation seemed to slip from enthusiastic encouragement to actual preaching. With laypeople and itinerants proclaiming their insights left and right, what would happen to traditional ministerial authority?

By the mid-1740s, when Whitefield made a second visit to Massachusetts, times had changed. Whitefield again preached across the river in Hadley, but the Williams family, now led by the increasingly powerful Israel Williams (presumably working alongside Reverend Woodbridge), kept him out of the Hatfield pulpit. Woodbridge was a relative newcomer to Hatfield when Whitefield first arrived, having been installed not even a year before, but when Williams died, Woodbridge took over the pastorate, and he shared the growing fear of Whitefield's agenda. But Hatfield people did not let Woodbridge prevent them from witnessing the excitement; they had ample opportunity to hear Whitefield in the surrounding towns. What's more, when Whitefield returned to Hadley, his outdoor lectures were allegedly audible to curious Hatfield residents across the river—including, perhaps, seven-year-old Rebecca Dickinson. If Hatfield families were willing to put a toe in the evangelical water, they nevertheless sought to keep the floodtide at bay.

In time Edwards fell out of favor with his Northampton congregation. Unsure what to make of the many alleged conversions, some of which he suspected were "counterfeit" (i.e., more about emotion and overexcitement than the true voice of God), he reinstituted a practice that had long been abandoned by the congregation, requiring evidence of a conversion experience, that is, a complete (and compelling) account of how one came to perceive God's active presence in one's life, before that person could be admitted to full church membership, including communion. The offering of some convincing, fairly detailed public testimony describing one's conversion had been a requirement of church membership from the beginning of New England's settlement, but over time the clergy had relaxed their demand for this proof. Edwards had adopted the practice of his grandfather, Solomon Stoddard, allowing everyone but the clearly and stubbornly unconverted to partake in communion. But now he changed his mind, clamping down, and his congregation didn't like it. In the wake of an incident in which he publicly chastised certain youths in the community for reading improper books, and amid tense negotiations over salary (when the community already thought the minister and his family lived a little large for local taste), this development caused Northampton churchgoers to perceive a certain arrogance in their pastor. The minister's flock turned against him. When Edwards was dismissed from his pulpit in 1750, Rebecca's own pastor, the Reverend Timothy Woodbridge, was among the council members who voted to relieve him of his duties.[5] Hatfield's chapter in the "Great Awakening" drew to a close, and Woodbridge helped close the book.

Little Rebecca Dickinson was only dimly aware of the complex theological debates swirling around her town in these years. She was seven when Whitefield was denied access to the Hatfield pulpit and eleven when Jonathan Edwards was dismissed from Northampton's. But Reverend Woodbridge had a hand in those proceedings, and his worldview—as it emanated from the Hatfield pulpit over Dickinson's first twenty-nine years—necessarily shaped Rebecca's own. Woodbridge, Williams, and the other men who directed the course of these events remained influential in Hatfield for many years The tumult of the Great Awakening may have represented a challenge to the old order, but Israel Williams and his peers survived, and even affirmed their power.

These events had such a great impact that people remembered them for decades. Some eighty-five years after Edwards left Northampton, Rebecca's sister Miriam, then eighty-eight years old, in an interview with a local historian, could still recount the drama of Israel Williams riding to Northampton to advise Jonathan Edwards in no uncertain terms that Whitefield would not be welcome in Hatfield. She remembered conversations with Reverend Williams's wife, Christian Stoddard Williams, who "told [her] many things" in the years between these events and Mrs. Williams's death in 1764 (when Miriam was in her teens and Rebecca in her twenties).[6] Miriam was not yet born when the evangelist's visit first rocked the community, and she was little more than a toddler when Edwards left his pulpit. That she knew this story and thought to recount it so many years later attests to its importance in the collective memory of the town. That same moment, with all its implications, surely lingered in Rebecca's mind as well, as she could claim to have some direct memory of the dramatic events. This was the first controversy that she saw convulse Hatfield, but not the last.

2

Entering the
Female Economy

Hatfield in the 1750s was a farming community. From the late seventeenth century, in addition to a number of crops, beef production drove the local economy. Animals raised and fattened in western Massachusetts were taken to Boston to be butchered, preserved, and shipped. Even in town, agriculture was everywhere. Most Hatfield families lived along the main street, but kept parcels of land elsewhere for planting crops, gathering wood, and so forth. Swine were free to roam at large, and flocks of geese honked at passersby. Men also worked in any number of artisanal crafts, as blacksmiths, furniture makers, and housewrights (home builders). Some kept shops; others became physicians, schoolteachers, or lawyers.

Rebecca's father Moses was a farmer and a dairyman, so she grew up around barns and milk pails. When she was a small girl her parents made sure she received some education. That she kept a diary at all tells us that Rebecca Dickinson could both read and write. In fact, reading and writing were considered entirely different skills in the mid-eighteenth century and were taught (if at all) sequentially: first reading, then writing. Born in 1738, Dickinson was part of a demographic phenomenon, a rising level of female literacy across New England. Some evidence suggests that whereas only about half of the women of Anna Dickinson's generation achieved literacy, perhaps 80 to 90 percent of Rebecca's generation would, though the likelihood depended greatly on where one grew up, because access to schools and local culture varied widely. In colonial Massachusetts, towns routinely hired schoolmasters to teach basic literacy and numeracy skills, while women led so-called dame schools for smaller children in summer. This latter institution has been described as a little bit day care and a little bit of instruction, with tutoring mainly in reading (so that one could read the Bible), but not necessarily in writing, considered a separate skill that girls were assumed to have less need for. Sometimes the keeper of the school was paid by the parents of the children enrolled, sometimes by the town. Young Rebecca almost certainly attended one of the schools offered in Hatfield in the 1740s and 1750s. Able to both read and write with ease, she was part of a longer-term trend that would encompass ever-larger numbers of women in eighteenth-century Massachusetts. She appears to have been at the forefront of it and likely possessed greater skill than many of her female neighbors.

The curriculum made available to girls was only part of the training that prepared them for adulthood. Women worked at all manner of occupations, generally following a course set out on larger family lines. The daughter of a midwife might well become a midwife; a girl who was raised in her parents' tavern might find herself running a tavern as an adult. The daughters of ministers often married ministers. Women in colonial cities had a wider range of options than those in rural places, but women everywhere found work in the clothing trades (as tailors, gownmakers, seamstresses, or milliners), healing occupations (as midwives or nurses), cloth production (as weavers, spinners, or fullers), and in other areas of the economy.

The relationships that these healers, gownmakers, spinners, housewives, and other women developed among themselves constituted a "female economy" that was separate from, yet intersected with, that of men. Women exchanged yarn for cheese and cloth for bread. They traded skill on the loom for skill with the needle. Although the evolving needs of a public commercial culture would over the course of the late eighteenth and early nineteenth centuries gradually replace face-to-face exchanges in favor of more distant and less familiar relationships, the female economy was less affected by this shift. For example, women relied on word of mouth more than the newspaper advertisements that became increasingly important to men's commercial lives, and they tracked their debts and credits in less formal ways than the ledgers kept by their better-educated and generally more numerate male counterparts.

As Dickinson neared her twelfth birthday, her parents contemplated her strengths and interests and decided to apprentice her to a gownmaker (sometimes called mantua maker, in reference to the stylish "mantua," a particular form of dress that emerged during this period). Today the production of clothing is so remote that it is easy to overlook the complexity of the clothing trades, both then and now. Romantic depictions of early America with mob-capped goodwives, needles perpetually in hand, have a tendency to conflate the wide range of occupations required to produce eighteenth-century apparel. Even in western Massachusetts, a multifaceted economy of tailors and tailoresses, gownmakers, staymakers, laundresses, shopkeepers, and milliners all helped families achieve the genteel appearance consumers craved. Sometime around the mid-eighteenth century Rebecca, an aspiring artisan, entered the female economy of rural New England.

Rebecca had probably already mastered the basic needlework skills that most young women achieved. Throughout Britain's Atlantic colonies in these years, needle skills formed part of basic female education, as these abilities allowed women to complete the everyday tasks associated with housewifery. Ornamental needlework allowed the young girls of a community's most privileged families to demonstrate a degree of gentility. The creation of decorative samplers or scenes signaled that a girl's family both had the means to send her to a school that taught these skills and could do without her labor while she was learning them. Behind every sampler and every crewelwork picture were the domestic servants and often slaves who kept households running smoothly while daughters of privilege concentrated on silk threads and stitch patterns.

But Rebecca was not so fortunate that she could concentrate on the ornamental at the expense of the practical. She had to work for a living. She must have demonstrated both aptitude and interest in clothing construction, because sometime around 1750 she and a girl named Catte (probably Catherine) Graves "went together to learn the trade of gownmaking," which Dickinson later described as being "of unspeakable advantage" to her, although of "no service" to Graves, who went on to marry and raise a large family (September 26, 1787). Apparently both sets of parents recognized the benefits that this marketable skill offered. Perhaps when their daughters reached an age at which they might be useful—probably around twelve or fourteen—the two fathers consulted one another about possible opportunities, approached a gownmaker, and entered into a formal agreement by which Rebecca and Catte might be taught to make, mend, and alter mantuas or gowns and other garments.

Trained gownmakers were important in colonial America. Though mythology about colonial America often suggests that most people wore clothing made by women in their own households, the creation of fashionable garments demanded more skill than most women achieved. The great cost of fabric meant that few housewives were likely to try their hand at cutting—and potentially ruining—expensive materials. Instead, skilled craftswomen who had mastered the ability to convert two-dimensional textiles into well-fitting, three-dimensional garments found work cutting out patterns for others in their communities, if not sewing them up (which some customers did themselves to save on the cost).

Having well-made apparel was essential to establishing one's position in the social order. A genteel appearance could only be accomplished by employing the services of many artisans, who dyed, designed, and printed fabrics; created laces; made wigs and shoes; fabricated stays; and formulated cosmetics. Gownmakers like Rebecca Dickinson were essential as men and women constructed wardrobes that matched the identities they embraced. This activity was by no means restricted to the wealthy; the hundreds of labor contracts that survive from this period also tell us that working men and women, at the close of their terms of service, were provided with two suits of apparel, one fit for the workday and one of better quality, "for Sunday." In their clothing suitable for Sunday church services, even less well off men and women could express at least some interest in fashion, which brought even these consumers to the door of the local tailor or gownmaker.

The wardrobe of a woman whose family's economic status, like Rebecca's, might be called "middling"—that is, neither especially well off nor especially poor—contained perhaps three to six shifts (the long, light gown that served as the century's foundation garment); two or three petticoats; three underpetticoats or skirts, sometimes quilted in silk or wool or made of linen and wool blends (such as linsey-woolsey); a number of "short gowns" (more akin to today's blouse than a gown, this was the everyday working shirt of the era); a cloak or cloaks; and assorted caps, kerchiefs, and aprons. The wardrobe of Hadley's Frances Spear, whose possessions were inventoried by the Hampshire County probate court in November 1770, suggests what was typical. In a chest itself valued at 3 shillings and another valued at 15 (much nicer, with two drawers), Spear stored her two black and green woolen gowns (worth 18 and 15 shillings), as well as a striped cotton gown, two calico gowns (one purple and white, the other blue, red, and white), three quilted petticoats and two pockets to wear beneath them, two cotton and three linen shifts, six aprons (in various cotton and linen weaves, some finer than others), handkerchiefs, and a single pair of linen stockings. She had a broadcloth cloak, valued at 19 shillings; a velvet hood worth just 4 shillings may have been an outdated piece of finery. A striped coat (probably another petticoat), a pair of stays, and a woolen gown stored near part of a woolen coat when the inventory was made suggests a mending pile.

Not surprisingly, the dress of the "better" classes was still finer and was particularly recognizable by its conscious use of color, texture, and fit—each of which indicated the amount of the work required to create a given garment, performed outside the household of the wearer. The bright colors, smooth feel, and polished appearance of commercially produced, imported fabrics indicated that the carding, weaving, fulling (i.e., preparing woven fabric for use by shrinking and beating it to the desired density and feel), and so forth required to create them was accomplished someplace else, and indeed, probably across the Atlantic. The more carefully fitted the garment, the more it shaped and reflected genteel carriage, the more likely it was to be the product of professional skill. Fitted garments in fine fabrics enabled both men and women to communicate the high proportion of their wardrobes that was created professionally.

The men and women of Hatfield, Massachusetts, had long-articulated, distinct beliefs about appropriate apparel, which was dictated by both gender and class. In the mid-seventeenth century the colony's leadership had expressed its "utter detestation and dislike that men or women of mean condition should take upon them the garb of gentlemen, by wearing gold or silver lace or buttons, or points at their knees (that is, ribbon or lace fastenings) . . . or women of the same rank" to wear silk or taffeta hoods or scarves, "which though allowable to persons of greater estates or more liberal education, yet we cannot but judge it intolerable in persons of such like condition."[1] Put another way, these men objected to people dressing beyond their station, taking a dim view of people who wore clothing more appropriate for comparatively elite persons. In the 1670s, as King Philip's War threatened New England's English settlements, the Hampshire County court attempted to enforce these sumptuary laws, hauling in some sixty-eight people for various transgressions, including the wearing of silk in a "flaunting manner" and "excess in apparel to the offense of sober people."[2] But it was a fruitless effort; the lure of luxury goods was simply too strong.

Over the course of the eighteenth century a rising tide of consumerism allowed and encouraged women to indulge in whatever fashions they could afford. But how did women learn what those new fashions were? No fashion press was yet available to tell New Englanders what to wear, or what not to. Style did not yet emanate from the minds of influential designers who set fashion for the coming year. Instead, it bubbled up from and was disseminated by consumers, who observed and copied the clothing of members of the cultural elite (who themselves were sometimes picking up cues and ideas from members of the working classes, as is true today, when celebrities and other fashion-forward members of the culture adopt and popularize fashions worn by social outsiders). Fashion information also traveled in correspondence, as upper- and middle-class women sent each other letters describing the newest fashions, emerging trends in color and trim, and other features of stylish dress. In some cases fashion news traveled with itinerant artisans, who made for clients in one community objects that they had produced for discerning clients in another. Merchants also instructed customers on what was most fashionable in other places, although their advice had to be taken with a grain of salt, invested as they were in convincing customers of the desirability of buying the goods they had on hand.

Transmitting information in this way, through a series of face-to-face exchanges, was in keeping with long-standing custom that regularly confined women to personal information networks. The spread of female literacy and the growth of a fashion press (generally associated with the appearance of *Godey's Lady's Book* in the nineteenth century) would in time provide greater numbers of women with direct access to more cosmopolitan information through newspapers, magazines, and books, but in the middle decades of the eighteenth century long series of mediations most often conveyed the fashions of Paris, London, New York, and Boston to the New England countryside.

In eighteenth-century rural Massachusetts, then, and certainly during the years when Rebecca Dickinson was learning her trade, fashion was not dictated to clients by designers or craftswomen. Instead, well-connected clients delivered fashion news to village craftswomen, who copied, interpreted, and tweaked it for local consumers. Gownmakers acted less as initiators of new fashions than as mediators of innovations introduced by others, and they needed the skills to implement variations when their clients described them. In the process, they acquired new knowledge and skills that could then be offered to other local women.

In early America a complex network of artisans satisfied the demand for apparel. At one end of this spectrum lay basic work open to almost anyone, tasks like the making and mending of household linens and everyday clothes, which consumed a great deal of a woman's time in early America. A slightly more skilled range of work was performed by generalists, women known in eighteenth-century western Massachusetts as "tailoresses" (akin to "seamstresses"; i.e., women with the skills to repair and construct simple garments, but not the training to create fitted apparel), who possessed a variety of comparatively modest skills and could be hired to do small jobs. At the upper end of the spectrum lay the specialists: the milliners, gownmakers, and staymakers, who produced fitted clothing for women, as well as the tailors (men, or more rarely, women), who produced fitted clothing for men. They had special training and special tools, and their products reflected more exacting, more demanding work.

Fundamental differences in construction separated the skills required to produce functional garments and the ability to create more complex apparel. "Short gowns" are a good example of the kinds of garments that most women knew how to make. In a basically two-dimensional conception of construction, they were made from a full width of material cut in one piece that stretched from one's waist at the back, over the shoulder, to one's waist in the front, eliminating the need for shoulder seams. An opening was cut to create the neckline, and rectangular pieces of material attached on either side created the sleeves. The garment's final fit wasn't the result of well-cut panels that enabled the fabric to hug the body (as in finer apparel), but rather the addition of either pleats or drawstrings that the wearer used to make the garment fit at the wrists and neckline. A whole genre of apparel was constructed in this way, including men's shirts, women's shifts, and women's skirts. These were the garments that most amateurs knew how to make.

But most women owned at least one gown of higher quality, which fit snugly through the bodice, shoulders, and arms before cascading gracefully to the floor. These garments required particular training and expertise. Unlike the essentially flat garments, gowns required the maker to be able to persuade flat textiles to cling to the rounded surfaces of the body. For example, fitting fabric to reflect the curve of the back required the gownmaking artisan to create a series of seams and darts designed to contract the material, a sophisticated manipulation of matter and geometry. Because many middling women owned only a single good-quality gown and acquired new ones infrequently, many were naturally reluctant to try to replicate this process. Even women whose family fortunes were what we today might call marginal hired experts to cut costly fabric.

For these reasons—to conserve the time and value invested in that material, as well as the time needed to attend to a host of other household chores, and to achieve an appearance reflecting some greater measure of refinement—many women turned to experts in their community for assistance in the construction of even everyday apparel. More fashionable clothing (which comprised a very small part of a working woman's wardrobe, a larger percentage of that of middling women, and a still larger one among women of the rural gentry) demanded levels of skill beyond the fundamentals most women learned.

Although some women possessed a natural talent for clothing construction and then cultivated it through experience, others, like young Rebecca Dickinson, served brief or extended apprenticeships with experienced needlewomen to learn the geometrical relationships that constituted the "art and mystery" (as labor contracts of the day phased it) of clothing construction. If an untrained woman sought to create for herself a fashionable garment, she often used another garment for a "pattern." With practice, she might learn to approximate the work of a trained craftsperson. Proficient amateurs could approach the work of a trained tailor, gownmaker or mantua maker, but truly fashionable garments required a more complex understanding of clothing construction.

In the creation of so-called polite clothing, needleworking artisans, like their woodworking counterparts, needed to understand geometry and how to translate two-dimensional measurements into three-dimensional goods. Clothing construction, like house building, involved more than just skillful hands and a knowledge of one's tools and materials. The best artisans could anticipate how cuts and seams would play out as the desired object took shape and knew how to take advantage of patterns and textures. In essence, needlewomen required a thorough understanding not only of physiology and geometry, but also of materials and motion; that is, of the particularities of the given fabrics as they assumed a fluid, three-dimensional form. With that expertise, a gown maker could use the special properties of expensive materials to best advantage.

In 1747 Waller's *General Description of All Trades* (a book for parents) advised that, for young women aspiring to become gownmakers, "there is little else wanting than a clever Knack at cutting out and fitting, handsome carriage, and a good set of acquaintances."[3] A "clever knack at cutting and fitting"—that is, mastery of those materials and three-dimensional relationships—depended equally on natural talent and proper training under the guidance of an experienced needlewoman. But also essential to success were a "handsome carriage" (an appealing personal appearance—no one would trust a gownmaker who wasn't herself well-dressed and well-groomed) and access to a set of contacts whose financial position and cultural sophistication would make them likely clients. Like the tailor's trade, the modest investment requirements of gownmaking (one need only acquire pins, needles, and an array of irons and shears; clients supplied the cloth themselves) enabled wives, widows, and single women to secure additional income to help support their families, or in some cases to support themselves. As the author of one trade manual assured readers, aspiring gownmakers should possess "a considerable share of taste," but needed "no great capital."[4] These requirements refer to both a familiarity with the "better sort" in one's community and an ability to mimic their appearance, to carry and clothe one's own body in ways that local gentlewomen would admire, and good enough relationships with them to secure their "custom."

When Rebecca Dickinson began her training as an artisan, she surely possessed at least basic needle skills, learned from her mother at home. What the needlewoman offered young Rebecca that her mother could not was an understanding of fabrics; their capabilities and limitations; and the creation, or, more literally the construction, of shape and form: the process by which two-dimensional lengths of costly fabrics were broken up into many pieces and reconfigured into a fitted, yet fluid, three-dimensional garment. As she worked alongside and observed the craftswoman (all the while engaging in useful labor), Rebecca began to learn how to measure clients correctly, how to cut shapes to assemble well-fitting garments, and how to plot their patterns so as to make the most economical use of the clients' expensive material. At the same time, she learned how to manipulate the grains of different fabrics, both bias and straight, and gained proficiency with a wider variety of skills and stitches, as well as the knowledge of how and when to employ them. A skilled artisan could execute the small, tight stitches needed to secure the sturdy seams of a close-fitting bodice as well as the longer, looser ones that allowed skirts to drape and move pleasingly. She knew how to combine sugar and water in just the right proportion to stiffen the material of flounces and frills. The gownmaker knew how to wield her irons to press those materials into their proper positions and possessed the "considerable judgment" required to keep the iron hot enough to perform its work without scorching her clients' expensive fabrics.

As she gained these various competencies, Rebecca Dickinson was mastering one of the most critical skills a gownmaker possessed: the ability to "flatter all complexions and favor all shapes." A skilled craftswoman observed the properties of her materials, the (changing) shape of her client, her client's posture, and even her walk and gestures, to create a garment that would at all times maintain the sought-after, fitted look that allowed for grace and fluidity. In sum, the fledgling gownmaker's career depended on her ability to produce fashionable and attractive gowns for her clients—and to make tacit adjustments when the desired style did not necessarily flatter the eager client.

How long did it take to sharpen such skills? What sort of training did Rebecca Dickinson and women like her complete? Without more systematic and comprehensive sources, it is difficult to determine. Although Rebecca recorded having "gone" somewhere to learn the trade of gownmaking, she noted neither the length of her own apprenticeship nor the durations of the apprenticeships she later directed. But there seems to have been a good deal of variety, probably reflecting a wide range in the rigor and extent of the training offered. Evidence suggests that the Hampshire County adolescents who aspired to the trade completed an apprenticeship of between one and two years.

Because Dickinson's teacher is not identified, we don't know whether she lived at home while she was learning or, as was common, moved in with her mistress during these years. That she used the phrase "went" "to learn the trade of gown making" to refer to her apprenticeship, however, implies the latter. Young Rebecca probably began by accompanying the gownmaker to the homes of clients, observing as the artisan measured clients, cut materials, and constructed garments. She may have begun her sewing by helping to stitch long seams. Perhaps the application of trimming followed. Finally, she would have assisted in the crucial work of fitting garments.

Gradually Rebecca learned the several methods in which gownmakers worked. These artisans did not rely on patterns as we know them today to suggest a garment's form; instead, they based their patterns on previous pieces they had made, taking into account any new requests or styles the client desired. Using the parchment measures as a guide, they worked, both sewing and cutting, toward a finished garment. For the bodice, gownmakers often draped and pinned some thin, malleable material— paper or a light fabric like muslin—over the client's shift and stays. This created a pattern from which to cut the garment's fabric, and, if cloth, provided the eventual lining. Finally, the client and craftswoman would have one last fitting in which the size and location of the back pleats would be determined and sewn in. All in all, it was a time-consuming process that meant much shared time and space between clients and craftswomen.

The fashionable gown that was the result of this cooperation was only one of the work's outcomes. For women like Rebecca Dickinson, the relative intimacy of this work would afford more than financial benefits. Gownmakers gained entry to the private spaces of their community's best houses. And they came to know the leading families. As a young apprentice, Rebecca Dickinson probably journeyed with her employer to the clients' homes, watching carefully as the craftswoman served, pleased, and negotiated with her valued clients. In time Dickinson would become friends with some of her own influential clients, relationships that would lead to opportunities both social and economic. Though she did not yet know it as a young woman just entering her trade, gownmaking skills would indeed prove of "unspeakable advantage."

3

A World at War,
a Soul at Peace

In 1754, when Dickinson was sixteen and possibly still serving her apprenticeship, war broke out once again in Europe and North America. This conflict came to be called the Seven Years War in Europe, but many on the North American mainland would remember it as the French and Indian War. While the war and its consequences were transforming life on several continents, Rebecca Dickinson grew through her teens and into her early twenties. And just as the war's outcome would set the stage for the independence movement of the 1770s, in those years Rebecca Dickinson set out on a course that would shape the trajectory of her life. Her soul stirred by spiritual conviction, she formally embraced the faith of her fathers, joining the growing numbers of women filling the pews of New England's churches. But if she conformed to the religious culture of her day, she did not likewise conform to marital culture. She joined the Hatfield Congregational Church at twenty-three, at the same age, she would later muse, when "other women choose a mate" (June 23, 1793). For Rebecca, a husband was not yet on the horizon; a spiritual marriage would have to suffice.

In the 1740s the British had engaged in yet another conflict with France, the War of the Austrian Succession (1740–1748); King George's War

(1744–1748) was the North American chapter of that longer story. The 1748 Treaty of Aix-la-Chapelle, which ended the war, did not resolve the underlying international tensions. Native Americans and their French allies continued to be of concern to English colonists, antagonism erupting along the western frontiers of Virginia and Pennsylvania. This time, instead of conflict in Europe spreading to North America, it was violence in North America that provoked another international war. After fighting broke out in summer 1754, when Virginia militiamen clashed with French forces in what is now Pennsylvania, Native forces in New England seized the moment to attack forts in western Massachusetts made vulnerable by the colonists' growing sense of security and lapsed vigilance. Hatfield's Israel Williams was commissioned as a commanding officer.[1] Troops were raised, and provisions secured. By summer 1755 some forty-five hundred Massachusetts men were engaged in the war, and by fall the number would be closer to eight thousand. Some of those men were, like Williams, Rebecca Dickinson's Hatfield neighbors.

In August 1755 British forces gathered at the southern end of a lake the French called Lac du Saint Sacrement but the English called Lake George. Their target, the French fort at Crown Point, was strategically important if the British were to squelch the French threat in Canada. Men from Hatfield again found themselves caught up in a global war for dominance. Oliver Partridge, having recently returned from meetings in Albany where he helped negotiate a treaty with the six Iroquois nations, served with the Hampshire militia. Ephraim Williams, a relative of Hatfield's Williams family, led a thousand men into a battle that proved disastrous; he and the troops were ambushed in an engagement remembered as the Bloody Morning Scout. Eventually the campaign shifted to Canada, and the English took Quebec and Montreal. By late 1760 fighting in North America was over. The families of Hampshire County endured their last Indian raid in the fall of that year. The war was not over, but the main theaters of battle had shifted elsewhere, to Europe and the West Indies, and Rebecca Dickinson's mind turned to other matters.

Sitting beneath the pulpit from which Reverend Woodbridge preached, Rebecca joined her congregation's prayers for the protection of their

friends and family at war and for England and its king. But her preoccupations lay closer to home. While England secured the safety of its
empire, Dickinson secured the safety of her soul. Years later, she would
annually recall the date in June 1761 when she underwent her conversion: that is, the pivotal moment in which she believed God stirred her
faith, when she moved from uncertainty to certainty, from hope to
conviction that she would be saved. The conversion made her a full,
formal member of Hatfield's Congregational church, able to participate
in communion.

During Dickinson's youth both religious and political authority had
continued to embrace a Calvinist orthodoxy that perceived of New England as a region in covenant with God, where providence steered events
and salvation came through faith alone, rather than any human effort or
works. Men and women were expected to attend weekly church services, but they did not achieve full church membership until and unless
they had passed through what was called a "conversion experience," a
dramatic, even traumatic series of events in which they both confronted
the full extent of their utterly sinful nature and grasped God's extraordinary mercy.

Dickinson's conversion occurred in 1761, her twenty-third year. Because Hatfield's church records from this period do not survive, we cannot know much about the context of her conversion. Statistically,
throughout New England in the decades before Dickinson's spiritual
rebirth conversion tended to come on the heels of marriage, men and
women alike joining the church a few years into wedded life (and so
typically in their late twenties). At twenty-three, Dickinson experienced
conversion at an age slightly younger than other women. She later came
to interpret the moment almost as a substitute for an earthly marriage,
but of course as a young woman seeking simply to take a step associated
with adulthood more generally, she could not yet know what her future held.

If matrimony did not prompt Dickinson's own experience, then
what did? The proportion of women joining the Congregational church
throughout New England was on the rise, the membership becoming
ever more female as demographic and cultural forces reshaping the role
of the church in the community heightened the importance of women

to the church and of the church to women. So in part, Dickinson was participating in a broad historical trend. But more specifically, her conversion might have been the product of a revival of religious enthusiasm that the members of the Hatfield church experienced in the winter of 1758 (itself perhaps linked to the stress of the global war unfolding around them). Many conversion narratives note a long period of indifference to matters of faith before a person begins to become aware of his or her spiritual shortcomings and grows dissatisfied with them; perhaps twenty-year-old Rebecca first began seriously questioning the state of her own soul during the 1758 revival (another period of religious enthusiasm in the area, stretching from 1762 into 1764, probably also buoyed her growing faith). If she followed the normal pattern, in these years she would have begun paying closer attention to Reverend Woodbridge's weekly sermons, perhaps seeking out readings on religious matters and talking more intently with others about their own spiritual lives. She would begin behaving more like those who believed themselves to be saved. Finally, she would have at last experienced the profound spiritual epiphany—something many believers described as a prolonged interior plunge into melancholy and helplessness as they scrutinized the true nature of their faith, followed by the acute pangs of spiritual death and eventual rebirth—that in the end affirmed her commitment to God and God's commitment to her.

Dickinson's conversion narrative—the testimony she was expected to give, articulating the progress of her conversion in such a way that her minister would find it convincing—has not survived. But it probably resembled those filed not long thereafter by other members of Hatfield's church. The men and women who shared Dickinson's place in the church were expected to assert their belief in "one, only, the living & true God, the creator and governor of all things, existing in three persons in one godhead, that each person in the godhead is equally and eternally possessed of all perfection, & worthy of supreme adoration & obedience," and that the Old and New Testaments were the faith's foundation. They agreed that man was at first sinless and placed under a "covenant of works" (in which his salvation was linked to his actions), but then he sinned, and having lost his innocence, "involved himself & his offspring in guilt & misery." Only "salvation . . . by Christ Jesus alone" could restore people's hopes, believers asserted; only through the "sufferings of Christ," and not by any of their own efforts, did the elect gain heaven. Christ's death, resurrection, and ascension into heaven; God's election of the saved into everlasting life; the role of grace; the inevitability of judgment day—to these and other Calvinist doctrines Rebecca would have given her "full assent and consent." A record of the required oath of confirmation preserved among Lyman's records reads:

> You do, now in the presence of God and this congregation, avouch the Lord Jehovah, Father Son and Holy Ghost to be your God, You give yourself to him forever, & promise to serve him with your body and spirit which are his. You engage by his grace to resign yourself to his will forever. You promise to give your infant seed to him and to train them up in the nurture and admonition of the Lord. You covenant to walk blamelessly in all the ordinances of Gods word and to submit yourself to the watch, instruction and discipline of the Church of Christ in this place. Sensible that it is an awful thing to transact with the living god thus you covenant.

Dickinson probably made this same affirmation, or something very similar, and would for the rest of her life observe her spiritual birthday— "the day which I was born of God or all my hopes of heaven are a delusion" (see, e.g., June 23, 1793)—annually.

Yet that sense of certainty that a parishioner possessed at the moment of his or her conversion could not be expected to persist day in and day out. Everyone had moments, even periods, of doubt, and Dickinson was no different. Despite her general confidence that "God in a wonderful manner showed me a glimpse of his glory as it is recorded in the book of life," Dickinson regularly had "some thoughts as [to] whether" she "was of God." She remarked on one occasion what a "sad day" it would be for her, or for those who have "cheated themselves out of the holy religion of Jesus Christ by the way of the new birth," by "thinking that I was born of God when my soul was a stranger to him" (July 27, 1788). Over the whole of her life she never stopped questioning her conversion. But at the same time, the prospect that she was "of God" provided tremendous comfort as the years rolled by and she did not add the joys of family life to her spiritual happiness. A quarter-century later she reflected on "how great the consolations of religion have been" in helping her cope with life alone (September 2, 1787).

Two years after Dickinson delivered her spiritual testimony, political resolution was achieved in the world war that had marked so much of her young adulthood. In 1763 the warring nations of Great Britain, France, and Spain signed the Treaty of Paris, bringing to a close years of violent conflict and along the way reconfiguring the globe. Britain had at last evicted France from Canada and acquired that nation's possessions in Dominica, Grenada, Saint Vincent and the Grenadines, and Tobago. From Spain, Britain acquired east Florida, which was the peninsula, and west Florida, which ran west along the Gulf Coast from Pensacola to Baton Rouge. Peace formally descended on Dickinson's Hatfield once more. The next decade witnessed a local boom. With the French threat removed, settlements at the edge of Britain's empire flourished. Yet though few were foresighted enough to predict it, long-standing patterns of influence and authority—between colony and empire, and among local elites—became increasingly strained. More immediately observable was that in this newfound atmosphere of safety, towns blossomed, spread, and sprouted up as young families in search of new opportunities looked westward, prompting a municipal meiosis that for Hatfield would spur growth in Whately and Williamsburg.

For her own part, in these years Rebecca Dickinson became an increasingly established craftswoman. She had completed her apprenticeship and begun seeking work around the county. Authors of eighteenth-century trade manuals agreed that a "good set of acquaintances"—that is, access to an affluent clientele—was essential if one was to succeed at gownmaking. One such writer advised that "young women ought, perhaps, rarely to be apprenticed to this trade unless their friends can, at the end of the term, place them in a reputable way of business, and can command such connections as shall, with industry, secure their success."[2] It appears that Dickinson had in fact cultivated such a network as she entered her thirties. She certainly traveled in the right circles. Her clients included Partridges, Porters, and other family members of the "River God"

families. In her diary she mentioned having dined with Israel Williams—
a man she would call a "kind friend" who made her "welcome [to] his
house and table"—and considered his daughters Elizabeth and Lucretia,
presumably her clients, "old friends" (August 2 and 5, 1787, and January
[], 1788).

By the war's end Rebecca Dickinson was working regularly in Hatfield as well as the nearby communities of Hadley and Whately, Amherst
and Williamsburg. She was also able to widen her range of influence
without having to travel. On occasion clients came to her via the traffic
that normally passed through the homes of the rural gentry, like the Porter
and Phelps families' large Hadley farm, Forty Acres, across the river.
Elizabeth Porter Phelps recorded that on one such occasion,

> in the eve Miss Rebeckah Dickinson came here to make a pair of stays
> for my mother and alter a gown. Tuesday Mrs Crouch and Moses
> Kellogg's wife came here—just at night Polly came to do some busi-
> ness with Miss Rebeckah. . . . I went [into town] returned that night
> found Rebeckah gone home. Friday she came over again—in the after-
> noon called upon us Esq. Porter with his wife soon left us—Gideon
> Warner's wife came for a visit. Just at night came up Mrs Porter and
> Mrs Colt, Polly and Nabby all for huckleberrying—presently up came
> Miss Pen [Penelope Williams] to see Miss Rebeckah—this day Miss
> Pen set out for home for Pomfret. Sat Miss Rebeckah went home soon
> after dinner.[3]

Some women clearly made it a point to come up to the Phelps house
while Dickinson was there, as Polly Porter and Penelope Williams had.
But it is also possible that Mrs. Crouch, Mary Sheldon Kellogg, and
Mary Parsons Warner, as well as Mrs. Porter and Mrs. Colt, also consulted with gownmaker Dickinson while visiting. They may at the very
least have seized the opportunity to secure a place on her calendar.
Penelope Williams then carried the fruits of Dickinson's labors back to
her home in Pomfret, Connecticut—where friends and neighbors who
admired the craftswoman's work might perhaps become clients themselves; "Mrs. Colt," another visitor from out of town, may have done
likewise.

Dickinson subsequently created the gowns that Phelps wore to weddings of friends and family. Weddings frequently followed Dickinson's trips to the Phelps home. On one occasion, following a visit from Dickinson, Phelps recorded that she and her husband had that afternoon attended the wedding of Mr. Chester Williams and Loice Dickinson of Hatfield. "Thursday," Phelps continued, "Miss Pen was married to Sam'll Gaylord, Timothy Eastman to Anna Smith, Eaneas Smith to Mary Dickinson, Hannah Montague to one Isaiah Carrier of Belchertown— so much for one day at Hadley."[4] Similarly, Dickinson labored at the Phelps home for the better part of the week of May 15, 1768, just prior to Elizabeth and Charles Phelps's departure for Boston during the spring elections, suggesting that she helped the Phelpses prepare to socialize in fashionable Boston circles as well.

Despite the status of these well-heeled clients and the quality of the garments she made for them, Dickinson's day-to-day work was probably more routine. While wealthy women bought fashionable fabrics and converted them into stylish garments, a gownmaker's work most of the time was less glamorous. Most days involved "making over" and "altering" clothing as families tried to make their existing wardrobes last as long as possible. Alterations were important, particularly so during periods of political and economic turmoil when commerce was necessarily disrupted, as it had been during the recent years of warfare. Hints in Dickinson's later diary suggest that she enjoyed seeing the results of her work; the look of attractive clothing as it transformed the bodies of her clients; and the prospect of numerous beautiful gowns gathered together, silks glittering in candlelight as her customers assembled for weddings and other festivities. But her daily work was surely less thrilling. And so she found other outlets for her skill and creativity.

Alongside the sewing Dickinson did in the course of her trade was needlework undertaken for personal satisfaction. None of the garments she created over the course of her long career is known to survive (gownmakers did not begin to stitch labels into their products until the midnineteenth century, so the makers of very few extant eighteenth-century gowns are known), but today some embroidered bed hangings survive to document Dickinson's skill and style.[5] Indeed, these works are so stunning and unusual that they offer evidence of real artistic sensibilities.

Dickinson's personality is partially revealed in several surviving pieces of crewelwork that capture her distinctive style. Crewel embroidery was enormously popular among New England's leading families. Well-bred wives and daughters deployed finely spun and dyed worsted wool threads, called crewels, across broad surfaces to create complex and colorful designs, giving leading families objects of beauty while demonstrating the talent, education, and taste of these women. In the eighteenth-century Connecticut River Valley, crewelwork was a necessary marker of elite status. Beds and bed hangings were objects of tremendous importance, stationed as they were in parlors and other public rooms, in view of family, friends, and guests, who were invited to appreciate the enormous amounts of time and of money expended on these textiles.

Bed hangings also helped display and advance a family's status, crewelwork hangings particularly so because they also affirmed that a woman had not only the financial means to acquire the materials but also the extraordinary amount of leisure time needed to make them. By the third quarter of the eighteenth century, enclosing the bed in curtains had become a popular choice, as the broad lengths of fabric conferred both warmth and privacy. By the 1770s in some towns as many as half of the households had at least one bed so enclosed, some even more. Using curtains entirely embellished by hand, rather than patterned or plain fabric, increased the impact of these important objects. Having appeared as early as the 1740s, bed hangings ornamented with crewelwork had become essential to the fashionable home. A complete set contained a "tester" (or roof), a headcloth (which hung where the headboard sits today), and four curtains. Often a set of valences was produced as well. Crewels were imported from England and purchased at shops. In Hatfield this probably meant a shop in town or in nearby Northampton, although Dickinson could have asked a friend to buy them on her behalf in Boston, as shopping by proxy was a common practice in colonial America.

Although some surviving pieces of crewelwork are done in a colorful array of threads, Dickinson's surviving pieces have panels worked almost wholly in shades of indigo. On one example, vines climb from the bottom to the top, with carnations, clover, and other flowers rendered in shades of blue. One observer of these embroideries notes the "nice sense of proportion" in Dickinson's designs, as well as her feel for color and design. The workmanship was superb as well: Dickinson's stitches were "so short and worked so closely" that she could squeeze together four bands of color in less than an inch, "interlocking them so smoothly that the transition from one shade to another is hard to see."[6]

One piece of crewelwork (shown on the cover of this volume) bearing the date 1765 is the most striking—and most cryptic—of her surviving work. As mysterious in its design as it is puzzling in its inscription, this headcloth was intended to enclose the head of the bed, its design ornamenting the interior. Unlike her other work, in which the vines and flowers typical of the era cascade along expanses of cloth, here, beneath a large and weighty fleur-de-lis, sits a large, full-rigged sailing ship, displayed beneath an arch of grape vines and above a three-scalloped line that suggests the ocean waves. This maritime imagery is surprising, because these elements do not commonly occur in the design vocabulary of eighteenth-century New England crewelwork. It is especially surprising in work by the landlocked Rebecca Dickinson, who so far as is known never saw an oceangoing vessel. To be sure, the literature with which she was most familiar—the Bible—included many references to sailing ships. Her journal entries contain phrases like "may my soul . . . always be in the trade wind for heaven" and "may my ship be richly laden with grace," but these lines reflect her familiarity with scripture, rather than real encounters with ships, sails, and docks (August [2], 1787). Why she chose this scene to depict in crewel is unknown.

Dickinson's ship also contains puzzles within puzzles. The fleur-de-lis so prominently incorporated into the design—a traditional symbol of the French monarchy, although it hardly seems likely that this association would be appealing to an English citizen in the 1760s—also marked north on early maps. Could this be its meaning here? Could she have been looking at a map for her inspiration? Also strange, the vessel appears to be sailing in two directions. A long angled element on the left is the bowsprit, with two of its stays leading up to the first mast, the foremast; the small, square sail toward the aft would then be a spanker sail (and perhaps the width of the ship to the viewer's right is an effort to capture the back cabin). The sails should billow in the direction the ship is headed; here, they billow in the opposite direction. The ship seems headed sternway (that is, backward)—an unlikely motion to wish to capture in thread.[7] Was the mistake her own, or was she copying a flawed print source, an engraving, map, or woodcut that made the same error? The answers to these questions also are not known.

To compound the artifact's mystery, an unexplained inscription is worked above the ship in cross stitch: F O A W T WA C O G V I U S A. Below these letters are two characters, M and D. Next, Dickinson stitched in her own name, "Rebekah Dickinson." She collaborated on this project with someone named Polly Wright, who also signed the work here ("Polly" is a nickname for "Mary," and both Mary and Wright are common names in eighteenth-century western Massachusetts, which makes identifying this woman difficult). Below her name are two additional characters, L and D, and below that the year "1765" (though the latter was perhaps rendered by another hand). If the imagery here is surprising, the series of letters is downright baffling. Was the significance of the inscription obvious to eighteenth-century observers, who all noticed the sailing ship and knew in an instant the poem or Bible verse she intended to reference? Or was it a riddle even then, a puzzle that the amused creators could enjoy watching their perplexed friends and relatives attempt to solve?

The answer to these questions may never be known, and this fact reminds us of the limits of the historical enterprise. For all that we can learn about Rebecca Dickinson from her own, very intimate diary, she still took plenty of secrets to her grave. For some reason, in an era that witnessed global warfare and not long after she underwent a profound religious experience, Rebecca Dickinson designed and executed this stunning and unusual headcloth. Whatever its meaning, this careful and inventive artwork reminds us that these skills proved valuable to her in more ways than one. It hints at both a commitment to craftsmanship and an expression of creativity, which rendered her talents a source of pride and an outlet for her artistic sensibilities.

4

The Unraveling

The year that Dickinson made the bed hangings—1765—is also the year that historians today often use to mark the beginning of the American Revolution. In that year debate over new tax policies erupted into mass political protest. Soon "no taxation without representation" became a rallying cry for Americans who saw dark implications in England's new revenue schemes. The inhabitants of Britain's North American colonies had only just celebrated their long-awaited victory over France when the cloth of empire began to fray and then unravel. And for twenty-seven-year-old Rebecca Dickinson—an artisan whose livelihood was threatened by the increasing public upheaval, entwining her ability to work and her need to do so as an unmarried woman with larger developments in imperial policy—it wasn't just the political situation that seemed to be tearing people apart. As the decade wore on, her own future seemed to be coming undone as well.

The victory over France, welcome though it was, had left England with a massive debt; with more territory to manage in North America, costs were also increasing. People in England found their taxes rising. Unrest mounted, and British administrators decided that the residents of the colonies should shoulder a larger portion of the collective burden. To cover the greater expense associated with its expanding empire, and namely costs associated with the roughly 10,000 troops needed to help protect British claims in North America, Parliament passed "An act for granting and applying certain stamp duties, and other duties in the British colonies and plantations in America," or "Stamp Act," in 1765, which would raise money through a series of taxes on paper items. Magazines, newspapers, licenses and legal documents, among other things (even playing cards), would all now have to carry the revenue stamp. Although stamp taxes in and of themselves were nothing new, some members of the colonial leadership, accustomed to controlling taxation themselves, bristled at what seemed a worrisome new precedent in the form of taxes levied in Britain on colonists abroad. In Massachusetts, Bostonians were particularly outraged. There, in an attempt to discourage consumption of fashionable but expensive items imported from Britain, about fifty leading men signed an "agreement to suppress extravagance and promote frugality," while some artisans began emphasizing the local nature of their wares, in effect urging people to "buy American." These were not the first efforts to organize resistance to imported goods—even before the Stamp Act, Bostonians had gathered together to pledge mutual nonconsumption of certain imports to boost the local economy—but in the context of the debate over tax policy, such actions took on new political overtones. Riots large and small erupted, none more stunning than the attack in August 1765 on the mansion of Lieutenant Governor Thomas Hutchinson, in which crowds methodically smashed the household's furniture, dismantled parts of the building's interior and cupola, and destroyed Hutchinson's papers. A group emerged to stoke the fires of dissent, calling itself the Sons of Liberty.

In October, in New York's City Hall, a formal meeting, or "congress," was held with delegates from nine concerned colonies, including Massachusetts, who gathered to plan a coordinated response to the proposed taxes. Rebecca Dickinson knew one of the men her colony sent. Hatfield's Oliver Partridge traveled to New York to represent Massachusetts in this debate over how best to react to these new and unwelcome policies. He was appointed to the delegation in part because the governor believed that he was a "prudent and discreet" man who would "never consent to any undutiful or improper application to the government of Great Britain."[1] After twelve days of deliberation, the Stamp Act congress issued a document, "Declaration of Rights and Grievances," in which the representatives asserted their belief that Parliament lacked the right to levy such a tax, as the colonies were not represented there. Partridge's Hatfield neighbors probably largely approved of this outcome. According to several historical accounts, the Stamp Act—both its implementation and repeal—attracted scant attention in western Massachusetts, although the comparative quiet should not be mistaken for lack of interest. To be sure, little occurred in the way of the dramatic public protests that helped secure the act's repeal, in part because the region's leadership also opposed the Stamp Act, so in Hatfield and its environs there were not the obvious targets of frustration that attracted unruly attention elsewhere.[2] Although we do not know what Rebecca Dickinson made of the talk once Partridge returned home and described events in New York, or just when news of the repeal reached her ears, across the river in Hadley, Josiah Pierce noted in the pages of his diary that "the repeal of the burdensome Stamp Act laid upon the American colonies by British Parliament . . . was [passed] and assented to by the king 18th March 1766 to take place 2nd May 1766."[3]

Rebecca Dickinson may have given little thought to the Stamp Act; it is easy to imagine the goods Partridge carried home from New York generating at least as much excitement in some Hatfield quarters as whatever news he conveyed of the deliberations there. Things were going well for her, an active craftswoman with a thriving circle of clients. But soon another attempt to raise revenue, the 1767 Townshend duties, disrupted that calm. Parliament, having been defeated in its aim to raise revenue with stamps, tried again with a set of duties proposed by the chancellor of the exchequer (akin in the United States today to the secretary of the treasury), Charles Townshend. The fairly modest sums anticipated to be collected would be applied to the cost of the royal payroll (including the salaries of colonial governors and judges, which some Americans correctly understood as a worrisome effort to shift the loyalties of these important officials away from the colonial assemblies to whom they had long looked for their incomes). The outcry over the Stamp Act had suggested to some imperial administrators that although the colonists objected to a direct tax (which the stamp tax was), they would accept duties on imported goods as a legitimate source of government revenue. So Townshend proposed new taxes on paper, paint, lead, glass, and tea. But Townshend misjudged the American mood. This plan proved no more popular than the one before it. Throughout the colonies, objections arose loud and fast.

Almost immediately opponents of the new policy concluded that British administrators might be more attentive to their complaints if the men and women closer to home felt some pain in their own wallets. They also realized that the colonies' dependence on imported goods would always be a problem. The solution? A boycott. They would show England the importance of the American market while at the same time encouraging American manufactures, and so decrease their dependence and indebtedness. In October 1767, in a meeting at Boston's Faneuil Hall, Bostonians asserted that "the excessive use of foreign superfluities" has been "the chief cause of the present distressed state of this town." They voted to forego the use of a long list of imported goods, including everything from carriages to loaf sugar. People should do without imported clocks and watches and fine dishes. Using snuff, mustard, malt liquors, and English cheese was discouraged. Much of the list named elements of finer wardrobes: men's and women's shoes, hats, and ready-made apparel would be off-limits, as would gold and silver thread and lace and gold and silver buttons. Fine fabrics, including velvets, silks, lawns, cambrics, and broadcloths that cost more than ten shillings per yard, should all be avoided if the colonists were to make their point.

In August 1768, some sixty Boston merchants drafted a nonimportation agreement: as of January 1, 1769, and for one year, they would stop importing English goods (in the end, only sixteen merchants and shopkeepers would fail to join this effort). Most of the merchants who signed these trade agreements were men, but women also ran shops and imported goods and so also found themselves having to take a side in these debates. Seven businesswomen signed on to the 1768 "List of the Subscription of those *Gentlemen* [emphasis added] immediately concerned in importing goods from Great Britain" while in July 1769, some ninety-five men and eight women joined another "Non-Consumption Agreement."[4] For women who for whatever reason did not comply, life as an outlier could get tough. In Boston, shopkeeping sisters Ame and Elizabeth Cumings, who chose their livelihood over the protest, quickly found themselves ostracized by some (though cheered by others), while

Jane Eustis—who had signed one agreement but not another—suffered enough persecution in the court of public opinion that she published a front-page notice in the November 6, 1769, *Boston Gazette* announcing that she had decided to give up altogether and sail for England.

For a boycott to work, the effort had to involve more than just politicians, merchants, and shopkeepers—it required the participation of the thousands of women who did their households' shopping. Targeted efforts sought to engage the political commitment of women as well as men. As part of an attempt to promote American-made cloth over that imported from abroad, some New England women (more than sixteen hundred between 1768 and 1770) joined spinning bees, lugging their spinning wheels to collective political gatherings that produced home-grown skeins of linen yarn to be woven into cloth. America, these women asserted, need not rely on imported wares; if they had to, they could, and would, produce their own fabric. As they gathered together, the spinners' gesture was as much religious as it was political, and offset rowdiness with reserve. That is, while men's political action often involved taking to the streets, spinning bees were held at the houses of ministers, who then received the work, enabling participants to display faith and patriotism at the same time. A combination of religious expression, political theater, and labor with real impact, these events aimed to draw both sexes into the protest activity. No such gatherings took place in Reverend Woodbridge's Hatfield; most such events were held in and around Boston. But Hatfield women may well have heard firsthand about the May 1769 gathering just downriver in East Windsor, Connecticut, where many in town had family and friends, or the August 1769 meeting that drew fifty-five women in Brookfield, forty miles to the east, along the road to Boston. Women everywhere were drawn into the campaign. As newspapers shared and applauded news of these events, they infused the protest movement with feminine skill, virtue, and resolve.

Women's support was sought in other ways as well. "Address to the Ladies," published in the November 16, 1767, *Boston Post-Boy & Advertiser*—in the form of a poem—urged the "young ladies in town, and those that live round" to cast aside imported brocades and "wear none but your own country linen," for "once it is known this is much

wore in town, / One and all will cry out, 'tis the fashion!" In order to establish manufacturing independence from England, female readers were
encouraged not to marry men who wore cloth from London factories
and to "love your country much better than fine things" by trading their
hair ribbons for "twine string."

As lighthearted as this verse is, for a self-supporting gownmaker like
Rebecca Dickinson, this development in the political sphere was no
laughing matter. Would her clients really exchange imported fabrics for
"country linen" and homespun cloth and quit buying the brocades, silks,
and ribbons that formed the foundation of her livelihood? The ban on
imported ready-made apparel may have been welcome, because for
women in the clothing trades it eliminated one source of competition,
but would her customers really eschew gold and silver thread, lace, and
buttons? Would they stop buying expensive broadcloths and forego velvets and silks? Dickinson knew that the clients she served were unlikely
to start making and wearing garments out of homespun, as the poet envisioned (they certainly weren't about to start wearing twine in their
hair), but she had every reason to fear that they might well try to make
do with the clothing they already owned and hold off on having anything new made until this latest crisis blew over. The financial implications for self-supporting craftswomen like Dickinson were considerable.

Watching closely the actions of her neighbors and friends, Dickinson
might have been relieved when Hatfield on the whole gave a cool response to Boston's attempts to stir her town's emotions. Passed in June,
the Townshend duties took effect on November 20, 1767. A series of
"Letters from a Farmer in Pennsylvania," written by a Philadelphia law-
yer named John Dickinson, began appearing in the Boston papers, fan-
ning the flames of dissent. In January 1768 the Massachusetts House of
Representatives petitioned King George to repeal the act and in February circulated letters to the leadership of other colonies suggesting they
do likewise. The letter asserted that the Townshend Acts were unconstitutional, and that colonies could only rightly be taxed by their own
assemblies. When Lord Hillsborough, secretary of state for the colonies,
learned of the action, he demanded that the Massachusetts assembly re-
scind the letter. But the assembly refused to comply in a 92–17 vote.
Hatfield's own representative, Israel Williams—whose political and eco-

nomic ties to the imperial leadership provided strong motivation to protect the status quo (and whose daughters were surely among Dickinson's most important customers)—was one of the soon-to-be infamous
seventeen "rescinders." But the ninety-two carried the day, and in response, an angry Governor Francis Bernard dissolved the body.

With the American Customs Board now housed in Boston (another
product of recent innovations in imperial management, this body would
help collect the hated duties), trouble was bound to erupt there, and it
soon did. Troops had been requested to help keep order, and when word
got out that they were en route, Boston's town leaders decided to convene an ad hoc meeting of representatives from as many towns as would
send someone to coordinate some joint response to the deepening political crisis. But again, when Hatfield received this invitation, the town's
response, shaped by Oliver Partridge and Israel Williams, was critical
of the whole idea. On September 22, when the townsmen met to discuss their reply, the letter from Boston was read aloud: Would the town
send anyone to a convention of towns? The answer was a firm "no."
Hatfield voters appointed a committee to draft a reply on behalf of the
town, which declared that Hatfield did not share Boston's concerns.
"We are not sensible," the letter reported, "that the state of America is
so alarming, or the state of this province is materially different from what
they were a few months since, as to render the measure you propose either
salutary [i.e., beneficial] or necessary."[5] Parliament's effort to raise revenue seemed to the good people of Hatfield a foregone conclusion, and
objections had already been raised appropriately through formal petitions.
The proposed meeting, they felt, would do more harm than good.

Furthermore, Hatfield questioned Boston's fears about troops being
stationed there. These men, settled as they were at the edge of British
settlement in a town with a long history of borderlands warfare, concluded that the soldiers could well be dispatched for the colony's protection should war break out again. If Bostonians were worried that the
king intended to turn his troops on his own subjects, maybe (they im-
plied) it was warranted: "If by any sudden excursions or insurrections
of some inconsiderate people the king has been induced to think [the
troops] a necessary check upon you, we hope that you will by your loyalty and quiet behavior soon convince his majesty and the world" that

troops were unnecessary. The statement did not mince words. "We are sensible," the town affirmed, that "the colonies labor under many difficulties and we greatly fear what the consequences of the disputes with our mother country will prove; however, we are far from thinking the measures you are pursuing have any tendency to deliver the good people of this Province, but on the contrary immerse them in greater, after all we should hope (were it not for your present attempt attended with a bad complexion) we might soon have deliverance from our present troubles and things restored as at the first."

Hatfield's response suggested that imperial administrators had responded appropriately to the concerns raised, and now "our duty is to wait with patience . . . unless we are determined to take the alternative: how far passion and disappointment and private resentment may influence any to hurry their neighbors into such mad and desperate measures we don't know but pray God to prevent." Indeed, "in our opinion the measures the town of Boston are pursuing and proposing unto us and the people of this province to unite in are unconstitutional, illegal, and wholly unjustifiable." The letter closed with the townsmen declaring "our loyalty to his present majesty, and fidelity to our country, and that it is our firm resolution, to the utmost of our power, to maintain and defend our rights in every prudent and reasonable way, as far as consistent with our duty to God and the King."

This statement reverberated throughout the colony, appearing in the October 6 *Massachusetts Gazette* and the October 11 *Essex Gazette* (published in Salem, Massachusetts). It even made the international news when the *Massachusetts Gazette* article was reprinted in the *London Magazine*. The Hatfield letter was among sixty documents on American affairs that Lord North presented to the House of Commons in November 1768. Readers in England must have been pleased to learn that in its sentiments, Hatfield was in step with its neighbors. Although some Hampshire County towns may have sympathized at least in part with Boston's concerns, only three of forty-one sent delegates to the September 1768 convention, which drew representatives from some ninety other Massachusetts towns.

Hatfield—like the other places that took a skeptical stance on the protest movement—had good reason to respond with caution, so thoroughly colored as it was by the influence of Israel Williams and his kin and peers. But political winds began to blow in a new direction, and in 1768 and 1769 there was a subtle shifting of the tides as consensus based on opposition to the Stamp Act was replaced by division over the Townshend duties. Importantly, the established gentry leadership, in a series of crisis moments, lost the confidence of their western Massachusetts communities as they seemed to abandon the public good in favor of more personal interests, introducing fissures that weakened long-standing political structures. When the nonimportation movement took hold in Massachusetts, Israel Williams opted not to participate. At the May 1769 election for the General Court, he failed to receive an outright majority of votes cast, only a plurality. Even though a majority was technically necessary, the moderator (friend Oliver Partridge) ruled that a plurality would do. So Williams prevailed. But change was in the air. Williams was not only a "rescinder"; he had also, by violating the nonimportation agreements, put his private interests before those of the community. It was a breach of the public trust that would not be overlooked. (For his part, Williams was undeterred: the *Boston Evening Post*'s February 26, 1770, edition carried a list of the "names of those who *audaciously* continue to counteract the *united Sentiments* of the Body of Merchants throughout North America, by importing British goods," and only two merchants beyond Boston were named: one in Marlborough, the other "Israel Williams, Esq., & Son, Traders in the Town of Hatfield.")

Because women—the invitation to boycott notwithstanding—were not welcome participants in any formal political discussion, it is often difficult to reconstruct their feelings about public affairs. Though for the most part women were held at arm's length from these policy controversies, they nevertheless formed strong opinions about the issues under discussion. Certainly these events generated heated debate, among women as much as men. Nights like the one that kept Hatfield schoolteacher Jonathan Judd Jr. and Lois Dickinson up until 2:00 AM "discoursing" on "political facts" were surely not as unusual as we today sometimes assume.[6] Had Dickinson not destroyed her earlier diaries, we might know how she felt about the dramatic events that gradually constituted Hatfield's revolution. What we do know is often captured in sideways glimpses, rather than direct evidence, and demands some inference, even speculation. While many craftsmen embraced the boycotts as an opportunity to cut foreign competition, as a gownmaker, Rebecca Dickinson may well have been apprehensive about the movement and likely greeted calls like "Address to the Ladies" with some alarm. But fortunately for her, most of her closest clientele appear to have remained aloof from these appeals. The memorandum book of Elizabeth Porter (soon Phelps), for example, notes several visits from Dickinson in these months, during which the craftswoman created gowns from now-suspect fabrics. On July 17, 1768, Porter recorded in her diary having Dickinson come to make a gown made of dark calico, an imported cotton. And later, in the nonimportation pact's waning days (though the nonimportation agreement was set to expire on January 1, 1770, in spring of 1770 some Boston merchants were busily urging its extension), as Elizabeth Porter prepared to marry Charles Phelps, Rebecca Dickinson again created apparel in the imported cloth selected by her wealthy clients. An entry dated June 3, 1770, confirms that Porter apparently felt no hesitation in choosing brown ducape—a heavy fabric of corded silk that was stiff but still soft to the touch, especially fashionable that year—for her own gown. A light brown taffeta gown (another imported silk) would flatter Phelps's attendant Dolly Phelps, her fiancé's sister. Just four months earlier, in Boston, several hundred "mistresses of families" had pledged to support the resolutions made by that city's merchants and abstain from the drinking of tea, to help "save this abused country from ruin and slavery" (a gesture followed by a similar pledge from more than one hundred "daughters" of "patriots," who swore off foreign tea "in hopes to frustrate a plan that tends to deprive the whole community of their *all* that is valuable in life").[7] But at least by June, Phelps, who had probably bought her fabric earlier that spring, was apparently unmoved by calls to join in the protest. Was Dickinson nervous about her client's politically charged choices? Disappointed? Relieved? We cannot know, but she most certainly felt some impact from these events on her own pocketbook, and her response to them could not have been a simple one.

While colonists responded to both the Townshend duties and the ensuing protest, events on the ground in Boston continued to strain imperial relations. On October 1, 1768, British soldiers, or "regulars," had begun arriving in Boston, sent at Governor Bernard's request in the wake of the unrest that accompanied the Townshend duties. But Bernard would not remain to witness the consequences, having returned to England after radicals published letters in which, among other things, he recommended changes to the Massachusetts charter (the document on which the colony's government rested) intended to make the unruly colonial council more compliant. Boston erupted in celebration at Bernard's departure; Thomas Hutchinson would now preside over deteriorating conditions there. Uneasiness between colonists and the soldiers had emerged quickly and grew over the ensuing months. Bostonians were angry about the various economic and social disruptions caused by the presence of troops in the city and fearful about implications for the future.

In time a number of conflicts—some petty, some not—arose, and bloodshed seemed increasingly inevitable. In early March 1770 an argument on King Street between soldiers and townsmen—tension grounded in smoldering antagonism about work (soldiers had been moonlighting at other part-time jobs in their off hours, and Bostonians resented the competition as much as they did their police presence) was sparked by several days of escalating disputes between soldiers and citizens over money, all deeply colored by larger political objections—finally exploded as people, some carrying clubs and sticks and others throwing snowballs, gathered to insult and taunt the guards near the Customs House. In the tumult shots were fired. The clash ended in the deaths of five civilians. After the silversmith (and activist) Paul Revere produced an engraving that depicted soldiers firing into an unarmed crowd, this riot on King Street came to be called the "Boston Massacre."

The very day that blood spilled on Boston cobblestones, across the ocean, in response to the colonial outcry, Lord Frederick North (the successor to Townshend, now dead; by 1770 North was Great Britain's prime minister) proposed that the hated Townshend duties be repealed—with one exception. The tax on tea would be retained, as a gesture to affirm Parliament's right to tax the colonies in this way.

In hindsight, the leaders of revolt in Massachusetts would recall the King Street riot as a turning point in the colony's readiness for rebellion, but at that point no one was yet talking about any movement for political independence. Most Hatfielders probably followed these developments with interest, even alarm, but at some distance, as some local controversies seemed more immediate. In the late 1760s Hatfield, like many towns now almost a century old, was experiencing growing pains. As the population became denser in outlying areas farthest from town centers, and in the wake of France's defeat, these communities within communities began petitioning to become towns of their own. Both Whatley (where Rebecca's father and brother had land) and Williamsburg (perhaps named after Williams himself, and another place where the Dickinson family had an interest as property holders) became new towns in 1771.

For Dickinson, these were exciting years on a more personal front as well, years during which she contemplated independence of another kind. She turned thirty during the Townshend Act crisis and was already older than most yet-unmarried women, and she was not getting any younger. About this time a pivotal occurrence set her life on its own special course. Our insight into these events is indirect at best, but we get a small glimpse into one important chapter in her romantic life when, almost twenty years later, she chronicled the events of an evening spent in the home of her sister Miriam. The usual boarders, Patty Church and schoolteacher Isaac Curson, were present, as was the blacksmith, Jesse Billings. Billings, she wrote, "put those sad thoughts into my mind." She returned home and "lighted no candle, for the darkness of my mind was beyond the darkest dungeon. There was no hope for me in the things of time" (August 12, 1787). She recorded that she "awoke after a strange dream" involving Billings. "I thought that I was on a journey with Jesse Billings' mare, with one rein of my bridle broken, myself lost—entangled among horses, where I had to lead the creature rather than have any service from her. My desire was to go to meeting, but [I] was not able to find the way. The first of my thoughts this morning was 'be still and know that I am god,' but the truth of those words has been disputed by me a great many times this day" (August [], 1787).

Dickinson woke up and went straight to her diary. It was not yet 8:00 in the morning. "So great a mystery I am to myself," she wrote. "The few days and months past," she mused, she had felt "quiet under the happy shade of God's government," but "the last night" she couldn't help but "rebel." The "prosperity of the wicked and my own wicked heart," she moaned, "with the smallness of my faith have once more led me astray." Why did seeing Billings bring out these "sad thoughts" and spark "strange dreams?" And what did she mean by the "prosperity of the wicked?"

Although the passage makes no further specific, emotional reference to Billings, another clue appears when, on another occasion, Dickinson mentioned the body's ability to "forget" pain, something that the mind, she added, is unable to do: "The soul or thinking part will remember. Some sorrow of the mind which was twenty years past is more fast on my mind than the pain [a bout with colic] which I felt the week back" (October 30, 1790). Just about "twenty years past" at the time she penned these words, in March 1770 (just days after Bostonians rioted on King Street), Jesse Billings married Rebecca's cousin Sarah Bardwell. Is this the "bitter stroke" of which she would so often write in the years to come, that "mowed down" her "earthly hopes"?

Although Dickinson was thirty-two years old in 1770, and so already beyond the age when most women married, Billings was in his late twenties and Bardwell was twenty-seven, which suggests that Dickinson could have reasonably entertained notions of marrying him. She routinely visited his blacksmith shop just south of Miriam and Silas's home (Jesse and Silas seem not to have been closely related, despite sharing a last name) for the maintenance of her sewing tools (September 5, 1787). Billings would seem to have been a catch. In one 1772 tax record from Hatfield, his was among the highest assessments in town. His decision to marry Sarah seems to have hit Rebecca Dickinson hard, remaining "fast on her mind" for the rest of her life.

A fair bit of speculation of course colors this interpretation of Dickinson's diary, and a bit more suggests that the drama that certainly came to encompass Billings in these years may have affected Rebecca Dickinson as well, perhaps in ways that entwined the personal and the political. Billings would find himself caught up in the political whirlwind only to land on the wrong side; perhaps this is the reason Rebecca Dickinson seems to call him a "wicked" man—though just why remains unclear. Maybe it was her broken heart, or because he proved insufficiently religious; maybe it was his politics. Probably it was some combination thereof.

Whether Dickinson articulated some romantic misfortune as the source of her singlehood as early as the 1770s or crafted this narrative only in retrospect twenty years later, we cannot know. But there was certainly some drama on both personal and political fronts at the start of the 1770s. As the decade began, Hatfield learned about the deaths of Boston residents at the hands of British troops, and Dickinson absorbed the fact of Billings's marriage. Two years later other developments began altering the town's spiritual life, as Reverend Woodbridge was succeeded in the Congregational pulpit by the energetic Joseph Lyman.

After a long vacancy following Rev. Woodbridge's death in 1770, the congregation hired Joseph Lyman, a young minister and patriot, whose vigorous activism in the pulpit would help cultivate revolution. Dickinson cared less for Lyman's political agenda, however, than for his orthodoxy and zeal at the lectern. Lyman's interpretation of God's word concurred with Dickinson's own: "Not one time can I remember him to interpret the word of God contrary to the truth as it is in my own mind." Lyman was, she gratefully recorded, "as strict a Calvinist as I could wish" (March 1, 1789).

Some historians today credit Lyman for fomenting revolution in Hatfield, though the truth is more complex. Like all Massachusetts towns, Hatfield had taken great pride in its status as part of the world's greatest empire, and its leadership had long been invested in protecting the status quo. When relations with imperial administrators began to sour, it took time—years, even—after the early rumblings of discontent were first heard for those rumblings to ripen into rebellion. Perhaps Rebecca Dickinson was among those who initially hesitated to support the colonial protest movement, but then came around thanks to Lyman's vigorous advocacy.

The 1770s in Hatfield saw a clash of two strong personalities. Lyman's mother "wrote him to 'walk softly,' and not stir up the spirit of rebellion, and to 'lay aside all political disputes,'" one local history recounts, but

her "entreaties fell on deaf ears."[8] Unafraid to contradict the powerful Israel Williams, Lyman is remembered to have said, "There is a man here
now he cannot rule."[9] It is especially unfortunate not to have Dickinson's record of Lyman's arrival in the community in 1772. We do know
that Israel Williams's influence, once so certain, had already begun to
wane, at least in part a casualty of his choices during the Townshend
Act crisis. Broad forces were converging that would undermine the long-
standing authority of the River Gods in the Connecticut Valley, and the
revolution in Hatfield cannot be reduced to a simple contest of wills.
But personalities can prove catalysts in volatile situations, and Lyman offered another source of leadership in Hatfield, one that Dickinson and
others found compelling. As Massachusetts colonists grappled with the
puzzling and unwelcome series of administrative measures, Lyman
urged his congregation to resist tyranny.

Eventually supporters of the growing political protest movement
gained sway in Hatfield. At about the same time as Lyman arrived in the
Hatfield pulpit, Massachusetts residents were debating the plan to pay
governor's and judges' salaries from Crown revenues instead of by the
colonial assembly, rightly fearing that the officials' sense of duty or obligation would consequently shift from the people of Massachusetts to
distant imperial administrators. Boston's Committee of Correspondence
saw an opportunity to address this together with the mounting list of
colonial complaints, publishing a pamphlet in which they once again articulated their grievances. They sent a copy to every Massachusetts town,
asking them to join in protest and to form their own Committees of
Correspondence. Hatfield framed its reply carefully. In May 1773 a
town meeting was called, and the reply was read, "after which many
things were said in favor of it and a great deal against it."[10] Finally after
"a long debate" the group voted, with eighteen in favor of the report
and sixteen against—a nearly even split. The move toward rebellion remained incremental. Although more than half of the towns colony-wide
responded supportively to Boston's increasingly radical leadership, only
seven towns in Hampshire County replied at all, and Hatfield seems
not, in the end, to have been among them. But more than one hundred of these Committees of Correspondence indeed formed across the
colony, the infrastructure of revolution growing bit by bit.

That same month John Dickinson (no close relation to Rebecca), not Israel Williams or another member of one of the "River God" families, was elected to represent Hatfield at the General Court. And now Massachusetts experienced another tax policy crisis, this time over tea. In the aftermath of the protests against the Townshend duties, Parliament had once again yielded to public opinion in the colonies and withdrawn the loathsome duties, but it had retained the tax on tea as a symbol of its authority.

While Hatfield men debated their response to Boston's newest provocation, on the other side of the Atlantic, Parliament was working on yet another measure concerning taxation in the colonies, and returned to the problem of tea. This new act, which the Crown approved in May 1773, was designed in part to address the financial distress of the East India Company (brought on in part by surpluses created as potential buyers preferred cheaper tea smuggled in to avoid British duties), a massive organization whose collapse would have been disastrous, its impact rippling throughout Britain's economy. The Tea Act granted the East India Company the right to ship its surplus tea directly to the American colonies. Eliminating any landing in England meant that the tea could be sold quite cheaply; no new taxes were imposed, but the duties still in place in the wake of the Townshend Acts crisis would be applied. The tea would still be priced more competitively for consumers. Colonists, however, interpreted the reduced price as a bribe to get them to concede the duty on tea.

Once again, while politicians responded with the tools of their trade, everyday men and women protested with their pocketbooks, as they chose what to wear, buy, eat, and drink. Consumers continued targeting tea in their boycotts, and here again, women were critical to the success of the effort. Three years earlier, hundreds of Boston women had pledged to quit drinking tea to signal their support for the political protest; now, newspapers again contained accounts of women who served alternatives in their own homes or otherwise supported the boycott. Offering tea or not offering it, accepting tea or declining it—all were political acts.

Late in 1773, as the first of the ships carrying the taxed tea made their way to Boston's wharves, the increasingly radical members of the city's circles of protestors planned a dramatic action. In December some 150 protestors gathered and dumped 342 chests of tea into Boston harbor. A half-century later, this act would come to be remembered as the Boston Tea Party.

Boston had to wait several weeks to learn how Parliament would respond to this gesture, and when the news came in May 1774, the city's residents were simply stunned. Parliament, incensed at the destruction of £18,000 worth of goods, put its collective foot down, directly on the necks of the unruly colonists. It passed a set of Coercive Acts meant to put these malcontents in their place. One act closed the port of Boston until the tea had been paid for, throwing the city's economy into a tailspin. Another affirmed the government's right to quarter troops where needed, while another allowed the governor to move trials involving royal officials to another colony or even to Great Britain if he believed that a fair trial could not be obtained in Massachusetts. To nip all this dissent in the bud a fourth act, the Massachusetts Government Act, replaced some of the colony's highest elected officials with thirty-seven royal appointees (named among these "mandamus councilors" was, unsurprisingly, Hatfield's Israel Williams) and forbade more than one town meeting a year, unless specific permission was sought from and granted by the colony's governor.

Another act passed in that same session, the Quebec Act, was not intended specifically to punish Boston, but to the people of Massachusetts it felt like part of this collective threat. Here Parliament addressed several matters concerning the governance of Quebec, and colonists in New England were both angry and alarmed by the guarantee that residents could practice their Catholic faith. The hated "papists" next door had only recently been enemy combatants in a war that was still very fresh in many colonials' minds. But it may have been the Massachusetts Government Act that at last turned indifferent colonists into indignant rebels. Town meeting was an old and cherished tradition in Massachusetts; if colonists had not yet been persuaded that new taxation policies constituted a secret plot to reduce the colonies to "slavery," this assault on established systems of self-governance seemed clearer and more frightening. Public reaction to these events would for all intents and purposes bring royal authority in Massachusetts to an end.

All of Boston would soon be reeling. With the port closed and wharves empty, residents lost work. Shops closed. Donations of food, livestock, and goods trickled in, but the city began a long period of real suffering. No one could now deny the trouble coming. Though before now Rebecca's client Elizabeth Porter Phelps had barely noticed the gathering storm in the pages of her memorandum book, on June 19, 1774, she wrote, "The people of this land are greatly threatened with cruelty and oppression from the Parliament of Great Britain—the Port of Boston is now and has been ever since the first day of this month shut up and greater calamities are daily expected." If she had been perhaps slow to warm to nonimportation as a gesture of protest during the Townshend duties crisis, she was convinced now.

As usual, people turned to their faith, hoping that a fast day would be declared. These official public days devoted to prayer and contemplation were a New England tradition, and men and women across Massachusetts felt one was sorely needed now, but the governor refused to make the declaration. And so congregations began declaring them for themselves. On July 10, Phelps noted that Hadley would indeed "keep a day of fasting and prayer on account of the dark aspect of our public affairs," and across the river in Hatfield, Rebecca's congregation did likewise. Reverend Lyman, taking as his text Isaiah 58:5 ("Is not this the fast that I have chosen? to loose the bands of wickedness, to undo the heavy burdens, and to let the oppressed go free, and that ye break every yoke"), helped his neighbors prepare themselves for the coming bleak occasion.

As towns across the commonwealth debated whether to join this increasingly volatile movement, patterns began to emerge. In the old towns, led for over a century by a handful of established and interconnected families, these initiatives were largely viewed with suspicion, while the smaller, newer towns, encumbered with less cultural baggage, proved more eager to flex some political muscle. In three-year-old Williamsburg, so recently created from Hatfield's western lands, townsmen reported to their Boston counterparts, "We are almost unanimously of the opinion by all means to resist Great Britain in their unconstitutional measures by which they usurp upon our [charter] privileges even to blood. . . . If you (being in the front rank) need our assistance in opposing them we stand ready to grant it according to the utmost of our small capacity."[11] Across Massachusetts the tide seemed increasingly to be turning toward revolution.

More gestures of protest would apparently be needed to reverse Britain's frightening course. Boston's Committee of Correspondence sent out another circular letter, this one proposing a "Solemn League and Covenant" in which all towns (and conspicuously, "all adult persons of both sexes" in them) would forego commerce with England. In Berkshire County nineteen towns—including Pittsfield, where Rebecca Dickinson had friends and family, and perhaps occasional clients— joined in their own pledge to suspend use of imported goods and to boycott neighbors who refused to cooperate. Hatfield men likewise assembled to consider "what might be proper for the town to do with regard to entering into a covenant to withdraw all commercial intercourse with Great Britain by a disuse of their manufacturers till such time as the general interests of the colonies are settled or our charter rights restored."[12] That summer some Hatfield residents speculated that the town's Whigs [the increasingly organized opponents of crown government, "Tories" being the term applied to those loyal to the king] were "laying some great plan," while gamblers laid odds ten to one that the governor "would be removed before next Candlemas day"—that is, by the beginning of February. Rebecca Dickinson surely noted that once again, consumer choices were front and center in the political crisis. And now her participation was being directly solicited, both as a consumer and as a craftswoman.

In August a convention met at Hadley. In the wake of the Massachusetts Government Act, one question was whether to stop the courts from meeting, as an act of protest. Delegates from twenty-five towns met to discuss their positions and in the end drafted a message to the justices of the county court asking them to state whether they believed their authority was grounded in the colony's charter, in place since the reigns of King William and Queen Mary (i.e., for most of the past century), and not in any way by the recent and repugnant acts of Parliament. When the county court convened at Springfield on August 30, the proceedings were brought to a halt by a crowd of more than a thousand people—some estimates said as many as three thousand—who wanted an answer to that and other questions. Israel Williams, as well as Springfield's John Worthington (another man who had been appointed a "mandamus councilor" under the odious new act), were asked by the crowd to renounce their allegiance to general and now governor Thomas Gage (sent to replace the unpopular Thomas Hutchinson). Williams declared that although he did not necessarily share his neighbors' views, he would "join them in the common cause."[13] As crowds across the colony closed courts and forced resignations, royal authority further dissolved and local authority gained strength. Whether or not she yet knew it, Rebecca Dickinson was witnessing the collapse of an empire.

As August became September, a series of events largely unremembered today, the "powder alarm," proved decisive in Hatfield. Governor Gage had grown concerned that the powder supplies were in danger of being seized by hotheaded colonists. On September 1 he ordered that powder in a Charlestown storehouse be brought into Boston. Word that the British troops had marched and taken the powder hit the streets, and rumor quickly spread upon rumor, escalating along the way. By the time that news reached western Massachusetts, the story was that fighting had broken out between the regulars and the colonists. A messenger in nearby Deerfield said that "Gage had ordered his troops to fire upon some people in Boston"; soon another claimed that some 106 men had been killed. "Our people soon took a start," one diarist noted, adding that everyone was now "wide awake, some for going away directly, others not."[14] Although the false alarm was corrected by the end of the day, the choices men made when the startling news arrived proved revealing.

The alarm and people's responses to it (or lack thereof) had made political positions visible. Two days later word spread that "all the western world was coming down to mob Col. Williams and others." A crowd had gathered in Williamsburg ready to seize Israel Williams, Oliver Partridge, and Hatfield's other known Tories. Williams was a constant source of tension, but when the alarm came Partridge had apparently refused to lend his gun to the community response, and now people were seething. Clearly, when pressed to take a side Partridge would choose the British government over his friends and neighbors. What if local men really *were* called to arms? "It would not be safe," one man observed, "to go to battle and leave a mess of Tory men behind to destroy the people at home."[15] A day of fasting and prayer had also been called for in the wake of the alarm, and word was spreading that Williams had instead thrown a feast, complete with a fiddler.[16] Men wanted to "know the truth of it and find out our friends from our foes."[17] A proposal emerged to get to the bottom of things. Some men, who had caught wind of a rumor that the targets of this action knew they were coming and would be armed, had brought guns, prompting others to insist that the weapons be left home, lest things get out of hand. At the appointed hour men gathered around Williamsburg's liberty pole, preparing to march. This was no impromptu action; on Sunday a group of men who had gathered in Hatfield were already talking about the anticipated crowd expected on Tuesday.

As the hour of action approached, the crowd sent Benjamin Read ahead to Hatfield to perform a little reconnaissance. Constable Israel Chapin knew trouble was coming, too; he met Read on the road and asked him whether the men "were coming to rectify private damages especially to punish Col. Williams relative to an old difficulty" (i.e., some lingering issues left over from the division of land). When Chapin learned that, quite to the contrary, it was a political gesture, not a private matter, he not only stood aside but also added that he himself thought "there was a corrupt vicious . . . crew in Hatfield and that they ought to be dealt with."[18]

The word "crew" sheds a little light on these events as they may have been interpreted by Rebecca Dickinson—and perhaps also illuminates the reasons behind her churning emotions about Jesse Billings—because it apparently included not only Williams and Partridge, but also David Billings, Obediah Dickinson, Asa White, and Jesse Billings, all men who "deserved to be dealt with in severity."[19] Later, when Benjamin Read was called to testify about these events, he noted that the mention of Jesse Billings's name as a possible Tory had surprised him, because he had "always heard that he was a high liberty man."[20] But Constable Chapin felt that Billings had behaved incorrectly when he got caught up in crowd action targeting David Ingersoll Jr., a justice at the Berkshire county court whose house had been attacked earlier in August. Driven out of Great Barrington, Ingersoll passed through Hatfield on his way to safer haven in Boston, but he was quickly driven on by another crowd of some two hundred angry men. Ingersoll had left his coat and pocketbook (akin to a briefcase) with Billings for safe-keeping, "for fear if the mob should attack him they might not get them," and Billings later made sure these were returned to the disgraced judge. For aiding Ingersoll in this way Billings came under suspicion of being a Tory himself.[21] Chapin told Read that if the men controlled themselves, the people of Hatfield (excepting Israel Williams, Jesse Billings, and the handful of men named) would rally to support the action.

The archival record is quiet on what happened next. But one might well wonder, if the townspeople were so angry about Williams and the "corrupt vicious . . . crew" in Hatfield, why did they need outsiders to launch some sort of action? Why not take matters in hand themselves?[22] In fact, the mob was all but invited in. Just days earlier a number of men in Hatfield had been complaining about Williams and his allies, but decided not to act themselves, because "it would break neighborhood and therefore would not do as well as for . . . strangers."[23] In other words, it was one thing for people to rise up against longtime authorities who were also friends and neighbors, and another for those same men to be challenged from outside. Hatfield men were ready to join, but someone else would have to start it.

As word about the impending action reached Deerfield, another crowd gathered to meet it. More men from Hadley, and another seventy from Amherst, rushed to Hatfield to protect the opposition. In the end, cooler heads prevailed. But there was another outcome: people had scared themselves. In the wake of these bullets literally having been dodged, a general covenant in opposition to mobs was drafted and signed, but Williams had to have seen the writing on the wall. Things would get worse before they would get better.

5

Revolutionary Hatfield

The powder alarm may have come to naught, but some surprising lessons had been learned. Before month's end the town began stockpiling powder and lead. Rebecca Dickinson and her family were drawn in as people were forced to choose sides. In fall 1774, when the local militia was called together (as it regularly was, volunteer military service being expected of healthy adult men), many Hatfield men refused to serve under the leadership of Colonel Williams or under the authority of Parliament. But they nevertheless wanted to serve the interests of their town. So on October 4, 1774, Rebecca's brother-in-law Silas joined more than two dozen Hatfield men who pledged to serve the town, but not the empire. The company, called "minutemen"—that is, men ready to respond in a minute should the colonists find themselves threatened—was reorganized under the authority not of the Crown, but of the colony. Dickinson, her family, and especially her brothers-in-law found themselves bracing for battle.

Rebecca Dickinson would face the coming upheaval as a single woman. By the close of 1774, thirty-six-year-old Dickinson was a mature working woman in Hatfield, still living in her parents' house. Samuel, Miriam, and Martha had married and begun families of their own. Around 1772 Martha had married a man named William Mather and moved with him seventy miles north to new settlements in Vermont. Miriam had stayed closer to home after her November 1773 marriage, traveling just a few doors away to set up housekeeping with her new husband, Silas Billings. Samuel wed Mary Dickinson (her maiden name and married name were the same) in February 1774 and went to Whately, where the couple ran the family's dairy. Meanwhile, Rebecca remained in the home of her birth, watching as her brother and these sisters courted, married, and began raising children. Anne and Irene were still at home, though both would in time become brides as well. (Anne would marry a man named John Ballard, with whom she would have six daughters and a son; they lived in Hatfield at least through 1791, but also spent some time in Pittsfield, almost fifty miles to the west in Massachusetts's newly established Berkshire County. Irene and her husband, Lucius Graves of Williamsburg [a town carved from lands taken from Hatfield in 1771 and incorporated in 1776], married in November 1780 and took up residence in that town.) For the time being Rebecca, her younger sisters, and her parents went about their daily business, all the while watching and worrying as conversation in the public sphere grew increasingly shrill. In these dramatic years the prospect of American independence was raised, and the question of Dickinson's own independence revisited.

In September, while Hatfield grappled with the meaning of the powder alarm, 250 miles south in Philadelphia, the first-ever Continental Congress was convening, with twelve of England's North American colonies sending representatives. Among their other actions that fall, they created a Continental Association to implement another mass boycott, hoping to continue to pressure British administrators to reverse course on these new policies. The agreement banned the consumption of tea together with all other British goods, beginning December 1, 1774, and proposed local Committees of Inspection charged with monitoring compliance. If all of this failed to work, in time they would ban exports as well.

A full-on rebellion was taking real form. Significantly, at the last town meeting of 1774 Hatfield voted to transfer payment of taxes from the imperial administration to the government of Massachusetts. In so doing the townspeople withdrew their financial support for a political authority that no longer seemed to be serving their interests. On December 15, proclaimed a day of thanksgiving by the Provincial Congress (formed after Governor Gage dissolved the legislature), Reverend Lyman preached a forceful sermon in which he prepared his congregation for the sacrifices to come. Surely Dickinson's ears perked up when he compared God's will to soap: just as clothes go through a vigorous washing to remove dirt and grime, Lyman said, so too should Christians prepare for a "cleansing trial."[1] The ordeal would be worth it: "Good obtained through suffering," he assured his listeners, "is the most delightsome." Some Hatfield residents were so pleased with Lyman's remarks that they carried a copy of them to Boston and had them published by Edes and Gill (the patriot publishers of the *Boston Gazette*) on Boston's Queen Street.

Lyman's sermon helps us understand the way many New Englanders came to embrace something as drastic as rebellion. Although much revolutionary rhetoric was aimed primarily at a male audience, under the steeple of the Congregational meetinghouse, men and women contemplated spiritual and political messages (which clergymen did not hesitate to deliver) side by side. Rebecca Dickinson did not hear the loud debate that rang through the room when men in town gathered to discuss their responses to the crises of the day, but she sat together with her whole community when Reverend Lyman spoke about them from the pulpit. On this occasion, after reminding his listeners that at any time "in this life" they might "be called to severe trials of their faith," Lyman urged the town to "gird up the loins of our minds, and prepare" for the inevitable battle to come. Only God knew "the events which await us," but it "is certainly our duty to be up and preparing for the worst." God, he argued, as "righteous punishment" for colonists' "luxury, lust and dissipation" had "raised up adversaries against this land."

Men who have had designs of their own, incompatible with the general interests of the British empire, moved with a jealousy of the liberties of the American colonies, which stands so much in the way of their ambition, have, by the sufferance of Gods holy providence, been able to procure measures, wholly repugnant to the civil rights of the inhabitants of this country. The British administration by the force of great abilities, perverted to base purposes, and by their command of the national treasure, have influenced the Parliament to enact the most grievous edicts against us. Laws made, with the feigned pretense of protecting and securing us, and for the support of civil government, have been the most direct invasion of our property, and subversive of every idea of English freedom.

These adversaries had been allowed to "lay us under tribute [i.e., extract undue taxes] when we have not even a distant restraint upon them [i.e., no representation in Parliament]." The colonists were entirely without a voice in their governance, Lyman asserted, and their oppressors too far away to hear their groans. He focused particular attention on the alleged plot to undermine loyalty to colonial affairs by changing the way in which officials were paid: "They have applied our monies for the purpose of supporting civil officers independent of our grants, thereby still further to detach from our interest men who have never . . . shown any such fond attachment" to the colonists. Instead, the interest of the governors and judges would be separated from those of the general public. The May 1774 Massachusetts Government Act prohibited "free deliberation," and once-legitimate remonstrances (documents in which grievances were formally presented to government officials) were now considered seditious. Lyman also articulated widespread anger when he complained that the English requirement that the colonists quarter troops was designed mainly to "keep in awe a people who have labored, who have fought and bled for them" (a reference to the colonists' involvement in military expeditions into Canada during the recently concluded and successful war against France). On his mind also were the "many and bloody Indian wars whereby not only our borders [were] enlarged, but their riches and power abundantly augmented." And of course his congregants needed little reminding that the British had "armed the soldiery to butcher our brethren in the streets" during the March 1770 "massacre in King Street."

Lyman's long litany of injustices went on. One can easily imagine his tone growing more insistent, his volume rising as he reached the crux of his message. Before he exited the pulpit he added a word of caution about what any public ill will could mean locally, "for since the beginning of this unhappy controversy, many rash, violent and unjustifiable measures have been taken by some amongst ourselves. In the heat of passion, and under the madness of oppression, many injurious attacks have been made upon the persons and properties of our fellow subjects. . . . In these things therefore, we have been permitted to become enemies to ourselves." In other words, though Lyman wanted his congregation to stand strong against their imperial persecutors, they should be careful not to give in to emotion or turn on one another.

But Lyman did not intend to close on a note of calm. Rather, after affirming that he had no doubt that their British adversaries would deploy the army, the navy, and all funds at hand to crush colonial dissent, he suggested that they might even "attempt, and God only knows whether they will succeed in it, to revive the late tragedy acted upon us by the Indians and Canadians, of dashing our little ones and ripping up the woman with child." Here, he may have been referring to the now-legendary 1704 raid on Deerfield, in which twenty-five children (and Rebecca's great-grandfather) were killed. Preying on long-standing prejudices against both Native Americans and French Catholics, he tapped into his listeners' basest aversions to secure their support, suggesting that the British were not above unleashing violent forces to compel submission. "This is no *imaginary* fear," Lyman assured his by-now alarmed listeners, "for the Quebec Bill was made, as it was said in Parliament, in order to be a curb upon the licentiousness of the other colonies." What he meant is that the act (one of those passed in the wake of the tea action, at the same time as the so-called Intolerable Acts) was designed by Parliament to restrain England's colonists in North America while protecting some of the interests of their Canadian neighbors, including the practice of both the Catholic faith and French civil law. In other words, England seemed to the Massachusetts colonists to have been accommodating, even favoring, papist practices—and right on their doorstep. Lyman wanted his "little flock" to be prepared, so that if these dire predictions did come to pass "you may not faint in the conflict."

Reminding the gathering that when their "civil liberty is once gone," their "religion will be driven into corners," Lyman concluded with some encouraging examples of other "nations, much weaker than we are" who had prevailed against enemies no less powerful, from Israel under the Midianites to the Netherlands' independence from Spain in the seventeenth century. "History does not afford us a single instance," Lyman closed, "wherein such a number of people, resolutely opposed to slavery, have been soon reduced under the yoke." With rhetoric like this, it's no wonder that Lyman succeeded in turning some still-reluctant Hatfielders into confirmed revolutionaries.

Lyman's concern about the potential mistreatment of local loyalists was well founded. In February 1775 tempers flared again when suspicion once more settled on Israel Williams. The month before, the town had formed a nine-man Committee of Inspection, charged with implementing the Continental Congress's association, limiting trade with England. A crowd was mustered to seize Williams, ostensibly on the basis of incriminating correspondence with Governor Gage. Some 150 men from all around western Massachusetts converged on Williams's house and took him and his son to Hadley. According to local legend, the crowd locked the men in a room, set a fire in the hearth, and then blocked the chimney, to "smoke old Williams to a Whig." But Williams himself told a different story. As he recounted it, he and Israel Jr. had been put under guard by men who threatened to blow their "brains out on the spot" should anyone try to rescue them; later, smoke from a stopped-up chimney drove the guards from the room, and after a sleepless night in the smoky room both Williams men were made to pledge not to oppose the Provincial Congress.[2] But of course neither man felt obliged to abide by such a statement, obtained under considerable duress. They figured that this rebellion would be put down quickly, so they placed orders for new inventory for their store to be shipped as soon as nonimportation was (inevitably) abandoned.

In April 1775 news arrived of dramatic events elsewhere. Fighting between the American colonists and British troops at last broke out in and around Lexington and Concord, in the first major clashes of the Revolutionary War. Riders carrying the news reached Hatfield the next day, about noon, and in a few hours Hatfield's men were on the march. Neither Samuel Dickinson nor Silas Billings seems to have been among the volunteers, but Lucius Graves (not yet Rebecca's brother-in-law) responded to the alarm with Hatfield's other minutemen, as a fifer in Captain Israel Chapin's company. He would stay on and witness the siege of Boston and the fighting on and around Bunker and Breed's Hills. Anne's future husband, John Ballard, lit out for Lexington also, with the other minutemen under Perez Graves, though they had only got as far as Ware when they learned the battle was over, and returned home. By summer Hatfield's Seth Murray took a full company of men to the camp assembling in Cambridge, just outside Boston.

Rebecca did not have to share her sisters' agonizing fear that war would carry away a husband, but she certainly joined all the women of the region as they worried about loved ones and braced for the effects of widespread violence. "Be not afraid nor dismayed by reason of this great multitude: for the battle is not yours, but God's," Reverend Lyman assured Rebecca alongside the other members of her frightened congregation; "If it may be thy will command a peace," Elizabeth Phelps, who attended Lyman's service, nevertheless pleaded in the pages of her journal.[3] But peace was not to be. Some women whose men had rushed to battle banded together. The roads in and around Boston filled with women and children seeking refuge. Other women—those who opted to stay behind and try to protect their family's property— found themselves isolated. Chaos made its own demands, testing everyone's mettle. Who could guess how they, or anyone, would respond to these unpredictable new circumstances? Marriages would be strained, and strengthened, as women found themselves necessarily taking on new roles.

Now that war had started in Massachusetts, towns across New England weighed their options. In Vermont Rebecca's sister Martha and brother-in-law William Mather were at the center of their own town's debate. When the men gathered to hold their first town meeting on May 8, 1775, William Mather was asked to serve as the clerk. It was he who recorded the will of the town as the colonial relationship with England deteriorated. Just two weeks later the assembly reconvened to determine "the minds of the people with respect to the impending war with Great Britain," and Mather found himself recording their frightening resolutions: "Resolved, we will, each of us, at the expense of our lives and fortunes, to the last extremity, unite and oppose the last cruel unjust and arbitrary acts of the British Parliament passed for the sole purpose of raising a revenue; Resolved, we will be contented and subject to the Hon. Continental Congress [i.e., the meeting of delegates from the various North American colonies gathered in Philadelphia to coordinate a response to the political crisis] in all things which they shall resolve for the peace, safety and welfare of the American colonies."[4]

In Hatfield men were coming to similar conclusions. In May 1775 the Committee of Safety visited perceived loyalists—Israel Williams and others—and asked them to sign declarations renouncing allegiance to General Gage as governor (and declaring him, for good measure, "an unnatural and inveterate enemy to the country") and pledge to "join our countrymen upon all occasion as in defense of the rights and liberties of America."[5] These suspected Tories were asked to promise to use their influence to resist the recent acts of Parliament and to bear their fair share in the inevitable need for both men and money.

Hatfield women were not invited to participate in these heated discussions—at least in a formal way—but they soon found themselves asked to contribute more materially as the colony braced for war. One way that many participated was to help meet repeated requisitions for clothing. In the weeks after the confrontations at Lexington and Concord, some twenty thousand militiamen had gathered outside Boston. They needed supplies. The first requisition for clothing in Massachusetts was made in June 1775, when the Provincial Congress called for towns in eastern Massachusetts to provide shirts, breeches, and stockings. In July they determined that no fewer than thirteen thousand coats would be needed to clothe the troops. These should be made of "good plain cloth," short and without lapels, and each one should carry a certificate, sewed in, identifying the maker, the town where it came from, whether the cloth was manufactured locally, and if so by whom (a requirement that was probably not altogether met).[6] A schedule that set quotas for each town aimed to collect just over twelve hundred coats from Hampshire County, thirty-seven of which would come from Hatfield. At the same time, the congress announced that "a large number of shirts, stockings and summer breeches are wanted immediately for the use of the army." Residents were "earnestly requested, as you value the lives and health of your countrymen," to round up at least two shirts, two pairs of stockings and two pairs of summer breeches for every coat they furnished and send them on. Accordingly, across the river in Hadley (its residents were tasked in the same document with supplying thirty-three coats), on August 13 Rebecca Dickinson's client Elizabeth Porter

Phelps recorded in the pages of her journal that she had learned how to make breeches for the soldiers from a local tailoress, and that "people are sent too to find 'em clothes." A skilled artisan in the clothing trades, thirty-seven-year-old Rebecca Dickinson almost surely found herself drawn into the gathering war effort through her artisanal skills.

Boston was besieged as militiamen from Massachusetts and other colonies encamped around the city trapped the British military and limited their access to supplies. Those who supported the patriot side rushed to get out, and those who remained loyal rushed to get in. Some ten thousand people fled Boston, while supporters of the Crown hurried toward the protection of the British Army. Hatfield people felt the effects of this massive dislocation of people. The Provincial Congress asked each town to help relocate those too poor to arrange to leave, to "receive, support and employ" a share of the almost five thousand refugees. Hatfield was scheduled to take in up to thirty-five people.[7] The refugees were lucky to leave the city, because reports throughout the spring described terrible scarcity and starvation. Crime was rampant.

The gathering American forces around Boston drove General Gage to try to improve his position. In June the British took Bunker and Breed's Hills (though at great cost). In July a Virginian named George Washington arrived to take charge of the newly created Continental Army, and men and materials began pouring in from other colonies. Months of misery had begun for those trapped with the troops in Boston. Hatfield residents joined with others in Massachusetts and other British colonies in collecting donations to help supply provisions.

By November that year Reverend Lyman had grown concerned about the effect of all this tension on his church. Church records report a meeting called to consider a petition seeking some means to address the divisions that were growing in town. As they worked to "prevent disorderly . . . division and separation," the committee reported that Israel Williams, "who had long withdrawn himself from the public worship and the administration of the Lord's Supper," appeared at the meeting to defend his conduct and declare that he had no intention of altering his behavior. The church members, asked to vote whether they were "uneasy" with Williams's general absenteeism from worship and communion, affirmed that they were. Asked whether Lyman should be directed to suspend Williams from the church, they again answered yes. Official notice followed. Before the revolution, whenever the Williams family had entered the meetinghouse, everyone present had remained standing until the leading family had taken their seats, and had remained standing again after the service until the Williams family had exited. But those habits were about to change. For her part, Rebecca Dickinson was perhaps unsurprised that Williams was removed from the meetinghouse: in a later reference to his daughter Elizabeth, Dickinson noted that the woman was "not used to religious conversation" in her father's house (August 2, 1787).

By the following summer, what had started as a political protest had become an all-out movement for independence. In January a pamphlet appeared in Philadelphia that electrified public debate. Titled *Common Sense* (and eventually revealed to be the work of an English radical named Thomas Paine), it laid out the case for separation so convincingly that fence-sitters began to take the patriots' side. Reprinted in Boston just weeks after it was published, it helped crystallize public opinion in Massachusetts as well. Meanwhile, during the winter men under the command of Henry Knox had hauled some sixty tons of artillery across the length of Massachusetts (captured at New York's Fort Ticonderoga the previous May, just weeks after fighting broke out), and in March 1776 those cannons succeeded in forcing the British to evacuate the city. Under the cover of darkness, two thousand men had built fortifications south of the city on Dorchester Heights; on the sixth anniversary of the so-called Boston Massacre, Britain's troops awoke to find themselves in an untenable position. The siege was at last over. The British Army abandoned Boston, taking some nine hundred loyalists with them.

The writing was now on the wall. On June 24, 1776, Hatfield men voted to instruct their representative to the Provincial Congress (i.e., the new state legislature) to support their delegates to the Second Continental Congress: "In case the congress should think it necessary for the safety of the American united colonies to declare them independent of Great Britain. . . . [The] inhabitants of the town of Hatfield with their lives and fortunes will solemnly engage to support them in the measure." Not only did those instructions make their way to the delegates representing the colony of Massachusetts, John Adams, Samuel Adams,

Elbridge Gerry, Robert Treat Paine, and of course John Hancock; the signers of the ensuing Declaration in Philadelphia also came to include William Williams, the grandson of Hatfield's Reverend William Williams and nephew of Colonel Israel Williams, then representing the colony of Connecticut at the gathering in Philadelphia. Towns elsewhere also issued such declarations. Predating the one made by the delegates to the Continental Congress together local declarations like Hatfield's cut the many ties that tethered the colonies to the empire, as much as or more than the famous document that severed the last remaining threads. When the men assembled in the Pennsylvania State House reached a similar decision in July 1776, they did so knowing that the people of Hatfield had their backs.

For the people of Massachusetts, then, by the time independence was declared, the British Army was already gone. It was the close of one chapter and the opening of another. In time war would bring food shortages, inflation, and other home-front challenges. Women in western Massachusetts escaped the trauma felt by those closer to the fighting: the destruction that battleground communities endured; the fear—and act—of rape by enemy soldiers; the threat to farms and homes posed by foraging, and desperate, combatants; and the need to attend to vast numbers of ill, wounded, and dead men. But enlistment campaigns threatened to draw away husbands, fathers, sons and brothers, while feeding families became harder as goods became difficult to get and prices rocketed upward. Just downriver in Hartford, Connecticut, where many in Hatfield had friends and family, women staged a raid on a merchant believed to be stockpiling sugar. In eastern Massachusetts, Abigail Adams described to her husband John a crowd of perhaps one hundred women who converged on a merchant who refused to sell coffee at a reasonable price, roughed him up, and seized the goods. Prices went sky-high, prompting many Massachusetts towns to pass laws intended to combat inflation and prevent price gouging. Basic household management became tougher and tougher. Women assumed responsibility for tasks usually managed by now-absent fathers, husbands, and sons. And they did contribute, at times, to the massive effort required to feed the armies traveling across the countryside and nursed soldiers injured in battle or who succumbed to the many sicknesses that swept through military encampments. For many, pride and confidence in their abilities grew.

In Hatfield, Israel Williams continued to be perceived as a threat to Hatfield's rebellion. Late in 1776 a very damaging set of papers that he had sent to (former) governor Thomas Hutchinson were intercepted. In these pages Williams reported (as one reader summarized) his "certain hope & expectation" that imperial forces "would very soon entirely defeat & fully subdue the Americans."[8] Hatfield's Committee of Safety also learned of a large order for British goods Williams had placed (clearly Williams expected the revolt to fail, and he wanted to be ready with fresh merchandise when it did). He and his son were confined once more. The members of Hatfield's Committee of Correspondence justified their actions by affirming that Williams "has been & still is a man of considerable influence with the people."[9] Williams would be tried in Boston, and then jailed in Northampton for several months, when he and his son would be released to house arrest. In just a few short years his fortunes had changed dramatically. The onetime "Monarch of Hampshire County" found himself imprisoned, and defeated.

The following spring, at a town meeting in May 1777, Hatfield men empowered the merchant John Hastings, their representative to the General Court, or state legislature, to take all "necessary measures for the immediate defense of the country and the unjust claims and cruel ravages of our hostile invaders"—a far cry from Israel Williams's testy response to Boston radicals just a few years earlier.[10] Hastings would be on hand as the newly independent Massachusetts, no longer a colony of the Crown, turned to the task of creating a new state government. Not long after the passage of the Coercive Acts, Massachusetts patriots had established its Provincial Congress as a legislature; its Committee of Safety served as an executive. Now, a new constitution would be needed for the colony-turned-state, but most people agreed that the General Court—given the relative inexperience of its new members and the demands of conducting the war—was not the body to draft one. But something had to be done, and so Hatfield residents conveyed their preferences to their new representative. Hastings's first duty, of course, per the town's instructions, was to the "public honor of God," but after that he was to attend to the "civil rights and privileges of the people." His neighbors directed him to use his influence to obtain a bill of rights and to ensure, among other things, that the expenses of the representatives would be covered by the state government in Boston (not the individual towns); that oaths of allegiance would be required of voters; that representatives would be required to own enough property to "make them naturally care" for the state's "prosperity and welfare"; and that the governor would be chosen by the "votes of the freemen collectively."

The people of Hatfield watched closely as events unfolded locally in Massachusetts and also in the Continental Congress. On January 9, 1778, the Articles of Confederation of the United States, passed by the Continental Congress, were read aloud and laid before the Hatfield town meeting for discussion. In fact, the Articles were by this time already in operation, but as they debated its merits, Hatfield men (and women) moved further toward a consciousness of themselves as members of the "United States of America" that it described.

As the colonies moved toward independence, Dickinson again contemplated giving up hers. In the midst of these trying months, Charles Phelps, a recently widowed bricklayer turned attorney from Northampton, Massachusetts, proposed marriage. Dickinson was almost forty. Charles and his wife, Dorothy Root Phelps, with their sons Timothy and Solomon, had some years earlier moved to a new settlement called Marlborough (or Marlboro), Vermont, about ten miles west of Brattleboro. (Another son, Charles, married Rebecca's client Elizabeth Porter.) Sometime during the winter of 1777 and 1778 (while the Continental Army so famously suffered at Valley Forge), Dorothy Phelps died, and the next year Charles Sr. was searching for a new partner to help him carve out a life on the margins of English settlement.

Was Dickinson surprised by the proposal? Perhaps not entirely. As the father-in-law of Elizabeth Porter Phelps, Dickinson's Hadley client, Charles would have encountered Rebecca regularly in and around their farm, Forty Acres. Rebecca was also tied to Charles Phelps through her sister Martha, who with her husband William had joined Phelps in the Vermont settlement. When the first Congregational church was established in the new outpost in October 1776, by Hatfield's Reverend Joseph Lyman, Martha and William Mather and Charles Phelps were among the founders. (Although most of Marlborough found the Phelps men full of hot air, Rebecca's brother-in-law William Mather was perceived as a valuable member of the community; he was the first man chosen to serve as town clerk, served as the first moderator of the Congregational church, and was a frequent member of town and church committees. Charles Phelps surely paled in comparison.) In addition, Dorothy Phelps had been a gownmaker in Northampton, and was when Rebecca apprenticed. It is entirely possible, then, that it was she to whom young Rebecca had gone for her training a quarter-century earlier. If this was so, then Charles, now about sixty-two, would have known Rebecca for many years and had even perhaps watched her grow up. That Charles proposed to Dickinson sometime during that same winter after Dorothy died suggests that the two were already well acquainted.

These events occurred a decade before Dickinson's surviving journal opens, so we can only speculate about her thinking at this time. But the very fact that she received, and declined, a proposal of marriage on the eve of her fortieth birthday hints that Dickinson considered some aspects of singlehood to be advantageous. At least she did not see the lack of a husband as such a desperate situation that she would marry any man who asked. Dickinson may well have given Phelps's proposal serious consideration, but something caused her to reject it. By now she knew from watching the women around her that no matter how conspicuous she felt as a single woman in her late thirties, matrimony was nothing to take lightly. Now a successful craftswoman, marriage would mean yielding control over her income to her husband, whom law and custom put at the head of the household. In eighteenth-century Massachusetts the legal status of a married woman—*feme covert*—provided that her public identity was in effect "covered" by that of her husband. (Other places in the British colonies had laws on the books creating a *feme sole trader* legal status that enabled married women to operate businesses, but Massachusetts did not adopt such legislation until 1787, and then only if the married woman had been abandoned by her husband.) Married women could not control real estate; their personal property became that of their husbands. They could not sign legal documents like deeds or contracts without their husbands' consent. Importantly for craftswomen like Dickinson, the laws of coverture would transfer control of any earned wages to the husband. Any prospective bride needed to be sure that the man to whom such power would be granted would use it wisely and well.

Phelps's advancing age, and the twenty-year gap between them, probably gave her pause as well. Or perhaps it was the prospect of moving, her sister's presence nearby notwithstanding, to a distant, unfamiliar, and unsettled place. Perhaps she was reluctant to abandon her established circle of clients. Perhaps it was Phelps's rather strong and, by most accounts, difficult personality that settled the matter—maybe she just couldn't stand him. She wouldn't be the first: years earlier, when Phelps had served on the local court, the sitting justices resigned en masse, calling him (as much in reference to his status as a onetime brick mason as to his by-all-accounts prickly personality) "such company as we never inclin'd to keep."[11]

Another factor may have played a role as well. Charles Phelps and his family were deeply enmeshed in a passionate debate about who should have jurisdiction over the land they had settled in what is now Vermont. The Phelps family upheld New York's claims on their lands, in opposition to others who favored the creation of a new, independent state of Vermont. Charles Phelps's outspoken stand would land him in jail. Although Dickinson described him as "a person well learned," she regretted that he "knew too little of himself . . . he was very great and very small" (April 19, 1789).

So that was that. Whether or not this was Dickinson's first real chance to marry, and whatever had or had not happened with Jesse Billings, she here received a genuine offer of marriage, but in the end decided that she was better off single. (Phelps did not suffer for long. Phelps family tradition says that he tried again, with a woman of Boston, who also rejected him, but at the same time mentioned that he might want to meet her visiting niece. Phelps, these stories claim, met her that afternoon, proposed immediately, and insisted that, should she be interested, the marriage must also take place immediately. It did, and by the afternoon of the following day, so the story goes, a new Mrs. Charles Phelps found herself in a wagon en route to Vermont.)

The year 1778 was not an ideal time to move to the northern outskirts of the British colonies. Things had been going badly for the Continental Army when a surprise Christmas 1776 attack on Hessian forces at Trenton, New Jersey, had begun to turn the tide. Britain tried to sever the unruly New England colonies from their neighboring colonies, sending General John Burgoyne south from Quebec to capture and control the Hudson Valley. Vermont became vulnerable to the empire's army as it descended from Canada. Burgoyne was finally defeated at the Battles of Saratoga in September 1777 (at Freeman's Farm in September and Bemis Heights in October). The captured British troops' march to Boston took them through Northampton and Hadley, a spectacle that drew crowds as locals got to see for themselves that the news of the defeat of the regulars was indeed true, buoying patriot spirits. Indeed, the only British troops that most men and women in Hampshire County ever saw in earnest were these bedraggled men, marching in defeat toward Boston. Patriots' morale was lifted once again when they learned that in the wake of American victories in Saratoga, the French, having secretly supported the American cause, had now openly joined the war effort, entering into a formal alliance with the American forces against the British. This would prove a turning point in the colonists' military fortunes. News of the French alliance, when it reached New Englanders, generated optimism that the colonies could indeed win their freedom. Hatfield taverns surely buzzed when the March 28, 1778, issue of the *Massachusetts Spy* arrived, reporting some of the first news that France had formally recognized the United States as independent of Great Britain. For those colonists who had launched a rebellion, things were looking up.

But though Vermont ceased to be a hotspot of military conflict, the looming presence of the British in nearby Canada and their control of Lake Champlain kept the residents in a constant state of alert. An oral tradition set down when Ephraim Newton years later penned *History of the Town of Marlborough* puts Rebecca's sister Martha at the center of the drama there. According to the story, at the end of October 1780 word

spread of an impending attack by a band of Tories and their Native allies. Observers had seen the glow of fire in the sky and believed enemy
forces to be encamped nearby, having apparently assaulted the town of
Newfane, about fourteen miles north. The militia quickly assembled
and marched out of town, while the town's women and children evacuated to a safe location. In her haste, Martha Mather left bread baking
in her oven. But no attack was made, and the local militia returned
home before the community's women and children and found Mather's
bread, now baked, in the oven. Famished from the march, they "left
not a whit behind." The whole thing had been a misunderstanding
born of fear. In an early freak storm, two feet of snow had fallen. "The
good people of Newfane, after clearing land on that last pretty day in
October, had simply decided to set fire to their own brush and log
piles; it seems the reflection of the snowy night sky gave the neighboring villages the false impression that the town was being burned by
the enemy."[12]

Of course this is the sort of oral tradition that cannot be confirmed
in traditional archival sources. It doesn't really tell us much if anything
about Martha Mather, the town militia, or the revolution as it unfolded
in Vermont. Instead, it tells us something about how the revolution
would in time—once victory was achieved and the new nation secured—
come to be remembered among New England families. The story survived in local history because it offered some humor in the wake of what
were in fact anxious times, when any light in the sky could signal big
trouble coming. That it all ended well, and nothing more was lost than
Martha Mather's batch of freshly baked bread, gave people comfort for
decades to come.

6

Rebellion, Redux

As Rebecca Dickinson watched the war press on, she and her community prepared for life in a new nation. The independence effort had gotten off to a shaky start, but with victories in New York and New Jersey, and the addition of the French alliance, prospects for the Americans had become brighter and brighter. The war was not yet over, but the theaters of war moved farther and farther from Hatfield. Dickinson was now in her forties. She had rejected at least one proposal of marriage—maybe more—and was single now clearly by choice.

These were years of transition for Rebecca Dickinson, her family, and the newly emerging nation. The question of independence for the colonies united in rebellion was closer to being settled—and so (it would seem) was the question of independence for Dickinson. Yet for both, appearances were not altogether what they seemed. Across Massachusetts, although the revolution itself came to a close, and the formal treaty finally achieved with Britain notwithstanding, lingering unsettled business prevented a true sense of peace from settling over the countryside. The 1780s in Massachusetts were filled with political and social agitation, some of it prompted by ongoing dissatisfaction with elements of the revised state constitution. Unrest came right on the heels of the end of the war and persisted throughout the events now termed Shays's Rebellion. At the same time, on the home front the death of Dickinson's father as well as her sister Irene altered the family's circumstances, and Dickinson continued both to resist and to embrace her unmarried status, feeling reconciled to the patterns of her life one minute and doubting them the next.

As the war dragged on, the seat of battle shifted ever southward. The British had evacuated Boston some years before, heading for the middle colonies, and in time attention turned to the south again, to Virginia, the Carolinas, and the Caribbean. People in Hatfield began to feel like the worst was over well before peace was secured. The rebellion and the sacrifices it demanded were no longer as acutely felt. As the fighting migrated farther and farther afield, Hatfield families were increasingly engaged less in actual warfare than in funding the war effort. In time a committee was appointed to tally up the contributions various families had made to the war effort and make any necessary adjustments. On June 24, 1779, the town voted to allocate a large sum (some £500) to enable the selectmen to procure shirts, stockings, and shoes for the Continental Army—an effort that may well have again drawn in women across the community, if they helped sew shirts or knit stockings.

Continued challenges associated with potential hoarding and price gouging as well as inflation engaged public attention in these months. Bostonians launched a proposal to convene in Concord to discuss matters. In July 1779 some 170 men from 120 towns met, setting price ceilings for an array of goods and urging towns to set prices for services and labor. Hatfield and Hadley both sent delegates to, and approved the work of, the Concord convention. The next month Hadley hosted a meeting of county towns to follow up on the need to set uniform prices. Figures were suggested for labor in a range of trades that employed both men and women, including artisans who worked in the clothing trades. In the rate documents that survive for nearby South Hadley, male tailors were advised to set their rates at two shillings, eight pence for a day's labor, whereas women were allocated half that. Gownmakers like Rebecca Dickinson conformed to such ceilings or risked running afoul of the revolution's local leadership.

Rebecca Dickinson also observed as strenuous debate about not one but two state constitutions unfolded. In 1778 the legislature had drafted a constitution to serve as the basis for the new state's government and submitted it to a vote at town meetings held throughout the state. But this constitution was rejected by a margin of three to one, in part because the document lacked a bill of rights, but also because the text was written by the sitting legislators, not by the separate convention that many citizens believed necessary to generate a constitution to serve as the state's fundamental law. So at a constitutional convention in fall 1779, John Adams, Samuel Adams, and James Bowdoin were charged with drafting a new document. John Adams alone would craft the text subsequently sent out to the various towns for consideration.

In Hatfield, first the assembled men (no women, of course, were asked to deliberate) voted on whether to accept the draft as written, a motion that was soundly defeated, 31–8.[1] The body then turned to a debate on the document's features. Most important, the Hatfield men suggested amending a line stating that "every denomination of Christians, demeaning themselves peaceably and as good subjects of the commonwealth, shall be equally under the protection of the law; and no subordination of any sect or denomination to another shall ever be established by law." Having fought so many wars against France's Catholic forces, Dickinson's Congregational community hoped to insert the word "Protestant" before "Christians" to ensure that no equality was conferred on papists. This measure passed 27–13. Similarly, the body wished to stipulate that the governor be required to declare not simply that he was an adherent of the "Christian religion," but specifically the "Protestant religion" (this passed 33–7). The delegates also came out in favor of term limits for civil and military offices, based on the logic that voters might not really know the people for whom they were voting, and it would be unhealthy for an incumbent to gain control of any office for too long. They also wished to prevent people whose jobs depended on their personal "connections" from acquiring long tenure, and recognized—pragmatically—that sometimes when "persons grow old they are fond of their offices" and remain so well after "everybody (except themselves) are sensible that they are unfit to continue."

Despite having joined a chorus of towns demanding revisions, Hatfield signaled its overall approval of the draft, and by June 1780 enough towns had given their consent that the new constitution was ratified.

(Most of the various amendments proposed here and elsewhere were not, in the end, incorporated and lingering dissatisfaction would reemerge before long.) The fight for independence was not yet over, but this new constitution, ratified by "We the People" of Massachusetts, became and remains the oldest written constitution in effect in the world today.

The document, as many soon argued, had the effect of abolishing slavery in Hatfield and the commonwealth of Massachusetts. Some enslaved men and women had of course already found ways to secure their own freedom, and the outbreak of fighting had offered some new opportunities. Some enslaved men seized the opportunity of the war to secure their own liberty. When the war began in April 1775, Hatfield's enslaved resident Asahel Wood, for instance, secured the permission of his owner, Elisha Allis, to join the colony's forces in Cambridge and would in time join the Continental Army; a man enslaved by Hadley's Phelps family, known as Caesar, also seized the opportunity to exchange farmwork for military service, joining the Continental Army in Cambridge and eventually traveling to Fort Ticonderoga. But even earlier, in 1773 and 1774, a number of captive residents began asking the General Court in a series of petitions to end slavery in Massachusetts, grounding their appeal in the same principles that the colonists were articulating in their struggle with Great Britain. In 1777 yet another petition from "a great number of blacks" asserted that "they have in common with all other men a natural and unaliable [inalienable] right to that freedom which the great parent of the universe hath bestowed equally on all mankind and which they have never forfeited by any compact or agreement whatever." Calling out the so-called patriots on their obvious hypocrisy, they sought an act ending the institution of slavery "so may the inhabitants of this state no longer chargeable with the inconsistency of acting themselves the part which they condemn and oppose in others."[2]

The 1778 constitution had accepted slavery as a legal institution—providing another reason for the growing numbers of slavery's opponents to reject that document. The 1780 version did not include any outright condemnation of slavery (as had the constitution for the new state of Vermont), but did assert that "all men are born free and equal, and have . . . the right of enjoying and defending their lives and liberty."

This phrase alone did not make slavery immediately illegal, but it did undermine its basis in law, and captive Africans and African Americans were eager to assert its implications by suing for freedom in the courts. It would take some time for those words to change lives; although some slave owners responded fairly quickly to the presumption of African American freedom, others resisted until they were compelled to do otherwise. When Quock Walker and Elizabeth "Mumbet" Freeman sued for their liberty between 1781 and 1783, their attorneys cited the language of the 1780 constitution; the court concurred, and the institution of slavery in Massachusetts began to be gradually dismantled. In the coming years it would fade from the region, though slowly. New Hampshire, like Massachusetts, would end slavery through a series of court rulings, whereas Connecticut and Rhode Island passed gradual emancipation laws in 1784 that freed slaves when they reached adulthood.

The decisions in the Walker and Freeman cases did not instantly liberate all of the state's captive laborers, but the language approved surely gave hope to Hatfield's enslaved men and women and conferred freedom on some right away. Seeing the writing on the wall, men like David Billings chose to free their slaves.[3] Silas Billings's father made a similar decision: Joseph Billings's 1781 will freed his slave Peter, as well as Peter's sons, Jonah and Peter. Two others, Eliphalet and Amos, were to be manumitted when they reached the age of twenty-one. Until then both would remain "under the control of and detained in the immediate service of" Silas, Rebecca's brother-in-law. The will was proved in May 1783; their age at the time of these events and the duration of their continued enslavement is unknown, but Eliphalet and Jonah seem to still have been in the Billings household some years later, when Rebecca noted their presence among others there. At least one appeared to be still in residence when the first federal census was taken in 1790, and perhaps both were when the second census was completed in 1800, because at least two free people of color were counted at that time. Whenever Eliphalet or Jonah claimed his promised freedom, their cases and others remind us how gradual and uneven such processes often were. Events in the courts aside, Israel Williams's will, written in 1783, bequeathed a woman named Blossom to his daughter Eunice. Williams lived until 1788, and whether Blossom ever achieved her own independence, we cannot know.

The 1780 constitution also addressed other matters involving property, establishing new thresholds for officeholding and voting. At that time Rebecca Dickinson had just acquired some property, though no one would have expected that she, as a woman, would then have become a voter, let alone officeholder, as well. (The only state to grant suffrage to women was New Jersey, where women were able to vote from 1776 until the policy was reversed in 1807.) In January 1780 Dickinson's father Moses, "in consideration of the love and good will" he felt toward his eldest daughter and "as part of her portion" (that is, this would be considered an advance on whatever part of his estate she would receive after his death), gave Rebecca some seventy acres of land in a part of Hatfield that had only recently become Williamsburg. No records survive to tell us whether Rebecca was able to derive any income from this land. The steep, rocky parcel, which lay just off the road west to Conway, was not viable as farmland. More likely it served as woodlot or pasture, perhaps cut over for potash (a chemical substance derived from plant ashes and used in making soap and bleaching fabrics) and rented out to a farmer who harvested wood, fattened cattle for market, or raised sheep there.[4] Perhaps Moses meant this to offer some sort of security to his unmarried daughter as she advanced in age; whether she gained regular income from renting it out to area residents or simply got some peace of mind from having this asset available for future sale is another part of the past that we cannot now recover.

News of the October 1781 defeat of the British Army at Yorktown, Virginia, was surely received with great joy in Hatfield, though little record survives of the moment word arrived. All told, about 124 men from Hatfield and environs had served in the war, including two of Rebecca's five brothers-in-law (but not, apparently, her brother Samuel). No one had seen more action than Hatfield's Joseph Guild, who was at the battles of Saratoga to help defeat the advance of General Burgoyne. Guild remained with the Continental Army as it wintered over at Valley Forge, marched to New Jersey's Monmouth Court House in June 1778, then headed south to confront British troops across the Carolinas and in Virginia at Yorktown. Guild later told his friends and neighbors that he had seen with his own eyes the moment when Lord Cornwallis yielded his sword, and that the great General Washington personally shook his hand when the army at last disbanded.

In the months following Yorktown, although fighting ceased in the colonies on the North American mainland, action continued elsewhere. In the West and East Indies the international contest over very valuable islands continued hot. In London the defeat in Virginia had brought about the collapse of the administration of Lord North. In April 1782 the House of Commons voted to bring the war to a close. Formal peace followed with the September 1783 Treaty of Paris; by the end of November 1783, the last of the British troops had sailed from New York.

Peace was restored, but the war left turmoil in its wake. The years during and after the revolution were difficult for Americans and for local and state economies. Some Hatfield farmers had profited from the sale of cattle to feed the troops during the war. (It helped that Epaphroditus Champion, a purchasing agent during the Revolutionary War, had provisioned the armed forces in part from the Hatfield tavern of his mother-in-law, Rebecca's friend Lucy Hubbard.) However, most Massachusetts families had seen the economy disrupted by the war and now struggled as the cost of the conflict was confronted. Taxes rose, and courts hummed as wholesalers sued retailers, and creditors sued debtors.

For many Hampshire County families, the squeeze was on. What could be done to relieve the pressure? In April 1782 men from three dozen towns gathered in Hatfield over the course of several days to discuss the mounting economic problems. A motion was made to request that the Inferior Court "forbear giving judgment in civil causes," except in limited circumstances. Delegates from Hatfield voted "nay" with the majority, signaling their support of court operations as usual, but just days later, crowds anxious to slow the progress of these lawsuits tried to prevent the Supreme Judicial Court and the Court of Common Pleas from sitting in Northampton. A leader, Samuel Ely, was captured and jailed. Two months later a crowd forced his release, but then the leaders of that action were captured and held in Northampton—essentially hostages until Ely returned to accept responsibility for his role in the disturbance. The unrest came to Rebecca Dickinson's front door on June 15 when hundreds of local men gathered in Hatfield's main street, ready to march to demand the men's release. A militia of another twelve hundred men convened to defend the jail. Eventually, after days of tense negotiation, the prisoners were freed.

Once again, towns opted to meet to discuss a collective response to the crisis. Conventions drew representatives from area towns to Hatfield on August 7–10, 1782, and again in March 1783. In October 1783 towns sent delegates to a meeting at the tavern of Hatfield innkeeper Seth Murray. Murray's tavern, often the scene of large public meetings, must have been a lucrative business; a decade later, when Dickinson made her first visit to the Murray home, she seemed truly taken aback by the affluence displayed there, noting "what a world of prosperity . . . [they] have enjoyed" (June 29, 1794).[5] Surely the taverns of Rebecca's friend Lucy Hubbard and her sister Miriam Billings were also, during these political conventions, crowded and loud with spirited debate. Taverns were central to public life in New England towns, and tavern-keeping families were key figures in the dissemination of news and information. Most tavernkeepers—or at least license holders—were men, but women too earned their livings behind the bar. Many husbands and wives worked side by side to run taverns and inns, and in Hampshire County some two dozen women held licenses in their own names. Lucy Hubbard and her husband Elisha had opened their tavern in 1768, when the unrest over imperial policy occupied public attention. When Elisha died in the prime of life, Lucy carried on alone. The daughter of longtime tavernkeepers, she was well prepared to oversee their Hatfield enterprise, and she kept the thriving tavern for more than a decade. Although the work was newer to Miriam than it had been for Lucy, she and Silas had the African American men Jonah and Eliphalet to help, and likely the labor of some women—black or white we do not know—as well. In moments of public debate, the Hubbard and Billings taverns, as well as Seth Murray's, were important nodes in local decision making, and women were central to their operation.

These conventions in the early 1780s kept economic questions front and center, but did little to resolve the issue. Closer to home for Rebecca, in the midst of this political and economic uncertainty, in

September 1785 her father Moses died, having reached the grand age of seventy-four. As he was approaching his death, Moses Dickinson sat down to write a will in which he provided for each of his "loving" daughters equally, bequeathing "the sum of sixty six pounds thirteen shillings and four pence of silver money that I have advanced to each of them to be accounted as part thereof the remainder [i.e., anything more than this amount that might be left over after the final bills of the estate were settled] to be paid by my son Samuel in two years after my decease."[6] He made no special provision for his unmarried daughter Rebecca, suggesting that he did not perceive her (perhaps because of the recent transfer of the Williamsburg property) as unusually needful at that time. When his family buried him, they chose a monument for their father that reflected much about Hatfield in the last decades of the eighteenth century. The slate marker that stands over his grave in the town's burial ground carries an angel in the tympanum, vines flanking the inscription "in memory of" Moses Dickinson. The stone marked more than the man's grave. Times were changing, and so were attitudes toward death and the afterlife. Once grave markers ornamented with death's heads strove to remind observers of their own mortality. Now attitudes were softening, and attention increasingly was directed not to the dead body, but to the person, the life to be recalled with affection. When Rebecca and her siblings instructed the stone carver to use these elements, they embraced and helped advance those larger transformations in the town and the nation's religious culture.

Rebecca Dickinson experienced other moments of loss in 1785, one involving the intriguing Jesse Billings. The revolution appears to have been sour for Billings who, as Reverend Lyman would observe in the church records, had taken overmuch to the use of "spirituous liquors" in the town's taverns. More important, he had been making himself scarce from church services, especially communion, and as if those errors weren't enough, he had begun speaking "irreverently and profanely of the holy scripture." Jesse Billings and his wife Sarah had been the first couple Lyman admitted to church membership after his arrival in Hatfield, but perhaps Lyman's pulpit patriotism had become grating for Billings, who had found himself on the wrong side of public emotion early on in the uprising. The members of the church had no choice but to admonish him. Billings was formally censured by Rebecca's beloved Reverend Lyman, and Rebecca would in time refer to Billings as "wicked." Whatever feelings Rebecca may once have had for Billings, and however mournful she may have been about the course of events between them, by the 1780s she judged him harshly.

Having buried Moses in late summer 1785, just five months later the family mourned another loss when Rebecca's sister Irene died in "childbed" in her house near the top of Petticoat Hill in Williamsburg. Irene and Lucius's first child had been born several months before their wedding, and Irene later gave birth to two and possibly three more sons before she and Lucius conceived a girl. Complications of this birth claimed the life of Rebecca's sister. The infant daughter was named Irene in her honor, but the child then died also. Later Rebecca would note that "Rene" "was sixteen years younger than myself, but she is gone, her place . . . filled by another. Her two little sons are comfortable beyond my hopes" (July [], 1790). Lucius had not remained a widower for long; Irene died in February, and he was remarried by midsummer, surely eager to find another mother for his family of young children. But things did not go well for the Graves family, and in time, to survive and pay his debts, Lucius began selling off his property, bit by bit, most of it to his neighbor, Joseph Wait. Hard times had come to the Graves home—as they had to much of western Massachusetts.[7]

In the mid-1780s Hatfield found itself caught up in another eruption of dissent, one that would reverberate well beyond Massachusetts. This "rebellion" is associated with the leadership of a Pelham farmer named Daniel Shays, but the discontent that drove this upheaval was widespread and involved hundreds of men across the commonwealth.

The state's economic crisis, occasioned by the war, had continued, and the Ely episode turned out to be the opening act in a longer drama. Conditions had not improved, and apparently people in the direst straits had begun to resort to out-and-out theft. At least in summer 1785, in Moses Dickinson's final days, Hatfield families felt sufficiently threatened (as the July 28,1785, *Massachusetts Spy* reported) to enter into a pact to support a force of eight men charged with pursuing thieves. But by and large, when financial distress led to courtrooms, it was not theft but rather debt that was the cause. Taxes had risen precipitously, while at the same time the cash needed to pay them became increasingly scarce. As the economy slid into recession, more and more families found themselves strapped. Petitions for relief went unanswered. People mulled over the causes of their suffering, and a widespread critique emerged that focused on the courts as central to the problem. Not only was the cost of the court system itself a burden, but it was the court that most immediately punished debtors and rewarded creditors. And so, as they had been during the revolution just concluded, the courts once again became the focus of public attention and mass action.

Towns continued contemplating their collective response to public events through mass meetings, or conventions, at which delegates sent by each community assembled to discuss shared concerns and formulate joint responses. On August 15, 1786, some thirty-seven Worcester County towns convened to discuss a response to the economic crisis, and on August 22 delegates from another fifty towns in Hampshire County gathered, once again meeting at the Hatfield tavern of Seth Murray.[8] The men talked for three days and in the end articulated seventeen grievances. John Hastings, still Hatfield's representative to the state legislature, helped define a series of complaints that criticized the ways state government undermined the economy and created significant inequities.

These gatherings attacked elements of the 1780 Constitution that had never sat well with some citizens. Indeed, one of the issues at stake during Shays's Rebellion was the legitimacy of the state government itself. More than simply the debt crisis or the current administration's fiscal or tax policies, the Constitution itself remained suspect, especially in Western Massachusetts, where only a fraction of towns had voiced approval of the document. Grumbling surfaced about the property qualifications necessary to hold office and about the very existence of the Senate, which struck many as an aristocratic vestige inconsistent with the values of a republic. Delegates gathered in local conventions proposed significant changes to elections in the lower house of the state legislature and suggested moving the whole thing out of Boston. They condemned the Courts of Common Pleas and General Sessions, questioning their existence too. In fact, the substantive questions raised at these conventions may have caused just as much concern in Boston as the later taking up of arms—itself more easily contained (once the militia was mobilized) than widespread discontent or (worse) rejection of the established government.

The men gathered also formally discouraged crowd actions, although "one of the chief effects" of these meetings, one chronicler would later suggest, "was to arouse the mob spirit to an attack on the courts."[9] Indeed, the listing of grievances seemed to some almost perfunctory. As one participant noted in the pages of his diary, the delegates knew the outcome going in: they would deliberate, articulate their complaints, and then "break up the court next week."[10] A week later, on August 29, the date the Court of Common Pleas and the General Sessions of the Peace were scheduled to open at Northampton, masses of men converged, coming down the hill from Pelham and picking up more in Amherst, a handful more in Hadley, and then, having crossed the Connecticut River into Northampton, found there an armed crowd numbering in the hundreds to greet them, likewise intent on preventing the courts from doing any business. When the justices appeared, clad in the accoutrements of their office—the robes and wigs that signaled their authority—they found the courthouse door blocked. They retreated to a local inn and met with a small delegation from the protesters. The men occupied the courthouse until midnight; the judges at last acquiesced and adjourned.

The arrival of delegates from more than four dozen towns and the crowd action to follow certainly set Hatfield in a stir—the taverns must have been bulging at the corner boards—but Rebecca Dickinson did not witness these events. On August 16, 1786, she had left to visit her sister in Pittsfield (August 16, 1787). Was it only chance that she was away from her home just as tumult descended on the town? Or did Dickinson, sensing impending violence, purposely make herself scarce?

Through September, courts across Massachusetts were prevented from doing their work. The insurgency's leaders were indicted by the Supreme Judicial Court, and when that court tried to meet in Springfield in late September, Shays and his fellow protestors decided to shut it down. William Shepard, a local militia leader, had rallied several hundred men to help protect the courthouse. In the end, the clash ended in something of a stalemate, Shays's troops marching in demonstration and the judges adjourning without doing any real business. Shepard's forces withdrew to the federal armory in Springfield. (The arsenal, erected in the early years of the revolution, held some seven thousand muskets with bayonets and thirteen hundred barrels of powder.) But with Shays and what were now some twelve hundred insurgents threatening public order and crowds continuing to close courts across Massachusetts, many men and women, having just endured the war for independence, felt that armed conflict was again looming.

A convention met in Hadley on November 8, 1786, to again debate the issues and—in keeping with the precedent lately set by their counterparts in Worcester County—when it adjourned, sent a letter to all the towns in Hampshire County suggesting that another convention be held to continue discussion on the first Tuesday in January, this time to gather again in Hatfield. The January 2, 1787, convention in Hatfield framed an address urging the insurgents to lay down their arms and pursue their complaints through the General Court. The newly established *Hampshire Gazette* (the county's first local newspaper, launched in part by Federalists eager to shape public opinion on the upheaval) captured the sense of the moment. "This Commonwealth is in a most alarming situation," the January 10, 1787, issue reported, "by reason of great uneasiness [about] the situation of our government," and residents were "exceedingly divided" about what to do. "Some cry one thing, and some another, and many flying to arms; yea, are we not in the most imminent danger of bringing on a civil war, which in all probability will involve us in everlasting ruin." In the interests of peace, the men assembled urged their readers to lay down their arms and "unitedly join with us in our prayers to the Legislature for a redress of our grievances." A "house divided against itself cannot stand," these observers opined.

By now Governor Bowdoin had succeeded in calling out militiamen from Suffolk County (which then included today's Norfolk County) and Middlesex County—some four thousand in all. These men, under the command of Benjamin Lincoln, marched west to confront the insurgents.[11] At the same time, attention remained focused on the federal arsenal in Springfield. In late January Shays and his men decided to attack. The arsenal was now defended by some twelve hundred men.

When Shays's men approached, Shepard fired into the crowd, killing four. After this clash the insurgents scattered. When the forces in Worcester received word of events in Springfield they headed west, catching up with the rebel troops in Petersham on February 4, 1787. Troops pursued and captured many of the protestors. One final skirmish, at Sheffield on February 27, resulted in the deaths of more protestors and one government soldier, and the revolt ended. Four thousand men would confess to rebellion and receive amnesty. But across the state more men had turned out to serve in the militias that put down the rebellion than did to support it.

This time Rebecca's family—or at least part of it—had been on the side of law and order, not dissent. A postscript to these dramatic events suggests Rebecca Dickinson's take on them. Her brother-in-law Silas Billings was a leader in the local armed forces. In October 1787 she noted that gathered at Northampton, apparently for a training exercise, was "Colonel [Seth] Murray's regiment, about seven hundred men." Rebecca's brother-in-law Silas Billings "was captain from this town"; together with Captain Chapin from Whately, he "made a grand appearance as the times go." But Dickinson's real interest lay elsewhere. "There happened a sad affair the same day," she noted: Eleazer Allis "was taken out of Captain Billings' company" for "going to see Electa Wait, a young woman of seventeen years of age." Allis was unfortunately a "married man who buried his only child but four weeks ago." His stunned and wounded wife, still grieving over the death of her child, upon learning of her husband's infidelity "attempted to drown herself and was in fits all the day." Dickinson hoped for the best. Her wish—"may not their marriage union be broken, but may order arise out of confusion"—could be said to stand for unity on both the political and the domestic fronts. Recalling Lyman's suggestion that it was the spiritual shortcomings of the faithful that visited on a wayward populace the trials leading to revolution, she asked for "help Lord, for sin and all manner of evils abound. Have pity on this land by reason of whoredom and fornication and all manner of impure doings." Put another way, in Dickinson's mind the disorder of the times was all of a piece: some analysts would point to the state constitution of 1780 and others to networks of debtors and creditors, but Dickinson's faith, age, and gender prompted her to interpret the chaos of Shays's Rebellion that had shaped the past year as a sign of God's chastising hand on a sexually errant people.

The confusion Hatfield was experiencing was also felt hundreds of miles away, in Philadelphia, where the threat of disorder was among the forces that pushed the assembled delegates to consider the creation of a much stronger federal government to link the former colonies. Critics of the Articles of Confederation that had organized the union of states throughout the revolution had launched a movement to supplant them with an entirely new and much stronger document. Though their path was not smooth, Federalist supporters were able to overcome the anti-Federalist opposition. A new U.S. Constitution was adopted in September 1787 and sent to the states for ratification. If and when nine of the thirteen states voted to ratify the document, that Constitution would take effect. Debate in Massachusetts was fierce; some 364 delegates gathered to argue the merits of the new form of government, Federalists supporting endorsing the document, while anti-Federalists worried that this accumulation of power in a strong central government threatened the very liberty everyone had just sacrificed so much to achieve. Finally, Governor John Hancock proposed that the state append a series of recommendations, including a Bill of Rights, to the document. With Hatfield's John Hastings voting "yea," Massachusetts then became the sixth state to ratify, on February 6, 1788.

A rare glimpse into Rebecca Dickinson's political inclinations appears in her diary entry for February 9, 1788: "God in a wonderful manner and after many great debates the joyful news that the people of this state had received the Constitution given them by the Congress. God has heard my request and my soul hopes for the blessing of heaven to attend it." In this she shared the views of her brother-in-law Lucius Graves, a passionate Federalist, and almost certainly those of brother-in-law Silas Billings as well. But we don't necessarily know why. Perhaps she was convinced that a strong central government was key to economic prosperity, or she may simply have desired a general restoration of order. Surely Reverend Lyman had been leading prayers on the Constitution's behalf under the shelter of the Hatfield meetinghouse, which Rebecca Dickinson apparently joined with fervor.

Israel Williams did not live to see that watershed moment. The month before, in a "sad accident," he fell down a flight of stairs and died. The aging colonel "was looking into a cellarway on the account of burning the chimney, his head swimming as is supposed, and he fell down to the bottom of the stairs and beat a hole in his head which bled a pint. He lived an hour but knew nothing what ailed him" (January 13, 1788). Despite her occasional criticisms of Williams, Dickinson noted his death with sorrow. He was, she now believed, "a person of great abilities and of great prosperity the forepart of his life" who had "greatly fallen in his old age"—something she hoped had "worked for his good." Indeed, "he appeared to get the good of his troubles in the last seventeen years of his life" (meaning that he had learned from the challenging experiences and was improved by them). But whether or not his earthly struggles had done anything for his faith, now "his soul is fled to God and of all his greatness nothing but the winding sheet and coffin, and this is the end of the great ones of the world." More important, Dickinson recalled, Williams had been "a great friend to the poor" who "has given of his money to those who called for charity and to those who did not ask" he still likewise "shared his bounty." She knew this firsthand. "He was a kind friend to me for a number of years back in my lonesome days," she observed, "making me welcome to his house and table."

Williams's funeral sermon was given by his longtime adversary, Reverend Lyman. The occasion brought Rebecca's dear friend Lucretia Williams home to Hatfield. The willful daughter of privilege seems to have remained unreconciled to independence. As a girl she had taken food to her father while he was imprisoned by the rebels, and in so doing was forced to "[submit] to the greatest indignities from suspicious opposers."[12] Though the Williams family does not appear to have been subjected to the property confiscations that many loyalists endured, loyalist women across Massachusetts—and the wives and daughters of loyalist men, whatever their own political inclinations may have been—did risk losing their homes and goods to the rebel government. Some became refugees, fleeing their homes and loved ones to start their lives anew in Canada, the Caribbean, or England. Hatfield men appeared among some three hundred individuals named in the Banishment Act of September 1778, which sought to either evict or prevent the return of people who had joined the enemy side. When the October 29, 1778, *Massachusetts Spy* had published the "act to prevent the return to this state of certain person therein named, and others, who have left this state . . . and joined the enemies thereof," it listed three Hatfield residents as threats. Thomas Cutler had joined the British forces; after the war he moved, with many other loyalists, to Nova Scotia. Ann Allis, who had married the physician Josiah Pomeroy in the summer of 1774, found herself in Montreal after her husband took a position as a surgeon in the British Army; their property in the United States was confiscated by the state. Abigail Dickinson's husband Roger (remembered in local history for having named a son Loyal George, making his own inclinations plain) took a position as a blacksmith with the British Army, although we don't know whether she chose to follow him and take up that itinerant life or to tough it out in Hatfield. Like many women married to loyalist men, she may have stayed behind to defend her family's assets from patriot clutches. Some women had actively resisted the revolution, serving as spies for the British Army; funneling supplies to British troops; and sheltering assets, documents, and men in support of the Crown's forces. Whatever her own experiences, for the royally inclined Lucretia Williams, the events of the revolution had been harrowing. As she returned home to bury her father, the ratification of the U.S. Constitution surely seemed no victory. While Rebecca Dickinson embraced the creation of a strong federal government, Lucretia Williams did not. Williams lived the rest of her life in western Massachusetts; family memory and local tradition held that she considered herself a loyal subject of the king of England until her own death in 1834.

7

Reproducing the Nation

As pleased as Dickinson was to see the new nation grow and thrive, she remained at a distance from some of the developments that accompanied life in the newly created United States. In the early years of the American republic women—so essential to the protest movement and then to the wartime military and home front—saw a new culture emerge that encouraged them (or at least middle-class and elite white women) to retreat from public affairs and make their contribution to the nation in more traditional ways. An emerging ethic of "Republican Motherhood"—a set of beliefs grounded in the premise that women in the new nation would exert influence not through the vote or any other direct political action, but rather by raising virtuous citizens—was reshaping women's lives across New England. This would, however, have only indirect meaning for Dickinson, for whom being a "Republican Aunt" would have to suffice.

As national focus shifted from female action to feminine virtue in the 1780s and 1790s, Rebecca Dickinson observed with some alarm changing patterns of sexual behavior. She was not a mother, but as the sole remaining child still at home with her own mother in the Dickinson homestead, she did grow into her role as an aunt and also acquired a nurturing, quasi-parental role as the mistress to the young apprentices she trained in her trade. It was a good thing that she began to have help, given the revolution in fashion that generated business in the last decade of the eighteenth century. Gownmaking continued to support a role for

Rebecca Dickinson in her community that replaced that of mother or grandmother, as she helped launch the new nation as best she could.

If former colonists celebrating the ratification of the Constitution is a scene easily conjured in our historical imagination, an entry in Dickinson's diary from around this time reminds us just how wide a gap separates us from the late eighteenth century, particularly in our understanding of health and the human body. "The corpse of the wife of Joshua Dickinson" (no relation), she wrote in summer 1788, "was taken up in order for the cure of her granddaughter after she had lain in her grave three years" (August 3, 1788). Her friend, tavernkeeper Lucy Hubbard, had passed on to Rebecca the "sad relation" of these tragic events, and given that Lucy's house stood next to the town burial ground, Hubbard was in a position to know. Perhaps she even watched as the grisly business unfolded. The trouble started when consumption (now known as tuberculosis) began raging through the family of the Reverend Justus Forward and his wife, Violet Dickinson Forward. Three of their girls were dead, and now a fourth showed symptoms of illness. A bloody cough, fevers and chills, a loss of appetite, and draining fatigue: the evidence was clear, and the tragic outcome predictable. Having exhausted the expertise of the local medical establishment, the family turned to folk tradition. They exhumed the body of Martha Morton Dickinson, Violet's mother, who had died in August 1785 of consumption, acting on the belief that her diseased body might somehow be drawing life from her living family members. If clotted blood remained in her heart, it would be burned to stop the course of the disease. But, Dickinson reported, "She was not what they had sought for her inwards was consumed or putrified." The body did not hold the hoped-for cure.

The family's gruesome action was not an isolated instance. "The week before last," Dickinson added, the heart "was taken out of the wife of Prinny Dwight who has been dead near six years." The "heart was whole after she was dead six years with fresh blood, but what use to be made of it I am not able to write." The phrase, "but what use to be made of it I am not able to write," might at first suggest that she did not know what use would be made of it, but she probably meant that she lacked the stomach to commit to paper what she heard had occurred. According to the folk belief at the time, the heart, if found to be bloody, must be burned and the ashes fed to the patient to ensure recovery.[1] It seems that the Dwights, in their sorrow and desperation, pursued this horrific course to the end, though "it appears folly to me," Dickinson observed.

That such an event could occur in the so-called Age of Enlightenment reminds us how uneven was the progress of scientific knowledge. Although great leaps were being made that would revolutionize medical understanding, great misapprehensions endured. But if some beliefs about disease, the body, and healing could persist over centuries, alongside continuity came change. Family size, in particular, was in flux during these years. In spring 1788 fifty-year-old Dickinson noted the death of Hannah Bardwell, a woman who "has had four children"; the "number so many pitch upon," she added, "as being a proper number" (March 17, 1788). New England families had once been quite large, ten and twelve children being unremarkable. But in the early republic rhetoric was encouraging families to control their fertility. Whether motivated by a desire to invest more resources in a smaller number of children or something else, the emerging ethos of Republican Motherhood and its emphasis on the nurturing of young citizens, or some other reason, couples began to purposely leave more space between children (e.g., women began breastfeeding longer, because they believed, with some reason, that lactation made pregnancy less likely), and women stopped having children earlier in their lives, in their late thirties rather than their early forties. Demographers suggest that the average number of births per family when Dickinson recorded her observation was closer to six or eight than four, but clearly the notion that smaller families were better was afoot. Dickinson's tone implies that she felt somehow annoyed by the calls for reform, but whether it was advocates at a distance or her own family and friends who were doing the "pitching" is unknown.

Another set of events in the public sphere reminded Dickinson and her counterparts across the region of the consequences of violating marriage and family law and custom. On Sunday, July 27, 1788, Dickinson recorded a dramatic event that had occurred in Northampton ten days earlier, when "there was hanged . . . a girl of near thirty years of age for the murder of a bastard child." Abiel Converse had ended the life of her newborn, was discovered, and was sentenced to execution. Just before she died, Dickinson recorded, Converse "confessed that it was the second that she had murdered." "She was conducted to the gallows," Dickinson further noted, by a "large assembly of people, the greatest on the like occasion." Converse "was of a very poor family"; "she came from Worcester County and was living at Norwich [today Huntington, Massachusetts] when the fatal accident happened which cost her life."

Unwed, Converse had become pregnant, but was unable to terminate the pregnancy—not necessarily because it was illegal, because abortion before the child had "quickened" (i.e., when the mother first felt the fetus move) was legal in 1780s Massachusetts—but because she lacked either knowledge of or access to effective abortifacients (plants like savin or pennyroyal). In general abortion was condemned not because terminating a pregnancy was a sin per se, but because it was a deception, an effort to hide sinful sexual activity. The commonwealth had only recently passed a law making the concealment of a death a crime—in part because juries had become reluctant to prosecute women accused of killing their children, since it was easy to argue (and tough to disprove) that the child had been born dead or had died of natural causes. But if a woman had taken steps to hide her pregnancy, that was evidence of wrongdoing in and of itself. The latter helped lead to the hanging of Abiel Converse, who had become visibly pregnant, but persisted in denying it. She gave birth to the infant, but then (the courts alleged) caused its death, thereby attempting to hide the evidence of a pregnancy outside marriage.

Earlier in New England's history, both members of an unmarried couple who engaged in unsanctioned sex would have been punished in the courts and reprimanded in church. Beginning around the 1740s, however, the courts gradually lost interest in prosecuting men. As concern shifted away from punishing fathers, whatever the circumstances of conception, toward ensuring the financial support of the child, women found themselves in court alone. But the threat of punishment did not stop women from willingly having sex outside marriage, and by the era of the revolution, as many as a third or more of brides in some New England towns were pregnant at the time of the wedding.

Whether Dickinson was present at or simply heard about the execution secondhand is difficult to say. She may not have heard the sermon delivered, but rather read it. The remarks the Reverend Aaron Bascom delivered and later published (in a document that can be considered religious in purpose as well as an early example of the emerging genre of "true crime" literature) exclaimed to the condemned mother, "You saw him, a helpless defenseless babe, who had neither injured you nor any of your fellow creatures: your own child, born of your own body, whom you had been wickedly instrumental of bringing into the world; yet you hardened your heart against him, and determined that you would not exercise so much compassion towards him as the sea monsters who draw out their breasts and give suck to their young ones, but with violent hands you put him to death."[2] Bascom charged that although Converse "thought that this crime of murdering [her] child was not so great as the murder of an adult person," in fact it was worse, because it was done without provocation. "Guilty of a most horrid, monstrous and unnatural crime," Converse was said to be "exceedingly fond of profane, wicked company." Bascom also noted the "horrid lies" Converse had told as she denied repeatedly being in a "state of pregnancy," right up to the child's birth.

Bascom did not miss the chance to instruct the large assemblage as well—the largest, Dickinson claimed in her diary, to ever gather at such a grisly event. His message was clear: "Let all young persons, and especially young women, take warning from the present spectacle, and see that they don't consent when sinners entice them." Failure lay elsewhere, also: "How many children are undone for the want of good examples, good government and instructions from their parents?"

Dickinson's position was unsurprisingly unequivocal. Other comments recorded in the diary suggest she was "tough on crime." One summer, when farmers began losing crops to thieves, she wrote: "This day I would plead with God" to deal with "those who are guilty of robbing or taking that which does not belong to them." "This week," she continued, "there was a woman stole who was in the negro's [or negroes'] company [whether the woman was African American or a white woman keeping company with blacks is unclear], but she was not whipped as she deserved" (July [24], 1791). This occasion was far more severe, and Converse's punishment, Dickinson believed, was justified. "How forsaken she should be by every good angel to kill two little babies," Dickinson asserted. But this death surely provided a valuable lesson to the assembled crowd: "The purposes of heaven must stand in regard to good and evil. The lord of his tender love strike all those people who saw her spring from off the cart and hasten to her own death. May the sorrowful sight affect the minds of the beholders and may the sin affect their hearts."

She often took a moment to observe such warnings when they came. On another occasion, she wrote, "This day was read the confession of Silas Porter and Mary Porter for the sin of fornication" (August [31], 1787). Apparently Mr. and Mrs. Porter had welcomed a child too soon after their wedding, suggesting that the baby had been conceived before they were married. She bemoaned "how oft that sad chore is to be done." Another time she noted "this day there was read the confession of Elisabeth Wait, who has been guilty of the foul sin of fornication" (March [], 1792). But such warnings seemed to no avail. One November she again recorded that "this holy day was read the confession of Augustus Chapin and Lucina Graves for the sin of fornication." Lucina was the daughter of Seth Graves, Dickinson observed, "who has had the misfortune to see his two oldest daughters in the broad alley [i.e., the broad center aisle of the Congregational meetinghouse] for the same crime within a year's time." She hoped that the "sad warning of the shameful death of Abiel Converse with the friendly admonition given by Mr Bascom at Northampton" would "sink like lead in their hearts" (July [], 1788).

Another time she noted the death of a young woman, elsewhere in the diary called a "helpless whore," who had had "four children, three by three likely young men." "The last," Dickinson added, was a "married man . . . who has forsook his wife." The woman was twenty-six years old and "died in great horror of soul." But for Dickinson, the tragedy was larger. "I would plead with God," she wrote, "for this people for this generation of women . . . may no whoredom stain their lives." Dickinson guessed that in these days of "iniquity," "more than half who marry are forced to join in wedlock," and although historical demographers would say she was exaggerating, new mores and standards were indeed reshaping sexual behavior everywhere. "How many there be," she mused, "who are defiled before they are wives. The Lord of his tender love send his Holy Spirit to cure this sad disease," into which "so many are carried headlong" (August 12, 1792; September 25, 1790).

Was Dickinson in fact witnessing a sea change, a rampant transformation of sexual mores—for the worse, it seemed to those of the Calvinist faith? Or was this simply a case of a member of one generation looking at the next with skepticism and disapproval, as often happens? It was probably a little of both. The last quarter of the eighteenth century did seem to witness a seismic shift in sexual values as young people, flush with the rhetoric of independence, rejected the values of their parents. As they watched the republic's youth seem to abandon some of the beliefs they so cherished, those parents, who had secured independence at great cost and were now in the midst of building a new democratic nation they believed dependent upon the virtue of its citizens, worried that their sacrifices would be wasted. The divergent value systems also seem to have broken down along class lines. Women from laboring families expressed far less moral discomfort with bearing children out of wedlock than did their wealthier counterparts. As the courts gradually stopped enforcing the sexual values of the past (though they continued to monitor the economic consequences of unsanctioned pregnancy, ensuring as best they could that some man—and not the public welfare system—would pay for the support of the child), women like Rebecca Dickinson wrung their hands in concern.

Whether or not the rising generation of women really had forsaken the values of their parents, Dickinson seemed truly grieved by these events. "It pains me when I think on the many fine figures of young women who are destitute of virtue," she sighed (July 27, 1788). "O that God would cure those distempered persons that the contagion spread no further . . . may the rising generation be afraid of that killing sin which draws two persons into such a sad sin against their own bodies." "Clothe the females with chastity and purity of heart and life," she prayed, and "may the spirit of God keep this people where I dwell from that foul sin and give true repentance." Converse's sad case made her especially concerned for her various nieces and nephews, who were about to enter adolescence—Joseph Billings was about twelve, and the others not far behind—and begged God to "remember my little friends and cousins. . . . [M]ay the fear of God be stamped on their hearts and may their lives be agreeable to the pure rules of the gospel" (July 27, 1788).

Dickinson of course had no children of her own and that would not change now that she had reached the age of menopause. But being an aunt to her sisters and brother's children was an important role for her. If the demands of Republican Motherhood were actively perceived by families in the early republic, Dickinson channeled that energy into helping to raise her nieces and nephews. Her journal, especially throughout her fifties, is filled with references to her seventeen "little cousins," as she called them. On one representative occasion she wrote, "God has added to my life my little cousins;" "May they grow in favor with God," she added, "and be useful in the world . . . and be fit for their Lord's Service" (August 12, 1792). When John and Anne Ballard were considering an invitation to place their daughter Emily (called Milli) with an area family, probably as a domestic servant, Dickinson prayed: "May my soul dedicate the child to God though she is none of mine" (March [], 1789). She taught her nieces how to sew and fretted over her nephews when they went away to school. These children were constantly on her mind and became increasingly important to her as she grew older.

Taking on the role of aunt usually gave Dickinson great satisfaction. For example, when Rebecca's sister Martha considered sending her daughter Anne to live with Rebecca while the girl attended school, Dickinson wrote eagerly: "I wish to know the truth for I feel out of employ" (July 27, 1789). But sometimes the care of these young charges became a burden. For several years Rebecca shared her home with her nephew Charles Dickinson, a "poor weakly boy" given to "fits" (December 2, 1787). Born in April 1779, Charles was the first child of Rebecca's brother Samuel. He and Mary probably sent their son to live with his aunt so that he might be of some help there, although a less generous interpretation suggests that the "feeble" boy, perhaps of little use around his father's farm, was best boarded out. Despite his "bodily disorder," Charles cultivated a "mischievous disposition" and was a handful as Dickinson struggled to manage her craft, her housework, and caring for her mother. One summer, for example, Dickinson was plagued again by that "distressing disorder, the colic," but could not turn for care to her "little family": "How sad to be sick [with] my mother here, almost eighty years of age, [and] our little boy sick with fits. But my illness is so that I can do for myself" (June 27, 1790).

Dickinson also found herself in a quasi-parental role when she took on apprentices. She had now reached the stage of accomplishment in her trade at which she was directing the apprenticeships of a new generation of aspiring gownmakers. In so doing she helped participate, in her own artisanal way, in the training of the "rising generation," the young women and men who would succeed her own cohort of craftswomen. Although popular historical imagination has long suggested that only men undertook or directed apprenticeships, in fact both women and men took on trainees, who worked around the shop as they learned a trade. Because women were far less likely to need or complete the sorts of contracts describing these arrangements that have survived in archives, these relationships have been somewhat overlooked, but women, including Rebecca Dickinson, refer to experiences and people as apprenticeships and apprentices. So it should not surprise us that Dickinson found herself on the other side of the apprenticeship relationship that she had first encountered thirty years earlier, in her own girlhood. She had good reason to take on students, because they could help with the more routine aspects of the work while also providing companionship. As she became older, she probably welcomed the assistance of younger pairs of hands and eyes; it is also possible that parents paid her for instructing their daughters. Those benefits aside, taking on these apprentices also gave Dickinson some access to the pleasures of nurturing young people that her sisters enjoyed as parents, reminding us that for some members of eighteenth-century society, relationships outside the nuclear family may have been as important as or more important than those within it.

Here, at least on some occasions, the roles of aunt and employer overlapped, because among Dickinson's apprentices was her niece Rebecca Ballard. Opening her home to her niece and namesake again allowed

Dickinson to indulge in her role as "Republican Aunt" while providing a service to her larger family. The Ballards, Dickinson observed, were "distressingly poor" (September 2, 1792); John Ballard sometimes left Anne and their several children on their own, presumably while he went searching for work. Often, the poorest families had trouble digging out of their circumstances because they lacked the financial means even to place children in apprenticeship, but Anne Dickinson Ballard had chosen to place her daughter with her sister so that the young woman might learn a useful trade. Another of Dickinson's apprentices was Patty Smith, the daughter of Hadley merchant Warham Smith and his wife Martha. Patty's apprenticeship was probably more typical of the times. In 1770 her father's holdings were valued at £120.14, when the average in Hadley was £71 and the mean value of Hadley estates was just £52. While the wealthiest families had little need to train their daughters in trades, and the poorest families had no means to do so, middling and well-off families like the Smiths could do without a girl's labor for a time and often sought to ensure that daughters obtained training in one of the handful of occupations available to women.

Dickinson may have been glad to have the extra help as she reached the top of her game. Hatfield's busy social life generated plenty of need for new and stylish clothes in the years following the revolution. A glimpse is captured in the diary entry describing the August afternoon when Dickinson "was at Sister Billings to fix Patty Church and Bets Huntington for the wedding reception of Oliver Hastings." "No doubt there was forty couples who was invited in," she guessed. "Some single, some married people—a very fine collection, all dressed out," the gownmaker was quick to observe, "to give them joy in their beginning . . . a great many fine people who was crowding in, the ladies with their silks, the men the happiest who could get the nearest to them" (August 2, 1787).

Clearly the economic distress endured by some families in the 1780s was not so widespread as to squelch shopping altogether; indeed, shifting fashions continued to drive business. As the century wore on, America's interest in the French Revolution launched a corresponding revolution in silhouette. French fashion, inspired by democratizing political impulses and an international fascination (sparked by the unearthing of Pompeii) with all things Greek and Roman, urged young women to don revealing white gowns that suggested the columnar marble statues of the ancient world brought to life. The broad skirts, heavy fabrics, and round gowns popular in the 1770s and 1780s were gradually replaced by the narrower drape and sheer materials of the new style, waistlines rising to just under the bust in what we today call the "empire" style. A major overhaul of fashionable American women's wardrobes generated plenty of activity for gownmakers like Rebecca Dickinson, and "invitations" to work in surrounding Hampshire County towns suggest that her skills were still valued throughout the county. Seeking this slimmer form, on August 3, 1788, Hadley gentlewoman Elizabeth Porter Phelps recorded engaging a craftswoman to "make [her] lutestring gown plumb"; that is, to reduce the bell shape of the glossy silk skirts in favor of a leaner garment that emphasized the vertical. That this particular gown was then about twelve years old suggests the degree to which alterations could extend the longevity of expensive garments. Indeed, the brown ducape gown that Rebecca Dickinson had crafted for Elizabeth Phelps's 1770 wedding was also altered to achieve a similar end in August 1788 when Northampton needlewoman Molly Wright revamped its lines to conform to prevailing style.

The income earned by rural gownmakers like Dickinson in these years is difficult to estimate, because few women in Massachusetts kept formal financial records of artisanal work. Moreover, exchanging labor for goods and services rather than cash was a central feature of the early American economy. Whatever items might have been acquired, payment might be rendered in wood chopped, cabinetry completed, sewing done, debts excused, or credit allowed. Debits and credits were often tracked over months and even years, the parties meeting only occasionally to compare records and settle accounts. Sometimes those relationships were triangular. For example, Dickinson appears in the account book of Hatfield merchant Oliver Smith, having purchased fabric—seven yards of calimanco (a worsted wool) and half a yard of cambleteen (another worsted fabric), amounting to ten shillings, seven pence—which was charged to her account and then paid for by Mary Smith, for whom Dickinson had performed some service, recorded elsewhere. The records of these transactions give us a sense of the value of particular skills or activities, but in the absence of a surviving account book, we cannot reconstruct Dickinson's earnings over a given year. What we do know is that while gownmaking was among the best prospects for women seeking to earn income, it seldom supported an independent living. The seasonality of the trade (which slowed during planting and harvest times and picked up again once crops were in the field or barn) and sporadic nature of demand made gownmaking unreliable as a steady source of income.

The value of the work is also difficult to gauge. As one advice manual, the *Book of Trades,* warned, "The price charged for making dresses cannot be estimated; it varies with the article to be made; with the reputation of the maker; with her situation in life; and even with the season of the year."[3] That uncertainty plagued Rebecca Dickinson. "How times vary with me," she noted one November afternoon, lamenting "how hurried [busy]" she "was formerly at this season of the year" (November 22, 1787). One eighteenth-century play captured the nature of the work in the lines of a character, who, like Dickinson, was an unmarried artisan: "What a present is mine, and what a prospect is my future. Labor and watchings in the busy season—hunger in the slack—and solitude in both."[4] On one occasion, though eagerly anticipating a visit from her sister Martha and her two children, Anne and Moses, Dickinson wrote, "[I] shall be glad to see them. I hope to be at home when they come to town, which makes me at a loss about going [to work in nearby Hadley], but my daily bread depends upon my labor." Torn between welcoming her anxiously awaited guests and "employ" for her "hands," Dickinson looked to her livelihood (September 10, 1787).

But work did more than provide the independent artisan with income. Dickinson's trade mitigated the loneliness that sometimes accompanied her life alone. Conversation over long afternoons of stitching and fitting was a godsend to the single artisan. For a woman as lively and quick-witted as Dickinson appears to have been, prolonged solitude must have been painful indeed. "How the person lives who lives alone," she sighed. "God only knows there is no one in the world [who] loves company more than me, but it is God's will or I'm quite undone. Surely it is more than I can do to submit to it" (July 13, 1787). In fact, her trade helped her create and sustain real friendships with her clients.

Elizabeth Porter Phelps, who initially referred to the gownmaker as "Miss Rebecca Dickinson," by 1788 was calling her "Becca." When her work was plentiful, Dickinson remarked "how my time flies," hinting that the long and lonely days that many entries record disappeared when she was actively engaged in her trade (September 10, 1787). As a gownmaker Dickinson took part in the joy that surrounded weddings, the excitement that preceded trips to Boston, and the plain fun that accompanied getting a new gown. Conversely, slack periods meant not simply a loss of income, but a loss of companionship. On one November afternoon Dickinson wrote, "This day I am out of employ the week before Thanksgiving . . . how like a being forsaken I live here alone, nothing to do but sit and mope the time away" (November 23, 1787).

At the same time, outings into her community sometimes grieved the aging gownmaker. "It is not worth my while to go from the house," she regularly observed, "it is so lonesome to return here again" (September 26, 1787). Weddings in particular proved sources of both employment and pain, because they reminded her of all that she felt she had missed. When noting one upcoming celebration, she wrote, "Fifty couples are to be there this evening—how gay the assembly will look. But I have no part, no portion there" (November 22, 1787). The delight the gownmaker clearly took in seeing a beautifully dressed assemblage could be quickly offset by the anguish such events produced:

> About dusk or the edge of the evening [I] set out to come home to this lonely house where I have lived forty-nine years, lonesome as death, to come here to spend the night alone, to reflect on my odd life and to ruminate the strange thoughts and schemes with which this mind of mine has surmised, to think on the many ways contrived by me for a portion in the world and with the world and like the world. But, after all, here alone as lonely as though I was cast out from all the rest of the people and was a gazing stock [laughing stock] for the old and young to gaze at. . . . Came home, crept into my window and fastened up my room, reeled down by my bed and after a poor manner committed myself to God. . . . O my poverty as to the things of time: when other people are seeing their children rejoicing with one another I'm all alone in the house and all alone in the world. (August [22/25], 1787)

Thankfully, as Dickinson herself said, those "dark hours" did not come every day. Indeed, her spirits seem to have risen and fallen with her employment, probably both because the income allayed her fears about the future and because the work kept her busy in the present.

Admission to the innermost spaces of a neighbor's family circle had other benefits as well. In the late eighteenth century gossip was a key source of information; it both built and destroyed reputations, making people with intimate knowledge about other households potentially quite powerful. In communities (and economies) highly dependent on reputation, few people had as much access to the households of the politically, socially, and culturally powerful as gownmakers like Dickinson. As they ascended to private chambers and settled in for long periods of measuring, fitting, cutting, and stitching, they had special access to information, regarding style, to be sure, but also gossip, an asset not to be dismissed lightly.

As an unmarried woman and an artisan with access to homes throughout the area, Dickinson may well have been an unusually important disseminator of public opinion in Hatfield. Needleworkers often played a special role in conveying information in a community. In the early nineteenth century Catherine Parsons Graves, daughter of Northampton tailor Catherine Phelps Parsons, remembered a customer of her mother who was "a great news gatherer," who "used to sit with the tailor girls for news."[5] Likewise, in *A History of Hatfield,* Daniel Wells recorded that as Dickinson "traveled from house to house about her work, she acquired a fund of information concerning her neighbors that was unequalled by any other person. A gift of making pithy, epigrammatic remarks caused her to be regarded as something of an 'oracle.'" The reminiscences of Samuel D. Partridge describe Dickinson as a "very intelligent woman" whose sayings "were frequently repeated" by townspeople.[6] Dickinson's diary provides a glimpse of this gossiping; when Hatfield's Asa Wells married Bets Smith, Dickinson recorded, "It is agreed by *all people* there never was a couple married with so poor a prospect of gaining livelihood" (November [], 1787; emphasis added). It is difficult to imagine that this opinion surfaced independently in conversations throughout Hatfield; it seems more likely that Dickinson, who presumably helped outfit guests, and possibly even the bride and her attendants, herself held, solicited, spread, and endorsed this appraisal as she made her rounds of the neighborhood. Potentially she was a real shaper of attitudes both toward and within Hatfield households, able to comment positively or negatively on family life in the houses she entered. More than any other fact—about her personality, circumstances, or needlework—it is her role as an observer, an accumulator and disseminator of information, that emerges from nineteenth-century reminiscences.

In the 1780s, then, Rebecca Dickinson was thinking hard about the future and trying to contribute toward it. Her role as an aunt became increasingly important to her, and the taking in of young trainees extended her income and her influence while alleviating at least to a degree the loneliness she suffered. As New England adjusted to life in the new nation, Dickinson seemed slowly but surely to be finding a place in this new order. But although she could have been expected to settle into a quiet groove at this point in her life, Rebecca Dickinson did quite the opposite. Reaching the half-century mark seems to have prompted a crisis for the never-married gownmaker, as she wrestled with uncertainty about her future. Just as the nation had grappled with the meaning and shape of its independence, revisiting the Articles of Confederation and arguing over a new Constitution, so did Rebecca Dickinson in these years contemplate changing the terms of her singlehood, or foregoing it altogether.

8

Singlehood and the "Bar in the Way"

On a rainy summer afternoon in 1787, Rebecca Dickinson took out a blank stack of paper and set it on her desk. It was time to open a new chapter in her journal. Soon she would reach her forty-ninth birthday. Dipping her quill into a pot of ink, at the top of the page she wrote:

This day is the 22 of July 1787. Here alone in this house. There has been a thunderstorm here this afternoon, some hard thunder and rain. It is good to be where God's voice is to be heard. There is no dread to me in that voice. Thunder never terrifies me but when it is very nigh and very loud. The Lord's voice is in the city. How many would fly away from this house alone? But it is good to be here. The Lord knows his saints and guards the place where they dwell, and if they should perish in the storm their death would be precious in his sight. There is no storm, nor no trouble, can send my soul from God. . . . No bar, no bolts, can bar the soul from God for it is a spark of heavenly fire which came from God and will tend to the center as the fire flies toward the sun, so the soul of the spirit flies to God. O my father make me to have more of thy one likeness. Cure me of my spot and blemishes and make me one with my father who is in heaven. The sabbath is gone and the Monday is gone; Tuesday is come this day.

Then her birthday came. "This is the 25 of July 1787," she wrote, "this day makes [me] forty-nine years of age. The goodness of God has suffered me to live in his world. It is God and God only to who I owe the length of my life." A nightmare lingered on her mind. "Last night had a sad dream which I hope will never come to pass," she mused: "methought that I was in a place where I could not escape." She didn't know why she was so plagued with these preoccupations; after all, "God has taken a fatherly care of me for near fifty years—why should I doubt?" Noting that she felt weak in faith, she added, "This summer has given me a sight of myself." "I know that I am not my own," she confessed. "The God who made me will dispose of me in his own time and way." There was nothing to do but submit: "I know that it is best that God should govern the world and dispose of me as he thinks best."

But submission would not come easily. She tried singing. Recalling lines from Isaac Watts's hymn book, she wrote, "[My] shepherd is the living Lord / now Shall my wants be well supplied / Providence and holy word / become my safety and my guide. / Pastures where salvation grows / he makes me feed, he makes me rest / There living waters gently flow / and all the food divinely blest" (August 5, 1787). But it didn't help. The verses from the hymnal were meant to reassure her that God had his eye on her, and that she would be cared for, body and soul. But she wasn't so sure, and the uncertainly itself reminded her how far short her faith had continually fallen.

If in some ways Dickinson in the early years of the American republic seemed to be establishing a place for herself in her community—as a respected artisan and tutor of aspiring craftswomen, beloved aunt and sister, and valued neighbor—her private moments were another story. The contours of permanent singlehood were beginning to make themselves plain, and Dickinson used her journal to respond to the worst of them: the loneliness, the vulnerability, and the public disapproval.

Summer 1787 was a sorrowful season. Just two weeks after she wrote the cheerless entry above, Rebecca described coming home from Miriam's house right before sundown into "this lonely habitation where there is no voice nor nothing but one old odd being" (August 20, 1787).

"It is well that those dark hours don't come every day," she mused. On three evenings over the past twelve weeks she could not suppress "those lonesome death-like thoughts." Her house, she wrote, "is a tomb," and she was "like one who has been a long time dead." She felt angry all the time, but did not want to be one of those people who "looks on the world with an evil eye and thinks those highly favored who have a portion here as children and friends, a home where company is, but mine is very different." "There is no one to speak to," she sighed, knowing that her sisters and friends didn't want to hear any more of her complaints. "How much company is wanted and how I have abused it that my God must shut me out from all the world to learn his holy will." The fault was wholly her own, she was sure. "God has done me no wrong," she wrote. Instead it was her "overfondness for the things of time" (i.e., for a husband and children) that had "brought all this evil on me."

Dickinson was feeling that she was a burden to her family and her community. "The winter is coming on when there will be no room for me," she mused. "This world is a crowded inn where we put up for twelve hours and no more," she wrote, thinking of "the tavern which is in the city of London where it is written over the door that none may exceed that term of time" (August 19, 1787). Whether or not she had kept any earlier diaries that engaged these questions, Dickinson's journal in these years became a place to contemplate "how my lot fell by myself alone, how it came about that others and all the world in possession of children and friends and a house and homes while I was so odd as to sit here alone almost froze with the cold" (August 20, 1787). It was late August in Massachusetts, and the aging craftswoman sat in her house alone, shivering and sad.

As crushingly lonely as Dickinson often felt, an even greater issue for single women, as she observed it, was their inability to control the circumstances of their lives. In late eighteenth-century New England being unmarried did not necessarily mean having liberty or feeling free. On the contrary, women without husbands were dependent on others—usually fathers, brothers, or nephews—who would decide their fate. Dickinson would have known this all too well if she recalled from her childhood the life Dorothy Allis led as a woman dependent on the support of the town; without the support of her family, Dickinson would have been just as vulnerable. Although she was pleased to continue living in the home of her birth, it was an arrangement that was fragile at best. She lived there at the pleasure of her mother and brother, who could decide at any time that the family's interests were better served by the sale of that property, leaving her to shuttle among her brother and her several sisters, sleeping in whatever space they could spare, squeezing into the interstices of other people's lives. Dickinson enjoyed the great luxury of remaining in her parents' home, even as it emptied out as her siblings married. Though she necessarily took on the care of her aging mother Anna, as an unmarried woman approaching fifty, Dickinson was able to move about her family home with comfortable ease, in rooms she had known her whole life. She had a good deal of privacy, and on a day-to-day level, autonomy. She was lucky, and she knew it. But at the same time, that independent existence was, she knew, highly vulnerable. Throughout autumn 1787, Dickinson worried that her aging mother would die, prompting another family conference that might leave her homeless. "What should I do was it not for this old house; it is a safe retreat from trouble"; "What shall I do or where shall I go? With whom shall I live when old and helpless?"; "They will put me where they please who have the care of me" (August 5, 1787; August 8, 1787; September 5, 1787)—passages like these capture Dickinson's sense of helplessness, her overwhelming fear of losing her home, and with it, her autonomy.

She had certainly had ample opportunity to witness the precarious positions of other single women. In the fall of her forty-ninth year, she noted, "This week died at Hadley . . . a girl of about thirty years of age—[she was] well and dead in a week. She had no home but was driven from one brother to another and lived with her sisters some of the time" (September 15, 1787). Another time she wrote, "This day have heard of the death of Patty Lymen, above thirty years of age." Dickinson called her a "disconsolate girl" and concluded, "When I compare my life with many of my acquaintances I am content and well I may be." "There is no unmarried woman" like her, with a "house to shelter my goods in when others run from place to place not knowing where to go nor what to do" (June [8], 1788). When observing her married sisters, Dickinson lamented her unenviable situation, but when she compared her lot with that of other never-married women, she recognized her circumstances to be better than those endured by most.

Keenly aware that a home of her own was a distinct advantage for a single woman, it appears Dickinson had engineered the opportunity to live alone in the place of her birth, a house that she both cherished and disparaged. She constantly complained that the house was "crumbling to pieces," that it "leaked like a sieve" and might "swim off" at any moment.[1] Still, in October 1787 she referred to her home as "the best place in the world but four years ago when it was better to be here alone than to have a family here with me," noting "how it was given me at my own request." Although it is unclear what this reference to a decision made four years earlier means, her drive to gain or retain an independent existence is striking. She did not legally control her residence in that house, but she had apparently talked her family into allowing her to remain there, with the understanding that she would care for her mother. Beyond a wish to avoid a life of dependency, she voiced a preference to live by herself, despite the eyebrows she believed this raised in her community. Significantly, what she apparently rejected was not moving in with one of her siblings, but "to have a family" there with her (September 22, 1787), presumably to have one of her sisters and her husband and children join her in the ancestral house. Somehow, she stayed in, and kept them out. Though she shared the house seasonally with her mother and with young nieces and nephews for whom she occasionally cared, the red saltbox was hers, for good or ill. In five hundred diary entries, Dickinson repeats the lament "here again in this old house alone" over 150 times. Yet despite the house's quiet and its deteriorating condition, she embraced it again and again.

Issues surrounding care—who should receive it and who should give it—constantly colored Dickinson's family relations. Unmarried women, viewed by their families as having no particular responsibilities of their own, were often expected to nurse aging or infirm relatives and to help with housework and child care: in essence, to remain "on call" as their families required. Failure to fulfill these responsibilities, whether or not the requests were justifiable, could cause a woman—perhaps aware of her comparatively, or allegedly, lighter load—to feel guilt, even shame. Serving in this role could also be rewarding, affirming one's purpose in the family and community. But like any work, it had to be balanced against other competing demands, including one's own household and livelihood.

Although Anna Dickinson's living arrangements are not entirely clear, it appears that after Moses's death she arrived each fall to spend the winter with her daughter Rebecca in Hatfield. Each spring she went to her "other house" "in the woods," the home of her son Samuel and his wife Mary just a few miles north, in Whately (perhaps to deploy her expertise in the dairy or to help mind the grandchildren while Samuel and Mary's attention was focused on the fields). Rebecca's siblings shouldered some of the burden of Anna's care, but Anna joined Rebecca during the season when both women were prone to illness. One might expect the arrangement to be mutually sustaining, because it offered both women companionship and care in their advancing age. However, a sense of duty and obligation characterized their relationship. Dickinson recorded a number of sermons reminding parents and children of their mutual obligations to one another, lessons she clearly took to heart. Her utmost concern was "my duty to my aged parent." Even as she sometimes longed to travel to Bennington to visit Martha and her family, Dickinson maintained that "my greatest scruple has been on my mother's account." She was "confounded between" her "schemes" and her "duty." Caretaking often proved emotionally and physically exhausting, and though Rebecca at times seemed to regret her mother's departure in the spring, she also expressed a certain vexation at her return in the fall. In October 1787 Dickinson wrote, "The 26 of this month came home my mother after an absence of some months. We have set up house keeping one time more. How we are to live I can't see but there will be a way. [Yet] there is a bar in the way."

Perhaps financial concerns contributed to her misgivings, but she sometimes hinted that the "bar" was her own reluctance to assume the responsibility. Contrite, she prayed, "may my stubborn heart be subdued to God's will and cheerfully engage in all that God shall call me to" (October 27, 1787). Just two weeks later, clearly at wit's end, she wrote, "My mother, seventy-five years of age, not able to take care of herself, in a puzzling fit broke my spectacles, a great loss to me for they suited me so well that 1 guinea should not have bought them out of my hand" (November 15, 1787).

Dickinson's own illnesses exacerbated her frustration. A "most distressing colic" had kept her confined the previous week. While she had "gained ease" when the local physician employed a popular technique— bloodletting—to relieve her distress, she was still dismayed by her family's obvious indifference: "How sad to be sick," with "no one to do the least kind office" (November 15, 1787). Indeed, "colic" seemed to plague Dickinson nearly every fall, and each year she nervously anticipated its reoccurrence. Anticipating another bout, again in November, three years later, she sputtered, "I can't be sick. I won't be sick. There is none of my fellow being to show me the least kind office. . . . My mother near eighty as stupid as can be [and] my body in sore distress." Her patience at an end, she fumed: "How can the stupid world not know my troubles? No one from my brother's house has been here but a boy of ten years of age [Samuel's son Moses]," and that only "after a great many words by me" ([late] November 1790).

One can only imagine the tension of this scene. Rebecca, already exhausted and feeling put upon, pleaded with her brother and sister-in-law for some support in caring for Samuel's mother. To her dismay, they responded by sending ten-year-old Moses, clearly more to appraise the situation and perhaps to provide some small help than to offer real care or assistance. The added presence of her mother was sometimes simply more than Rebecca could bear; as she later remarked, "We was too feeble to help one another. I thought I had better be in the house alone" (November [21], 1790). For a woman who constantly bewailed the lack of companionship, this is a strong statement. Perhaps it is no wonder that Rebecca wrote, after Anna's departure one spring, "My mother has been gone five weeks tomorrow and sweet content has crowned every day" (June 22, 1788).

Conflicts over caretaking—who would provide it and who would receive it—colored Dickinson's relationship with other family members as well. She and her sister-in-law Mary, in particular, enjoyed a less than cordial relationship. Dickinson described Mary as "the most unhappy of the daughters of Eve. She is passionate, covetous, jealous, sordid, [with] no love for her husband [and] mean as the dirt." "What a trial she has been to me," Rebecca concluded (June 29, 1794). One can easily imagine that ongoing disagreements over the care of Samuel's mother Anna generated anger on both sides. Here Mary's refusal to travel to Hatfield to look in on Anna, Rebecca, and even her own son Charles suggests that she suspected Rebecca of exaggerating her situation. This disparity between Dickinson's response to aspects of her singlehood and the reaction of family members to those same challenges surfaces again and again.

For Dickinson, her craftwork and her work in the family created opportunities and obligations that she both relished and struggled to meet. As much as she craved the companionship and community those activities provided, she resisted compromising her autonomy. She was unwilling to play the role of a dependent, and because she possessed an artisanal skill and had secured a roof over her head (such as it was), she did not have to.

As she aged Dickinson's worries multiplied, aggravated by recurrent bouts of "colic." As someone dependent on her own work for her income, these periods of sickness were a source of real concern. During the winter of 1787, for example, illness and "physic[al] overdoing" finally caused her to faint. Alone in the house, she took to her bed, but there she only worried about her financial affairs: "Have had an invitation to go to Hadley to work but no strength to move. . . . [I] must be content with what is already earned by me since my health and my strength is gone. I would beg of God that my estate [perhaps a reference to those seventy acres Moses had had the forethought to give her several years earlier] may be a comfort to me now in the time of old age" (December 2, 1787).

Even in times of relative health, Dickinson found herself increasingly unequal to the demands of her craft. On the threshold of fifty, she wrote that some years before she had been "hardly too scared to walk two miles afoot" (i.e., unafraid to set out on a walk of even two miles), but now, she fretted, "old age ha[d] crept up" on her (September 5, 1787). Exhausted one August afternoon, she dropped into her sister's tavern because she had elsewhere found "no rest for the sole of her foot"

(August 20, 1787). The number of her clients, she recognized, would necessarily decline as her geographical range narrowed. (Without a horse, Dickinson seems usually to have walked to anyplace local she needed to go.) Factors as capricious as the weather also limited her mobility and hence her income. Elizabeth Phelps described one stormy night when the sixty-eight-year-old Dickinson appeared at her door during a "hard shower of rain, dripping wet."[2] Walking home from Amherst, a ferry ride and good four-mile hike to the east, she had been caught in a downpour. Soaked to the skin through her red broadcloth cloak, she lodged with Phelps rather than complete the journey home. But if getting to (or home from) a job could be a trial, she was nevertheless glad to have that problem: "God has in great mercy this summer back given me work. He heard my cry and has sent employ for my hands. The God who heard my cry has given me work" (September 10, 1787).

It did not help that in those decades a stereotype was cultivated and nourished that cast never-married women in the worst possible light. Centuries earlier, in the Middle Ages, English culture took little notice of never-married women. When they appeared in literature they were generally envisioned as young maidens, with little thought, good or ill, about older women who were yet unmarried or who never wed. Sometime in the seventeenth century authors began to recognize that such women existed. The general sentiment at first was pity for what were depicted as somewhat hapless creatures. But toward the end of the seventeenth century a shift occurred. A noticeably derisive attitude emerged, and for the first time the word "spinster" took on a negative connotation.

One measure of this long transition is evident in a phrase invoked in the 1590s by (among many others) the playwright William Shakespeare: "They that die maids, lead apes in hell."[3] The origins of the saying are murky, but beginning around the mid-sixteenth century, in the middle of the English Reformation, it began to be repeated as authors disparaged women who died virgins, whatever their age. The notion can be linked to the English effort to throw off what religious reformers saw to be the corruptions of the Roman Catholic faith. Whereas the Catholic faith had long offered unmarried women a role as nuns, the gathering forces of Protestantism had nothing comparable in its structure or theology. In fact, in the ascendant Protestant faith matrimony—not celibacy, celebrated in Catholicism in the roles of both priests and nuns—was key to salvation. Any woman who remained single, and so celibate, was doomed, the adage suggested, to leading apes (perhaps an allusion to monks, or old bachelors, or something else altogether—the source of this element of the image is unclear) in hell.

By the late seventeenth century this aspersion against "maids" had evolved to mean "*old* maids"—that is, women over about thirty who had not yet married, unnaturally prolonging their virginity. The term "spinster" underwent a similar change. In the medieval period the term had been used in economic and legal contexts to describe an occupation: a woman who spins thread or yarn. By the seventeenth century it had come to be associated with unmarried women more generally, apart from occupation, but was still neutral and merely descriptive. It wasn't until the early eighteenth century that the term became connected with never-married women as a class, and by the nineteenth century it would overtake "old maid" as the term most often used to cue the set of negative ideas we recognize today.

These stereotypes in English Protestantism were exacerbated by distinct features of Puritan culture, emphasizing the ways in which women were subject to their husbands, as believers were to Christ. Puritan belief had little room for women outside family government. The pressure on seventeenth-century women who for whatever reason could or did not marry was significant. In Massachusetts the Reverend Cotton Mather in 1692 acknowledged the contempt that had attached to permanent singlehood when he censured girls who found it such a "*great curse* to be an *old maid*" that they would take a "*bad* husband merely to avoid the . . . reproach of having *none*." English author Mary Astell (sometimes considered England's first feminist writer) in 1697 likewise addressed women who, "quite terrified" by the "dreadful name of old maid," in order to escape the "scoffs that are thrown on superannuated virgins," instead "[fly] to some dishonorable match as her last, tho[ugh] much mistaken refuge."[4]

These writers thought it was far better to remain single and reject cultural disapproval than to spend life in a miserable marriage, but that was easier said than done. Stereotypes about single women were ugly and not so easy to shrug off. Some historians of the witchcraft hysteria that plagued Salem, Massachusetts, in the 1690s have speculated that unmarried women became targets of persecution in part because people feared their independent status and therefore literally demonized them as witches. By the mid-eighteenth century other assumptions had come into play. Never-married women were regularly accused of having pre-posterously high standards as well as pitifully hard hearts, which to-gether prevented them from accepting reasonable suitors. An especially derisive poem printed in a 1744 issue of *American Magazine* expressed this argument in lyric form. Entitled "The Heron: A Tale for Old Maids," its stanzas recount the actions of a finicky bird who, having passed up a variety of tasty meals, was forced to eat snails.[5] Verses ap-pearing throughout these decades continued to deride the "old maid." A woman working in the clothing trades would have been especially chagrined to encounter the short poem "To a Needle," in which the steel tip is urged against the rock-hard heart of the old maid who held it: "That blood from thence thy point had dy'd / Which Cupid's keenest shaft defy'd." Cartoon satires also painted never-married women in an unflattering light. Depicted as bony, pinched old women (visual short-cuts to cue their barren wombs), the "old maids" of popular prints and magazines were selfish, useless objects of mockery. Even the excessive affection for cats—still part of the caricature today—was present at this early date. With this cruel stereotype prevalent in popular culture, for women like Dickinson there seemed almost no escape.

At the same time, unfortunately for the aging craftswomen, another set of cultural forces planted the seeds of the youth culture that Amer-ica knows today. In an energetic new society and new republic eager to establish itself on the world stage, the elderly, once revered, were in-creasingly moved to the margins. Perhaps the always-perceptive Dick-inson, acutely attuned as she was to the attitudes of people around her, picked up on these subtle changes as she herself aged, sensing another shift in the way people reacted to her as she grew older.

In this confluence of developments, the term "old maid" cued the bundle of negative stereotypes associated with the never-married in Rebecca Dickinson's lifetime. The set of ideas signaled had already taken the shape we know today: the spinster or old maid was either a dried up, prudish, humorless, and severe crone, or a silly, harmless-but-senseless, almost infantile woman who had never really come into her maturity.

Given that cultural context, it is no surprise that Dickinson seems to have embraced, at least at times or to some degree, her society's disapproval of never-married women. For example, one diary entry records the visit to Hatfield of "Billy Lymen with his wife Rachel" as well as "their sister, an old maid who is forty-seven years but does not know how old she is" (September 7, 1788). Dickinson also remained alert to other women who shared her circumstances. On one occasion she came home from a gathering and noted having seen "Anna Shadock, Eunis White and Liddy Wells—three unfortunate girls, a sight which I don't ever remember to have seen, three in one company who was forsaken by their companions" (September 5, 1787). Another time, recording the death of Hannah Meekins White, she noted that Hannah was an "old maid above forty years of age when she married" (June [], 1789]). Although Dickinson was only a child when Hannah, now ninety-two, had wed, she had learned this little biographical tidbit and thought to note it alongside news of Hannah's passing.

Dickinson may have embraced prevailing stereotypes in another way as well, as she crafted her own understanding of the "bitter stroke" that sealed her fate. Her assertion that an unrequited love had dashed her hopes for marriage and family may have been a story she gradually adopted (consciously or unconsciously) as an acceptable explanation for her life alone, the narrative of the jilted lover being one of the few "plots" available to eighteenth-century women to explain a failure to marry. The poet and author William Hayley, in his "Philosophical, Historical and Moral Essay on Old Maids" (which appeared in 1786, the year before Dickinson began the surviving portion of her journal), articulated a widely shared opinion when he urged the "old maid," "whenever she has occasion to speak of the nuptial state, to . . . represent her own exclusion from it, not as the effect of choice, arising from a cold, irrational aversion to the state in general, but as the consequence of such perverse incidents as frequently perplex all the patterns of human life, and lead even the worthiest of human beings into situations very different from what they otherwise would have chosen."[6] Eighteenth-century literature is filled with examples of discriminating between despicable women, who either rejected the institution of marriage or foolishly rejected valid and desirable proposals of marriage, and honorable women, who failed to marry out of concern for an aging parent, devotion to a dead lover, and so forth. Perhaps Dickinson began explaining her single state as the product of a "bitter stroke" in the wake of Jesse Billings's marriage because of some real or imagined disappointment there, the episode also providing the sort of cover Hayley suggested the never-married should seek to avoid public disapproval.

One challenge that Rebecca Dickinson did not have to cope with, that her modern counterparts do, was questions about her sexual orientation. Today women who never marry—especially if they are successful career women in the public sphere—often endure speculation about their sexual orientation. But in the eighteenth century no one was likely to have contemplated this as an explanation for someone having remaining unmarried. In general, English culture was not overly preoccupied with lesbian activity, and the term "lesbian" little used, English law on the whole being more concerned with sexual contact between men than between women. Religious proscription worried more about any sexual activity not directed toward reproduction than about lesbianism per se, and the era in any event distinguished engaging in any particular sex acts from possessing a particular sexual orientation. On this side of the Atlantic, in seventeenth-century New England, the set of laws that John Cotton proposed to the Massachusetts General Court contained an article stipulating that "unnatural filthiness" be "punished with death, whether sodomy, which is carnal fellowship of man with man, or woman with woman, or buggery, which is carnal fellowship of man or woman with beasts or fowls."[7] These laws were not adopted (although sexual activity between women was made illegal in the colonies of Rhode Island and New Haven), and lesbian activity was only very rarely noticed by early Massachusetts courts.

In the eighteenth century popular culture did include images of what we would today call lesbians, and recognized lesbian activity, but most discussions of women enjoying sex with other women (and these were infrequent) presumed that these same women would abandon that activity if and when a more appropriate union with a man became possible. For instance, John Cleland's 1748 novel *Memoirs of a Woman of Pleasure*—widely considered the first pornographic writing in English culture—introduced to literature the still-infamous Fanny Hill, who has a sexual encounter with a woman as part of the plot, but then moves on to heterosexual liaisons. In Dickinson's world questions about sexual orientation would not have leapt to mind as they do in the United States today; rather, observers would probably guess (as Dickinson well imagined) that it was some character flaw that led to her prolonged singlehood.

Over the course of her life, Rebecca Dickinson saw public conversation about her marital status grow harsher. Depictions of the never-married in art and literature caused her to question her own social value; popular culture proved as important as religious proscription as she struggled to sort out how to feel about women who never married, herself among them. Though there were limits to the stereotype, it was certainly no fun accepting the label "old maid." Given the challenge of living under that kind of pressure, it is a wonder that, when she once again got a chance to "change her name" at the late age of forty-nine, Rebecca Dickinson turned it down.

9

The "Most Dark and Puzzling Affair"

The revolution notwithstanding, the central drama of Rebecca Dickinson's life involved reconciling herself to a life alone, and as she approached fifty that struggle reached its climax. As she continued to grapple with the changing meaning of singlehood, in the context of both broad cultural forces and her own lived experience, in the late 1780s events forced her to confront that status, as well as her willingness, or unwillingness, to alter it. In 1788 she once again received an offer of marriage, and this just as she had decided to throw in the towel on her life in Hatfield and try a fresh start in her sister's community of Bennington, Vermont. As she weighed the costs of singlehood against the benefits of matrimony, the result may have surprised even her.

As the years rolled on, Dickinson had begun to concentrate more and more on the quality of her faith. Seeming to heed Cotton Mather's admonition that the never-married woman should "make the single state a blessed one by improving her leisure from the encumbrance of a family in caring for the things of the Lord," Dickinson confirmed that "what is wanting" in her "outward circumstances" could be "made up . . . in the blessings of the better covenant."[1] "There is something I have to learn or I should not be here in this house," she mused, "something I have to see or feel or I should not be here" (August 3, 1788). Unlike other women, who might understandably become preoccupied with the cares of this life, she wrote, "There is no excuse for me: I am wholly unconnected with the world. There are no children, no grandchildren, no house, no land for me to set my heart upon [i.e., no real property to care for; her own modest house and minimal property didn't rise to this level of preoccupation]. But may my spirit hold communion with God at all times" (May 3, 1789). Dickinson's strict Calvinism welcomed adversity as evidence of God's attention and recast hardships as a loving parent's corrective action: "It is good to be afflicted, for thereby I have learned to keep thy commands" ([late] October 1790). Likewise, in denying her the comforts of family life, God, in his love and wisdom, had protected her soul from competing earthly interests. Both clergy and congregation shared Dickinson's assumption that her lack of "dear connections as children and the care of a family to engross [her] thoughts and cares" heightened her ability to focus all her "affection on God" (August 1, 1790).

But if such divine intervention was a blessing, it also carried with it implicit criticism: Dickinson's poor spiritual state apparently needed unusually strict monitoring. After much reflection, she determined that it was her sinful preoccupation with earthly possessions, including a family—the "things of time"—that had condemned her to a solitary life. "God well knew how poorly you would have used the things of time," she reasoned, and "has saved thee a great deal of trouble by the loss of them" (September 4, 1787). Hoping to curb rising resentment at another evening spent alone in her "old house," she told herself that "no other place would do" to "wean" her from the distractions of earthly comforts like a husband and children (September [12], 1787).

Given her exceptional opportunity to cultivate a pious spirit and a contrite heart, so the theory went, Dickinson should have attained a level of spirituality unavailable to her married sisters. Her belief that she had failed to do so produced frustration, shame, guilt, and fear, for if she failed to make use of the opportunity God had presented to her—to be "so recluse and get no more good by it"—the consequences would be dire: "What a sad thought to be so miserable here and tormented in the world to come" (October [5–14], 1787; July [12], 1790).

An illuminating passage captures Dickinson's belief that those who remain single should be able to achieve a heightened spirituality. Recording the death of Abner Meekins, a member of an "afflicted family" in which "four . . . have lived unmarried," she empathized with his siblings: "May we who are single or unmarried wait on God, who orders all things for us." She closes the passage with the central lesson of her religious life: that God "knows the best time to mow down our earthly comforts" (August 10, 1794). She applied this standard to her own spiritual state and sought to match the faith and goodness she observed in other never-married women. "This week back," she reported, "came here in the newspaper the death of three women," including "an aged old maid who was a hundred years old and was called venerable," a "title" by which "I wish to live and die" (July 30, 1791).

Rather than envy the happiness of others, she strove to "bless God" with her whole heart, "for the many advantages for my soul while here in this house alone, which is the best school in the world for me" ([early] August 1787). Dickinson also suffered from the belief that spiritual shortcomings held negative consequences not only for herself but for those she loved. One especially poignant passage records just such an interpretation. Dickinson accepted her own lack of children as part of God's stringent but necessary plan: "God knew my tender make and doomed my darlings to death before they was my own [i.e., denied life to her potential children] for which . . . I give thanks" (April 12, 1789). But it was not only her own "darlings" who were imperiled by her weak faith. After her year-old niece Ruth died the following year of "eruptive sores," Dickinson speculated that her "fondness for her" may have been the "cause of her death" ([early] November 1787). Difficult as it is for us to imagine today, Dickinson wondered whether her excessive love for her adorable niece had compelled God to remove the child from the scene, to ensure that Dickinson did not become distracted from her faith. Witnessing Miriam and Silas's grief at the death of their beloved daughter, Rebecca couldn't help but feel at least partly responsible.

Dickinson's struggle to understand and accept the "portion" God had allotted her, a struggle that colors each and every page of her diary, shared the same concern that weighed on other aging women in early America: the increasing desire as one approached death to resign oneself to the will of God. Indeed, on the first page of her surviving journal, Dickinson wrote, "God has taken fatherly care of me for near fifty years; why should I doubt? . . . I am weak in faith. . . . I know that it is best that God should govern me [and] the world and dispose of me as he thinks best" (July 22, 1787). "May I learn to die," prayed Dickinson, after witnessing the dignified death of an admired acquaintance. "My wicked heart does still contrive how to dispose of my mortal interest when I would hope that all my wants are lodged in the hands of God" (March 22, 1789).

But the comfort of divine attention could not always assuage Dickinson's loneliness or her bitterness. At times her despair nearly surpassed her endurance. Deaths in the community caused her to wonder, "Why do I live while others die?" (May 25, 1788). Having "outlived all my friends and all my connections," she could only conclude that she was utterly superfluous in a world of couples, with "no part, no portion"— that is, no role to play in the "busy scenes of life" that surrounded her (September 2, 1787).

Given the tremendous grief that colors these pages, the agonizing daily dissection of evidence concerning God's will for her and the state of her soul, it seems surprising, even startling, that she refused another proposal of marriage in these same years. The story emerges during a period of turmoil that Dickinson referred to as "the most dark and puzzling affair" of her life ([late] March 1788). Those events shed further light on the ways in which her search for companionship and community collided with her pride and independence. In moments of clarity, Dickinson could acknowledge that her living situation was clearly better than that endured by most of the other unmarried women she knew. In 1787 and 1788, however, she contemplated a radical change in circumstances: leaving Hatfield altogether for a fresh start in Vermont. After several agonizing months, on September 10, 1788, she finally made her break, planning to move permanently to her sister's community. But by September 22 she was back in Hatfield, her plans abandoned.

These months represented a turning point in her life. She had destroyed some of her previous secular diaries in summer 1787 and begun her new, more theologically engaged reflections. She had also lost the company of two close friends, probably confronted menopause, and indulged memories of a long-lost love. She then entered into a period of anxiety, illness, and despair. Throughout the fall and into the winter months, work eluded her, and when it was available, she was often too ill to attend to it in her usual fashion. Sickness was compounded by fatigue, as she cared for her aging mother.

It is little wonder that Dickinson had started searching for an escape from Hatfield. She couldn't seem to keep her mind on anything else. "More than half the time this holy Sabbath," she wrote on August 27, 1787, "[I] have contrived for myself how to spend the winter coming." Later that week, she elaborated: "This week has been spent by me here alone. The bigger part of my whole time is spent in contriving to make my escape. . . . I have solemnly sworn to myself not to spend the summer to come here under the same circumstances as I have lived this summer, so lonely." Certain that "no way" had been left "untried," she sadly concluded that no matter "how many ways my foolish heart has contrived where to go and what to do," she was trapped (August 31, 1787). Despite her wish to "run from here," Dickinson remained in Hatfield, whether by choice or necessity, through the fall.

Dickinson may have had particular cause for sensitivity in her fiftieth year. In September she recorded a Saturday morning visit at the home of her minister, Joseph Lyman, and his wife Hannah. With them was Joseph's brother Eliphalet, himself a minister in Woodstock, Connecticut, with whom Rebecca had "been in company" a decade earlier. (Whether this meant some past romantic attachment or just that they traveled in the same circle is unclear.) She apparently had not seen him in some time. Recounting the awkward moment of their reintroduction, she wrote, "He has since very well married and has been blessed with several fine children. How poor I felt in his company—alone in the world, I thought to myself" (September 25, 1787). Eliphalet Lyman compounded her embarrassment when he bluntly asked if she had since "changed her name."

Nonplussed, she responded only with a "wicked thought" yet was "more poor" when Hannah Lyman quickly inserted that she was "about to change it"; in other words, that Dickinson would soon be married.

Her humiliation complete, she "felt like a foolish being—[I] could not say a word for myself, at fifty years of age. What could I say? The suitor not to suit, when it was to be the last?" (September 29, 1787). Hannah Lyman's assertion that Rebecca was "about to change" her name, coupled with Dickinson's comment about telling "the suitor not to suit," suggests that she was being courted during the year she considered a move to Bennington. The courtship evidently was not going well, and the Lymans may have been doing their best to encourage it. Hannah Lyman would not have spoken of an impending marriage if she had not believed or at least earnestly hoped that one was on the horizon; here she announced the engagement as if it were an accomplished fact. Dickinson's "What could I say?" query suggests that she herself had little enthusiasm for the courtship, but hardly felt in a position to dismiss it out of hand.

The next month, again visiting at her minister's home, Dickinson encountered newlyweds Elias Peck and Lydia Lyman Peck, a sister of Joseph and Eliphalet and another "old acquaintance" of Rebecca's. Dickinson records that as she prepared to leave, Lydia "followed me to the door and told me that she could not bear to have me come to this house alone." Thirty-six-year-old Lydia had herself found a partner relatively late in life; she may well have harbored a special concern for Rebecca's situation and been eager to see her wed. In any case, momentarily speechless, Dickinson replied, "Not so lonesome as the grave." Once home, however, she couldn't help but doubt "whether I was right to give such an answer" (October [5–14], 1787).

The events of the weeks between these two events are not known. But whether Dickinson had declined her suitor or he had failed to press his suit, she remained single, open to the thoughtless inquiries of strangers and the well-intentioned meddling of friends.

In January 1788, after another bout of colic had left her bedridden, she received an invitation from her sister Martha to live with her family, who about six years earlier had moved from Marlboro to Bennington, Vermont, another thirty or so miles to the west. Three months later Martha's invitation was still open, but Dickinson was paralyzed by indecision: "For two or three weeks back have been almost distracted with my own thoughts, not knowing where to go or what to do. My scruples are almost removed; I begin to think that I shall go to Bennington to live this spring" (March 2, 1788).

Whatever "scruples" (i.e., practical considerations) were hindering her move—her work, care of her mother, loss of friends—Dickinson also worried about her reception in the new community. "What sad thoughts arise, to quit the town where I have lived fifty years and try my fortune among strangers," she fretted (March 2, 1788). Confused, Dickinson turned to her sisters and brother for advice, but when they encouraged her to join Martha's household, she became perturbed, convinced that they simply wanted to get her "out of their sight." Her dread and irritation mounting, she argued against the move in the pages of her journal: "How dismal the thought, a woman my age in a strange place for the people to gaze on. How sad my case. I have thought myself to be poor but am poorer when I think of going seventy miles and to leave all my clothes behind me" (March 23, 1788). Perhaps she meant that she would not have had room to store all of her possessions (including the surely stylish wardrobe that she created for herself) in her sister's house.

By the following Sunday, however, noting that "the matter which has perplexed me seems to be a little over," she concluded, "it is wisdom for me to leave this house." Insisting that this was not a "move to get rid of trouble—that is not my motive," she reconciled herself to her present "duty." She clearly hoped that joining Martha's family would cause "many things that have been very troublesome" to "disappear," though "what new ones will arise," she wrote, "I cannot tell" (March [30], 1788).

Dickinson's misgivings renewed themselves, however, as she worried about assaults on her privacy and her pride: "How sad the sight to see a single woman above fifty and not married," her new neighbors were bound to conclude. "Something is the matter," they would surely think: "she is come for a husband having no luck in her own land" (April 6–17, 1788). Her mind was in a tumult all spring. By June she had begun to take her meals at Miriam and Silas's home, which went a long way toward easing her loneliness, and she was less inclined than ever to leave. Her siblings, however, perhaps anticipating more waffling, remained resolute. Frustrated and resentful at what she now perceived to be her complete helplessness in the matter, Dickinson fumed, "This week have had a message from my sister to be ready for a start. I threw my things on the chamber floor, but no man, no horse ever came. There they lie on the floor" (June 15, 1788).

Something had happened to delay her travels, and she was both relieved and disappointed. Then a late August storm gave her a serious scare. The violent gale rose up from the south about 2:00 in the afternoon and roared for over an hour, even two; in twenty especially intense minutes, the wind took down several barns and a number of "hovels," razed several roofs, and destroyed apple trees and stacks of grain. She stepped outside and was "surprised to see the steeple of the meetinghouse which shook with the wind." She turned back toward her home and "saw the roof of this old house begin to arise." Then, "before I could think," she wrote, "[I] was buried under the ruins of the roof which was scattered abroad," some of the rafters landing on the roof of a nearby barn. Across town (reported the *Middlesex Gazette* on September 8, 1788) a child had been killed by a flying board, but she was luckier (August 24, 1788). Her "breath was gone," but she "crept out from under the rubbish" and made her way to her back door and into the house. A neighbor who had seen the roof fall rushed over and sent for Rebecca's brother and the town doctor.

For three days she was "very sick," and "could hardly turn" in her bed in Miriam's "north room," but Miriam, the mother of three boys between the ages of eight and twelve, bluntly told her older sister that she "ha[d] enough" without her underfoot as well (August 30, 1788). Dickinson's house, containing the "whole of [her] worldly possessions," had finally failed her, and her sister's attitude stung. Finally Rebecca returned to her house "before the sun went down. Stayed here alone and cried myself to sleep, to think how I was alone in the world. It is not an imagination, but a reality." Perhaps it is no wonder that by early September 1788 she had again resolved to leave Hatfield and "go into the north country."

The plan seemed simple enough: Martha's daughter Anne would move to Hatfield to attend school, which would leave a vacancy in the Bennington home for Rebecca. But when Martha's husband William fell ill while Rebecca was en route, preventing Anne's departure, Rebecca arrived only to learn that there was, literally, no room for her in the household. Clearly her concerns about her status in the household had been well founded.

To make matters worse, more indignities followed. Dickinson immediately suffered precisely the assault on her privacy that she most dreaded. Fear became fact when a prying matron asked outright why she had never married. "A woman who had been exceedingly prosperous in the world asked me whether I was not sorry that I did not marry when I was young." "[I] was thunderstruck," Dickinson later recorded. "It was one of my youthful days carried into old age," she mused, perhaps remembering the romantic rejection that she sometimes considered the cause of her trouble. In an attempt to mask her mortification, and perhaps feeling real pride at the degree to which she had been able to provide for herself for so many years, she retorted, "My affairs might be in a worse situation." Although she thereby betrayed some satisfaction in her own accomplishments, she acknowledged in her diary that "to see an old maid after fifty is a sight that would make any woman wonder" (September 22, 1788).

The incident proved decisive. Now, "more than ever," she felt like a "poor bird who was picked of all its feathers." Dickinson spent the Sabbath in "earnest supplication at the throne of God" and resolved to leave Bennington and return to Hatfield, "contrary" to her "intent." On Monday she "cried all the day without cessation—the tears would flow without my leave." Her family was at a loss. Rebecca records that she was "called an odd being as ever lived by my two sisters [who] would be glad to know what I was crying for." Martha and Miriam found Rebecca's sudden reversal of intention, and ensuing grief, incomprehensible. Neither could imagine the feelings this sudden focus on her singlehood had produced in their sister.

A cryptic remark in this entry offers a small glimpse of the sometimes surprising ways Dickinson's singlehood caught her up short. When confronted with the question of whether she was "sorry" that she hadn't married while young, Dickinson leapt to her own defense—but, she added, she "felt the Pot on [her] head" as she did it (September 22, 1788). It's hard to know just what her metaphor meant, but it may be a reference to the cap she wore. Caps were deemed appropriate for mature women in eighteenth-century Massachusetts; brides tended to begin to wear caps after their wedding or once they became mothers, to signal their adult status. By the late 1780s a woman Dickinson's age typically would have worn a cap that covered her hair and framed her face, prompting the analogy to an upside-down pot, though one made of linen or cotton. If that's what she was thinking of, then Dickinson's embarrassment at having donned the trappings of age without having reaped its usual rewards was acute. Whatever the "pot on her head" may have been, her sense of conspicuousness verged on disfigurement.

Though she would return to Bennington several times after this incident, happy to see old friends there, she was only there for a long visit, even a season, not planning to move permanently. The autumn of 1788 clearly became a turning point for Rebecca Dickinson. The Bennington debacle is recounted in the entry dated September 22, 1788. Then, on October 2, Dickinson's diary records a proposal of marriage from Dr. Moses Gunn of Montague, a prominent man whose first wife had died. The couple had been childless. Perhaps Gunn was the suspected suitor who had either failed to press his suit or had been dismissed by Dickinson the year before; perhaps not. In any case, she spent some sleepless nights tossing and turning while she considered the proposal.

The physician had achieved some stature during the revolution, serving not only as a longtime member of his town's select board, but also as their representative to the September 1768 convention in Boston that considered the colony's response to the Townshend Acts, and as a delegate to the Provincial Congress in 1775. He had also served on Montague's Committee of Correspondence. A graduate of Yale College and about ten years older than Dickinson, by the 1780s Gunn's occupation and revolutionary service had made him a well-respected figure in the community. But she could not overcome her misgivings. "He was more agreeable than I could think of," she mused. "He would do if he was the right one," she wrote, "but I shall never change my name. I really believe there will always be a bar in the way" (October 3, 1788). Dickinson may have found the fact that Gunn had lost a leg "by a fit of sickness" distasteful or the move to his community unappealing. That she was beyond her childbearing years may also have contributed to her decision, because marriage would no longer produce for her the children who would care for her in old age. (This may not have been a concern for Gunn, given his interest in fifty-year-old Rebecca Dickinson, but he did indeed find a wife, marrying in the following year the thirty-four-year-old Elizabeth Ingram, who would give the doctor, in his seventies, two children.) In the end, for whatever reason, altering her lifestyle to accommodate the unknown trials of matrimony finally struck Dickinson as unthinkable.

And so, less than two weeks after her utter humiliation in Vermont, she declined this opportunity to finally change her name. Whether or not she had been waffling over Gunn's proposal previously, she now firmly rejected him. Fully accepting the decision as her own responsibility, she wrote in her diary: "Though I have no home, may it be on my mind that today I have had the offer of one" (October 2, 1788). *May it be on my mind*—here the diarist recorded a pointed and permanent reminder that she had elected to retain her independence. In moments of despair, Dickinson could return to this entry and remember that, having weighed her options with care, she had deliberately chosen to remain single, whatever the consequences.

In the following spring, the April 1789 death of her onetime suitor Charles Phelps gave her an opportunity to revisit that particular decision, too: "I have lived better than I could have lived with him for the last ten years of my life" (April 19, 1789), she concluded, surely in reference to Phelps's turbulent and ultimately unsuccessful campaign against the state government of Vermont (which eventually left him imprisoned and impoverished) as well as her own success as a local craftswoman. Dickinson had considered Phelps's offer, yet had chosen to remain unmarried, and she congratulated herself twelve years later that her judgment had been sound. Now she had rejected Gunn as well (and if Gunn was not the September 1787 suitor, that man also). Her reflection about Phelps, that she had "lived better than I could have lived with him" for the last decade, seems to summarize her decision to reject each of her various suitors. Again and again, Dickinson measured marriage against singlehood and chose the latter.

How do we reconcile the powerful emotions that color page after page of Dickinson's journal with these moments of choice that clearly reflect some satisfaction with her life? The loneliness and dismay captured in the journal are very real, yet passages throughout—including the proposals of marriage declined—suggest that Dickinson was not so anxious to exchange the single state for a married one that she would accept any suitor who came her way. The circumstances or sentiments that constituted the "bar in the way" that repeatedly prevented her from marrying are never spelled out, though on other occasions (e.g., October 27, 1787) the "bar" meant, to Dickinson, her "stubborn heart," perhaps a vague reference to a general disinclination toward marriage. She clearly perceived some attractions in singlehood, and were it not for her apparently genuine belief that she truly was disliked for having remained unmarried, may have been perfectly content to accept the challenges of a life alone, whatever the original cause. Yet this sense of shame and her sensitivity to it often squelched the positive feelings about singlehood that she occasionally expressed.

At times Dickinson looked at her married counterparts wholly without envy. Her references to the challenging situation of Rebecca's sister Anne Ballard, struggling to raise five children in abject poverty, register her understanding that wedded life was not always a picnic. Dickinson visited the Ballards in September 1787, when one of the children was sick and Anne's husband John had "disappeared," perhaps traveling in search of work (or perhaps due to some marital discord, but the former seems likelier, since he did in time return). "How dark it looks on the account of living," Dickinson wrote (September 8, 1787). "How much the assistance of the husband and the wife is wanted where there is a family of children," she mused, "but my sister is alone in the world as to the care of the family and he gone clear away from home." Families were blessings, yes, but also burdens. Just the month before she had observed that there are "a great many family blessings which I know nothing of, but the gifts of time always bring sorrow along with them." A "numerous family and a great estate," she knew, "bring a great concern upon the minds of the owners, more than a balance for all the comfort that they bring" (August 5, 1787). Put another way, as envious as she sometimes was of her friends and acquaintances with children and grandchildren, she understood—especially when she looked at her sister Anne, living hand to mouth and caring for several small children without the steady support of her husband—that marriage and family brought strain as much as joy.

By these years, too, eating at the Billings house had taken the edge off at least some of her dissatisfaction, providing some semblance of family life and conviviality. Rebecca took her meals at the tavern down the street and then returned home. "Have just now been down to brother Billings to breakfast," she wrote one morning. "There is a great family, but there is the house where I can enjoy myself"—adding, "the company is more then the provision" (June 22, 1788). The "provision," however, could also produce both delight and dismay. On a February morning in 1788 Dickinson wrote, "How dry I have been for two days back, and have hurt myself by drinking beer," adding "how foolish I was for a momentary gratification, to make myself sick" (February 24, 1788). Another 1788 entry paints a lively picture as Dickinson listed the "great family" of fourteen at breakfast. In addition to Miriam and Silas and their boys Joseph, Erastus, and Roswell, she saw Northampton's "Catte Olver" (probably Catherine Alvord), Patty Church ("whose parents are dead and she their only child, who is a boarder"), fourteen-year-old Rachel Randall (of Belchertown), a hired man from Chesterfield named "Gypsun," David Stoddard, a man named White from Northampton or Springfield, the former slaves Jonah and Liffe (that is, Eliphalet), and other "comers and goers" who "fill two tables" (July 27, 1788).

More often than not, the contentment Dickinson sometimes found in her circumstances went unrecorded in the pages of her journal. She didn't need her diary when she was feeling happy and confident: the function of the journal means that it largely captured hours of despair. But if actions speak louder than words, then Dickinson's choices in these pivotal years convey volumes. Time after time she rejected the "respectability" marriage would have conferred, as well as the companionship and maybe even the financial security. Plainly, despite her loneliness, despite her sense of community disapproval, she had strong feelings—a "bar in the way"—that did not lend themselves to marriage and was willing to withstand the skepticism, wonder, and even disapproval of her neighbors to sustain her single life.

10

Twilight

Dickinson's internal drama was invisible to her Hatfield neighbors; to them her world probably seemed steady and unchanged. She spent the entire autumn of 1789 in Bennington, and though illness prevented her making such a trip the following winter, she traveled to the "north country" again in 1791. In summer 1793 she made the 170-mile trip again, noting that in the course of her life she had visited Martha once at Suffield, seven times at Marlboro, and six at Bennington. And she would go again the following summer. In these years Dickinson began to take on a new role in her community—the sage elder—even though she was only in her early fifties. Relegated prematurely to a group whose members were older than she was, as she aged Dickinson was absorbed into the community of widows that made up the majority of women without spouses. Given the proximity of her home to the meetinghouse, it was a natural spot for people to rest between Sunday services, and these women proved sources of both companionship and irritation. "This day there are a great many women below," Dickinson mused one Sunday between services, "which makes me take to the chamber." Among her companions that day were Lydia Fitch, a "widow aged near eighty"; Rebecca's aunt Ruth (the eighty-year-old widow of Moses's brother Benoni); the widow "Beck" Dickinson; sixty-year-old Miriam Morton; and her mother, Anna—all widows (August [] 1787). Although Abigail Nash and her daughter Abigail Chapin, Abigail Smith, and seven-year-old Emily Ballard were there as well, Dickinson seemed to feel like one among outcasts. "How poorly the time spends," she sighed.

As the years passed, she noted the "furrows" that increasingly marked the faces of her acquaintances and mused, "How little old age is to be coveted and yet it is a blessing if God so orders it" (August 31, 1793). Past the age when she compared herself to other women who were mothers, she now noticed that she ought to be a grandmother, as others were. "How connected the world is," she opined. "Children and grand-children are the portion of many of the daughters of Adam, but God of his faithfulness has set me by myself" (July 24, 1794). Unlike her neigh-bors, she had "no children's children to be accountable for, no home, no habitation of my own." "I am fifty-three years of age tomorrow," she noted, and "goodness and mercy" have "followed me all my life long. No good thing has God withheld from me; light and life has daily been with me."

In the last years of her life Rebecca Dickinson began truly to find herself reconciled to her choices. Ironically, the fact that there are far fewer entries in her diary in these latter years points to her growing contentment. At least, once she relocated altogether to the home of her sister Miriam, she stopped writing in her journal during the winter, the lively atmosphere of the Billings household reducing her need to commit her innermost thoughts to paper, and in time she stopped writ-ing altogether.

While Dickinson's sense of satisfaction with her life alone rose and fell, financial insecurity continued to trouble her. Throughout 1789 fears of poverty had invaded even her sleeping hours. One passage cap-tures vividly the specter of unemployment and the tremendous relief of having a steady income. One night she was "awakened by a dream. I thought that I had stole from Mrs Hubbard. . . . [I] knew myself to be innocent but my credit was a-going" (July [],1789). Her subconscious mind imagined her reduced to a thief in Lucy Hubbard's tavern, sug-gesting that anxiety over money ruled her consciousness both day and night. Though she would live for many more years, Dickinson was by this time in her early fifties and perhaps found performing close needlework hard on her eyesight. The November 15, 1787, entry describing how her mother Anna, in a "puzzling fit" had broken Dickinson's spectacles, suggests that her work had by this time taken its toll on her eyesight.

Little evidence survives about when Dickinson retired from active engagement in her trade. Yet her journal makes no reference to her craft after 1790, and entries in the Phelps diary after this point do not specifically record her having worked for the family, although she continued to visit and may have continued to influence Phelps's wardrobe. On July 8, 1787, Phelps wrote: "Thursday the Widow Hubbard, the Widow Ellis and Becca Dickinson all here from Hatfield. Becca stayed—the rest went home. Friday she and I into town at many places." Two weeks later Phelps noted that she and her husband rode into Northampton to "get a black gown" (i.e., the fabric to make one) for Phelps's mother, whose sister had died. Perhaps Dickinson helped Phelps select the appropriate materials and trimmings for this mourning garment while the two women were in town shopping. That Dickinson's apprentice, Patty Smith, arrived Saturday to sew the gown suggests the extent to which Dickinson continued to participate in gownmaking at Forty Acres, this time in an advisory role. Whether or not she helped choose the fabric, she surely looked on as her protégée measured her esteemed client, cut the expensive material, and fashioned it into a gown suitable for the elderly Mrs. Porter.

As Dickinson aged, she began to witness the passing of the revolutionary generation. In a November 21, 1790, sermon Joseph Lyman observed the death of Benjamin Franklin, who passed away in April, and Governor James Bowdoin, who had died earlier that month— "two . . . wise and good men," Dickinson noted. Franklin was among the greatest statesmen of the age, beloved by Americans and Europeans alike. Bowdoin had been active in the revolution and had served as president of Massachusetts's 1779 constitutional convention. As governor during Shays's Rebellion, he had rallied the militia to quell the uprising (which cost him his office), although he returned to public service as a member of the state convention that ratified the U.S. Constitution. Other members of the revolutionary generation also began to fade. In July 1792 Oliver Partridge died. The man, Dickinson effused, "was in all places the most useful person that I ever knew. His worth was great at home [and] abroad." Apparently forgetting altogether the tension over Partridge's loyalty during the revolutionary tumult, she added, "Enemies he had none, or so few that they never appeared" (July 22,1792). A close friend of the family, she "stayed until five o'clock looking for his children" from Berkshire County "where live five daughters [and] three sons who have gave credit to their father who was wise and set good examples before them."

Long-standing fears about mortality closer to home came perilously near to truth in December 1792, when eighty-year-old Anna Dickinson nearly died. "My mother is very sick and it is likely she will not live long and where my home will be God only knows," wrote Rebecca (September 15, 1792). The two women's fates, Rebecca knew, were entwined, and two weeks later, with Anna still failing, Rebecca fretted, "I have no house or home to find or hide me in" ([late] September 1792). Finally Anna's health improved, and she was well enough to move into Samuel's house, at which time fifty-four-year-old Rebecca, secure in the knowledge that she could return in the spring, promptly left her own home and spent the winter with the Billings family (December 9, 1792).

Three years later Rebecca Dickinson moved entirely out of the home in which she had lived most of her years. The condition of the ancestral house had continued to deteriorate. "This old house is crumbling to pieces," she wrote in summer 1794. "It seems [as] though it would swim off [in] every rain." Dickinson had "no house to flee to" (that is, none she owned), but assumed that "God knows all my wants and will provide" (July [], 1794). All around her were symbols of mortality. One day in the summer of 1794 she learned of the death of eighty-year-old Mrs. Ashley of Sunderland. To Dickinson it seemed like an "admonition . . . to be ready." Again, she had some startling dreams. In one "very strange dream the sun fell from the sky." Dickinson said to herself "amen"—just as "the God who has set the sun in the firmament knows the exact time to be removed" so too her own "sun has often set in regard to the things of this life." Indeed, her whole "lonesome life" was a "daily admonition that my sun has set" (July 24, 1794).

Though Anna Dickinson would survive until 1804, in August 1795 Samuel and Mary Dickinson finally sold the family homestead on Hatfield's Main Street, after which Anna moved permanently to their home in Whately, and fifty-seven-year-old Rebecca moved in with her sister Miriam and brother-in-law Silas in a house that they had built just two years before. That Dickinson wrote comparatively little in her journal after these events (she didn't write at all during the winter of 1793– 1794, which she may have spent at Miriam's) points to the close link between the journal and her "house alone" and provides further evidence of the diary's role as a source of companionship.

As the eighteenth century drew to a close, Rebecca witnessed a development that Hatfield people would long remember as extraordinary: the first formal public education for girls. Boys had long had access to schools. Some attended simple grammar schools, while others prepared for college. Just a few years earlier, in 1792, Miriam's son Joseph had begun preparing for a career in the ministry by reading with Reverend Lyman, then entered Yale College. (He taught briefly in New Salem, but realized in time that his speech impediment would always be an obstacle to either a ministerial career or life as an educator, so instead he went into commerce, running a store in Hatfield for a few years.) Girls had previously attended so-called dame schools in private homes, usually led by women schoolteachers. For example, Patty Reynolds, whom Rebecca mentioned from time to time as a companion at meals in the Billings tavern, came to Hatfield during summers to teach school. (Rebecca's sister Martha Mather sent her own thirteen-year-old daughter down from Vermont to attend a school kept by an Englishman named Isaac Curson.) But in the mid-1790s the town of Hatfield decided to fund a public school for girls, four months of the year, in summer.

Of the many outcomes of the revolution, none had been increased political or economic power for women. Although Abigail Adams privately urged her husband John to "remember the ladies" and help rewrite the oppressive legal codes that kept wives under the thumbs of their husbands, he declined to become a champion of women's rights. Few other public voices took up that cause. Neither Abigail nor the vast majority of other leading women of her generation pressed for women's participation in political arenas. An exception was Judith Sargent Murray, a Massachusetts playwright and essayist who in 1798 published "Observations on Female Abilities," arguing that educated women were as capable as men of "supporting with honor the toils of government." In this and others essays in *Massachusetts Magazine* and *The Gleaner,* Murray urged readers to remember the many women throughout history who had contributed to the life of their nation. Her essay "On the Equality of the Sexes" asserted the equal capacity of the female mind. No records today tell us whether Murray was read in Hatfield parlors, but closer to home, perhaps Reverend Lyman helped shape public opinion on that score. In a 1799 sermon given at Deerfield's Dickinson Academy he praised not just those who sought education, but those who provided it, "knowledge" being "essential to wisdom," and "the arts and sciences" being "handmaids to virtue." God "makes provision," the clergyman asserted, "not only that the fathers, but that the future mothers of the race may be richly furnished to train up their children to learning and virtue."[1]

The relative capacity of men and women was a topic more generally on the minds of citizens in the new republic. In 1805 the Massachusetts Supreme Judicial Court considered a case that required them to articulate whether or not the wives of loyalists who had fled during the war could have a citizenship status separate from their husbands. As some families across Massachusetts had escaped the revolution—leaving for England, Canada, the Caribbean, and elsewhere—many married women, obligated to follow their husbands, necessarily forfeited family property. After the war the success of attempts to reclaim this property hinged on whether these married women had been free to stay if they wanted to. A landmark case, *Martin v. Massachusetts,* addressed the issue. Ironically, to save the seized assets, lawyers advocating for the woman's heirs had to argue that she had no meaningful autonomy in the matter. Could married women have responded independently to the revolution and chosen for themselves which government to follow? In a decision that would stand into the twentieth century, the court concluded that they could not have: a married woman's citizenship followed that of her husband.

This setback on the legal front was closely related to the creation of the ideal of "Republican Motherhood"—women's civic participation would take other forms. In deciding to educate girls, Hatfield families (as Lyman's sermon suggests) again participated in the development of that ideology, which held that, for the new republic to flourish, its citizens needed to be knowledgeable, informed participants in public life. Heightened investment in mothering afforded women a sense of contribution without seriously challenging the existing social order, and education was key to that enterprise. Though female literacy had been rising already, the next generations would look markedly different than Dickinson's own, and with unexpected consequences: the daughters of her nieces, with their expanded skills and broader horizons, would launch the reform movements of the nineteenth century.

In funding the school, Hatfield embraced a trend that had in fact been unfolding across Massachusetts for some time in terms of increasing educational opportunities for women. Change came unevenly: surprisingly, while some towns expanded female education as early as the 1760s, nearby Northampton did not institute regular public schooling for girls until 1807. While one might guess that a town as sophisticated as Northampton would have valued and promoted education more generally, that community's interest in university training worked to the detriment not just of girls, but even of boys not headed to college. As late as 1788, the town specifically voted "not [to] be at any expense for schooling girls," and in the 1790s it was fined by the state for failing to provide this service.[2]

Perhaps Hatfield residents were more influenced by the Massachusetts School Law of 1789, which for the first time referred to both the town school "mistress" and the school "master." In fact, the expansion of access to education for girls was likeliest to occur when and where a small group of elites no longer dominated public life, middling families had enough wealth to exert influence of their own, and no single religious institution controlled spiritual matters.[3] In Hatfield the decision was not without controversy: for years afterward, residents remembered the debate that ensued surrounding efforts to "teach the shes."[4]

Other developments suggested the advent of a new era. Dickinson had already begun to witness remarkable transformations in her trade, as America's first industrial revolution was just making itself felt. In her youth, beautiful silks and damasks landed on Massachusetts wharves from manufactories across Europe, while more serviceable goods emerged from the wheels, looms, and fulling mills of her neighbors. By the time Dickinson reached late middle age, new enterprises at Byfield and elsewhere had brought factory production to her state. Social relations of work were changing in other ways, too. One wonders what the craftswoman made of the news in spring 1796 as the house joiners and cabinetmakers of Hampshire County gathered in a general meeting and agreed on set prices for their work—the dawn of collective labor action in western Massachusetts.

The landscape itself signaled new economic systems in the form of new roads, stagecoach routes, and bridges. A lottery was held to raise funds for a bridge across the Connecticut River, linking Hatfield to Hadley and facilitating commerce across the state and the region. The ferries that for so long had linked towns set on their paths toward extinction. The political landscape was also evolving, as formal parties—the Federalists, who believed in a vigorous central government and robust support for commerce, and the Democratic-Republicans, who preferred that power reside in the states and resisted the growing influence of banks and merchants in favor of agricultural interests—solidified. In early nineteenth-century Hatfield, "party spirit ran very high." One resident recalled that the "Federalists would have their Thanksgiving Ball in one place, while the Democrats had theirs in another."[5]

In these same years Hatfield was also taking on an aura of antiquity. One traveler called it a "handsome old town," hinting that, as the market revolution gained velocity, Hatfield felt more like the past than the future.[6] On July 7, 1805, the *Massachusetts Spy* described Hampshire County's festive observance of the "29th anniversary of our national freedom and glory" (that is, of the 1776 Declaration of Independence). At sunrise Captain Edwards's artillery company gave a salute, and at lunchtime a procession marched from Asahel Pomeroy's Northampton home to the town's meetinghouse, at which Hatfield's Rev. Dr. Lyman (now in his post for more than thirty years) offered a prayer. The public memory of the revolution was taking shape, as only some events and figures, not all, entered the collective consciousness, codified by monuments, memorials, poems and parades. At the same time, the aging Rebecca Dickinson herself was edging toward relic status.

In the Billings household Dickinson was now an intimate member of the family, and this seemed to ease her mind considerably. The 1803 will of Rebecca's brother Samuel also suggests that she had reason to relax. When Samuel died that summer, she was among his largest creditors (to the amount of $97.00). Perhaps Samuel never conveyed to his sister the funds due after Moses's demise, or perhaps she had found other ways to assist his family. Whatever the reason, the fact that Samuel owed her this much money suggests that she never suffered the straitened financial circumstances she had so desperately feared. (Tension over money may help explain Dickinson's poisonous relationship with her sister-in-law Mary, whom she believed "passionate," "covetous," and "jealous.") Indeed, Rebecca was soon the senior member of her immediate family. In 1804 her mother Anna died; her room at Samuel's house contained only her riding hood and a silk cloak, two gowns, her bed and the coverlet that warmed it, and a brass kettle.

Rebecca outlived other members of her family as well. John Ballard died on February 22, 1806, of palsy, and fifty-five-year-old Anne followed on March 29. The cause of death recorded, "general decay," suggests that a hard life had taken its toll. In 1808 Silas Billings died (of peripneumonia). The elderly sisters Rebecca and Miriam moved into the home of Miriam's son Roswell.[7] In 1809 the women received word that sister Martha, by then living in Wethersfield, had died as well.

If the world began to pass Dickinson by, some things remained unchanged. In religion, as in politics, the town was conservative, in the word's literal sense. For generations New England towns had engaged in the process of "seating" the meetinghouse: assigning the best seats to the best families, then moving out and down through the social spectrum as the remaining places were dispensed. Even before the revolution, Massachusetts families began questioning, and even rejecting, what seemed increasingly like an old-fashioned habit, a vestige of a more hierarchical world now gone. But Hatfield continued this practice into 1807 and beyond, long after many towns, sensitive to the new republican spirit, had abandoned it. As changing values and beliefs transformed the region, most towns gradually discarded this custom in favor of new, more democratic practices. But in Hatfield, old ways died hard.

In April 1810 Rebecca Dickinson, preparing for the inevitable, wrote her own will. "Being of sound mind and memory," and finding it "fit to dispose of my worldly substance," to her nephews Joseph, Erastus, and Roswell Billings, she bequeathed the seventy acres of land in Williamsburg that her father Moses had given her years earlier. For Samuel's boys in Whately she excused their father's sizeable debt to her. Joseph's wife Polly received her "suite of bed curtains" (i.e., her extraordinary embroideries), her flame-stitched fire screen, and her pocketbook, while Erastus's wife Abigail was given her scarlet broadcloth riding hood. Hannah, the wife of Roswell Billings, would receive a round maple table, a half-case with drawers, and her wool riding hood, whereas niece Anna Davenport got a blue bed quilt, her two best blankets, and her black silk gown. The rest, she thought—aprons and shawls, table linens and towels, teaspoons and a canister and teapot, and the bed in which she died—would be meted out among the family.

The garments she had made over those many decades continued to serve the women in her community, and eventually their daughters and granddaughters. In 1812 the brown ducape gown that Rebecca had crafted for Elizabeth Phelps's wedding was remade yet a third time in forty-two years. Created in 1770, it had been altered eighteen years later, in 1788, when Northampton craftswoman Molly Wright extended its life for another twenty-four years, and now here again, Hadley needlewoman Hannah Stockwell further prolonged the garment's usefulness by remaking it once more, four decades after its original construction. Certainly it was a testament to both the skill of the maker and the stewardship of the Phelps women that the cloth survived for so long. Did Dickinson absorb the news with pride, or did she cringe to hear that the gown she had so carefully crafted decades before had been so radically transformed?

At the age of fifty-six, Dickinson had once again "resigned" herself to her singlehood, sighing, "I have this day concluded that I must finish my days with the title of old maid, an unenvied title but surely there is no hope for me" (August [], 1794). Even this phrase, "surely there is no hope," hints at *some* hope, but over time she indeed seemed more reconciled to the single state. If the story of her "bitter stroke"—that is, whatever event she considered the reason for her singlehood—served as a useful, even critical, passage in Dickinson's larger narrative, it is ultimately an unsatisfying explanation for her singlehood. In the midst of her story, she also conceded that "my lot is of my own choosing and of my own contriving" (August 12, 1787). Apart from any unrequited love, Rebecca Dickinson bore greater responsibility for her singlehood than she generally acknowledged, and she enjoyed more autonomy than she was able to admit. No single incident destroyed her chances at marriage. Rather, as one historian has observed, "unmarked by ceremony, gifts and congratulations, the choice to be single is usually found in small acts, seemingly insignificant decisions that move one in immediately imperceptible ways from marriage—sometimes even before one has rejected marriage per se."[8] Although we have no record of the choices, small or large, that Dickinson made in her youth, we do know that later in life she consciously decided to retain her independence. That she was a decade past the usual age of marriage when she felt the bitter stroke suggests that she may have already begun to move "in immediately imperceptible ways" away from marriage, and later in life she declined marriage in ways entirely perceptible to all.

"This morning," she wrote one summer day as she was "recollecting on the affairs of my life back," she noted that a particular "song has been in my mouth": "In all my fears / in all my straits / my soul on thy salvation waits" (August 8, 1787). In Dickinson's later years, she constantly strove to achieve contentment. "How good and comfortable it is," she observed, "to wait on God. May the happy state of mind abide with me . . . there is no company here, no voice to be heard. The birds sing around me, but what is all the music of the groves to that small voice which whispers peace to my soul?" "My boughs have been trimmed off, but the tree is not hurt," she observed another time. "Though I stand in the forest with my branches off and look not like the rest of the trees, yet my mountain stands strong," Dickinson asserted (August 12, 1792). Her lack of children notwithstanding (i.e., the boughs trimmed off her family tree), she "stood strong." In fact, through her singlehood God would "surely bring [her] feet to the gate of heaven." "There are a great many family blessings I know nothing of," Rebecca had once written, "but the gifts of time always bring sorrow along with them. A numerous family and a great estate bring a great concern upon the minds of the owners—more than a balance for all the comfort that they bring" (August 5, 1787). Throughout her life Dickinson struggled to cling to that insight, to look at a neighbor and conclude that "she has her fortune, I mine—very different and both right" (May 31, 1794). At the throne of her Calvinist God, Dickinson was not an old maid but simply another penitent soul striving toward heaven. "My days glide quietly along," the aging artisan wrote in the summer of 1794. On that Sunday afternoon she rededicated herself "to live in the light of spiritual life." "Hoping, waiting, doing God's will to the end of my mortal life is the desire of Rebecca Dickinson" (August 3, 1794).

But in summer 1794 Dickinson's end was not yet especially near. Some two decades later, on a Saturday in March 1815, her onetime client Elizabeth Porter Phelps—now a woman of advanced age herself—made the trip to Hatfield to look in on her old friend, who wasn't well. On March 25, 1815, Phelps recorded an event that is all too familiar to aging women today: when she "rode to Hatfield to see Becca Dickinson," she found that Rebecca had "fall[en] down & hurt her hip badly." Perhaps it was the last time the two women spoke. At the year's end seventy-seven-year-old Rebecca Dickinson succumbed to influenza. She was laid to rest beside her parents and among her family in the Hatfield burial ground.

CONCLUSION

Remembering Independence

Rebecca Dickinson and King George III were born just weeks apart, in summer 1738. They witnessed the very same revolution from very different vantage points. As a young woman Rebecca lived proudly in a North American colony of Great Britain, a member of the greatest empire in the world. At twenty-two she claimed George III as her king with the same satisfaction as did her English counterparts worldwide. By the end of her life she would be able to reflect on a revolution and the creation of a new nation. She welcomed the new government with enthusiasm, while her friend Lucretia Williams is said to have regretted the loss of the monarchy to her dying day. This was the reality of the revolution and its aftermath in Hatfield and elsewhere across Britain's onetime colonies: some cheered, some mourned, and some shrugged.

Artisanry played no small role in events as they unfolded. In the movement for independence, craft and consumption moved to the center of the revolutionary boycotts. It was equally critical in Dickinson's personal movement toward independence. Craft skill enabled her to fend off the poverty so often associated with never-married women and helped her withstand the loneliness and sense of purposelessness that she so often battled. Dickinson may well have taken special pride in the quality of the clothing she created. During the crisis over the proposed move to Bennington, her complaint that leaving Hatfield would mean, among other things, that she must "leave all [her] clothes behind" (March 23, 1788) hints that she may have created a personal wardrobe in which she took real pleasure. Or perhaps simply seeing the clothing she made worn by her clients each Sunday in the meetinghouse or at various events produced true delight. Gownmaking provided much of Dickinson's social life, too, and created a place for her in the community that stood in for parts of family life. Indeed, her trade and marital status, and the very nature of gownmaking itself—from numerous fittings to time shared stitching together the pieces of a garment—lent themselves easily to an intimacy between craftswomen and their clients and community and could result in an honorary or symbolic familial status. It may well be her artisanal skill that permitted, or even encouraged, her to resist offers of marriage, because she could control her own income in a way many women could not. Importantly, it enabled her to find a positive role in her community that the "unenvied," "formidable" title of old maid did not encourage. The surviving examples of Dickinson's careful and inventive needlework hint at both a commitment to craftsmanship and expression of creativity that made her trade a source of pride and an outlet for her artistic sensibilities. For this single artisan, craftwork and artisanal identity provided the main means by which she formulated a place in her community and perhaps a good deal of her private identity as well.

Dickinson's life helps us understand both the independence movement and independent women in early America in new ways. "To old people who remember her," Hatfield historian Margaret Miller wrote in 1892, "or knew her by hearsay, she was a 'Saint on Earth,' [a] 'marvel of piety.'" Others remembered her as the "most industrious woman that ever lived."[1] Her extraordinary status in her own time made her a memorable figure—so memorable, in fact, that she became one of the few residents of early Hatfield plucked from the pages of time, preserved in the ongoing historical memory of the community. As a point of entry into women's lives in the decades between the Great Awakening and the

War of 1812, her experience prompts a rethinking of both the world of artisans in the run-up to revolution and Republican Motherhood as they affected never-married women. Her life illuminates the history of women, culture, and politics in the eighteenth and early nineteenth centuries. But the many ways Dickinson and her story of independence figured into the historical imagination of new generations also help us better understand changes in women's lives in the decades after her death.

When Rebecca Dickinson passed away on December 31, 1815, she left behind the usual remnants of a long life: cloaks of satin and broadcloth, gowns of calico and bombazet, a handful of aprons and shawls, a pair of silk gloves, scattered pieces of furniture, an assortment of household linens, earthen plates and her black tin teapot, a looking glass, and of course, her Bible. Some special objects were laid aside, passed down to favored nieces and nephews: her finer gowns, her better furniture, and those spectacular embroidered bed hangings. She was laid to rest in the Hatfield burial ground beside her old friend Lucy Hubbard's tavern, a plain headstone marking her grave. Her ramshackle house survived her; described as "old and neglected" in the 1810s, it continued to find use as the site of a private school and as a family home possibly as late as 1860. Around that time it was razed, as the old made way for the new.

But Dickinson's death and the demolition of her home did not relegate her to obscurity. In the late nineteenth and early twentieth centuries, she was rediscovered by a community of Progressive Era women eager to harness the power of early American crafts to address the social and cultural turmoil of their Victorian present. Among the adherents of what we now call the "colonial revival" was Margaret Miller, whose early efforts to publish Dickinson's "dolefully dolesome" prose were so soundly rejected. Margaret and Ellen Miller were sisters who, together with another dozen or so leaders, helped launch an arts and crafts revival that would transform Deerfield, Massachusetts, the village just north of Hatfield that had been sacked in the 1704 raid. Deerfield had been famous in the eighteenth century as the scene of this legendary attack. In the decades since the revolution, Deerfield—passed over by the industrial development thriving elsewhere—had declined from a prosperous farming community into an economic backwater. Its past was beginning to seem more appealing than its present. By the third quarter of the nineteenth century the town had little going for it except a stunning collection of early houses little changed through the years, in part because the families who occupied them could ill afford to renovate or remodel. In 1848, when a house that had survived the 1704 raid was threatened with demolition, some residents rose up to try to save it—an attempt widely recognized as the beginning of the historic preservation movement in America. The effort failed, but in time a small community of like-minded people came to see that Victorian Deerfield's future lay in its colonial past: the houses, artifacts, and folk knowledge of its Yankee inhabitants, all extraordinary survivals from New England's glorious history (as people believed), were valuable resources in an age that feared rapid industrialization, accelerating urbanization, and wave after wave of unwanted immigrants from undesirable nations. The colonial revival would thrive in Deerfield, like almost no place else, and "Aunt Bek" would be rediscovered and reclaimed.

Appropriately, it was a community of never-married women who brought about this transformation. In the wake of the demographic catastrophe of the U.S. Civil War and the consequences of westward migration by men of marriageable age, late-nineteenth-century Deerfield found itself home to a sizeable community of never-married women who had large old houses to keep up. But cultural prescription had not caught up with economic imperatives: there were few ways for these women—genteel in their pedigree, if not their bank accounts—to earn the livings necessary to maintain their homes. At the same time, some women of means who lived in the nation's largest cities—Boston, New York, and Chicago—found Deerfield a restful summer destination, a place to escape the stresses of modern living. Their fondness for the town led to a desire to preserve it. But their aim was not wholly nostalgic. They actively sought to harness the virtues embedded in the tangible remains of the colonial past and deploy them as antidotes to the excesses of their times, from the shoddy goods crowding department store shelves to the shallow values associated with their fast-paced age. Put another way, their vision was of America's future as much as it was of the American past. They did not seek so much to escape the present as to transform it. As these women restored crumbling houses to their earlier glory and revived (and reinvented) crafts like basketry and needlework, they transformed "Old Deerfield" into a historic village and early center of heritage tourism.

Margaret Miller's family had lived in a number of places, but Hatfield, Massachusetts (just fifteen miles south of Deerfield), was Margaret's mother's childhood home. In 1863, about the time Margaret was born, the family settled there. From early childhood Margaret evinced an interest in local history, making "many friends among the old people of the village, going regularly to sit with them to listen to their stories of their lives, tales she never forgot, and which sometimes oddly illuminated the confused records of the town scribes, by hitching together their disconnected facts. Her regard for these favorite friends was shown in the party for her eleventh birthday which she celebrated with a group of old ladies all over eighty years of age."[2] It was from those elderly friends that Margaret came to her appreciate the colorful figures of Hatfield's eighteenth-century past, including Rebecca Dickinson and her memorable family. She never met Dickinson, but she knew people who remembered her well, and as another unmarried woman, seems to have felt a certain kinship with her.

Margaret and Ellen were both part of a large segment of educated Americans who toward the close of the nineteenth century embraced the "arts and crafts movement." The nineteenth-century craft revival evolved in part from an emerging preference for goods that, unlike the cheap factory-made goods, conveyed in their materials and workmanship an authenticity that many feared was slipping away from the industrial nation. In many ways, it was a development not unlike the craft revival of the early twenty-first century, in which consumers have taken up knitting and crocheting or have sought out craft commerce sites like Etsy to find unique handmade goods in order to establish their individuality in a world of mass consumption. Victorian women looked to and admired the handwork of the past and wished to embrace its power for their own time. In 1889 Rebecca Dickinson's bed hangings and fire screen were included among the "relics" on display at a meeting of an area historical society, the Pocumtuck Valley Memorial Association. (They were shown among a "collection of antiquities" of the "early settlers," including a looking glass said to have come over on the *Mayflower,* powder horns from both King Philip's War and the American Revolution, and other family, and now community, heirlooms.) Seven years later Margaret's sister Ellen, together with Margaret C. Whiting (the two women inspired by the colonial needlework they had seen, including work by Rebecca Dickinson), founded the Deerfield Society of Blue and White Needlework. The society's leadership looked to the needlework of the past for inspiration and then designed new versions of old patterns, to create something new from the best that past and present combined had to offer.

The needlework of the colonial revival encouraged women everywhere to embrace a legacy of art and craft that linked them to their colonial counterparts (while also finding means of fresh artistic expression). The Miller sisters, with their family connections, were familiar with Dickinson's crewelwork and had ample opportunity to examine it. Ellen Miller and Margaret Whiting made a careful paper pattern from one of Dickinson's surviving coverlets, and the Deerfield Society of Blue and White Needlework adopted Dickinson's flowers, clovers, strawberries, and pears into the goods—doilies, tablecloths, and other household textiles—that the society offered contemporary consumers. Also in Hatfield, Mary Wait Allis Hurlburt (descended from the same Waite as Rebecca's grandmother, Canada) seized an opportunity when she created a piano scarf—a popular craft project distinct to her own moment in time—that represented more than 150 years of female tradition in Hatfield. Having found a piece of linen woven by Content Hastings in 1824 from fibers spun four years earlier by Mary Hastings Wait, Hurlburt drew on the crewelwork Dickinson had created in the 1760s to create a new piece of ornamental needlework, in a new form, but from old patterns. The piano scarf, which proudly displays at its center a large fleur-de-lis adapted from Dickinson's own centuries earlier, honored the mind and skill of Rebecca Dickinson and the generations of women who followed her.

Margaret Miller, who first grasped the poignancy of Dickinson's journal and sought to publish excerpts of her prose, saw in Dickinson other meanings for her own time, grounded not in craft, but in singlehood. By the end of the nineteenth century, "spinsters" had become stock figures in art and literature. In countless works of fiction, unconventional and even peculiar "maiden aunts" provided comic relief or cautionary tales. Indeed, Dickinson's "eccentricity," as suggested in the 1910 history of Hatfield by Daniel White Wells and Reuben Wells, is especially interesting in light of the tendency of nineteenth-century novels and short stories to cast never-married women as curious, quirky figures. Put another way, Wells and Wells's portrayal of Dickinson in the official town history may owe as much to their own cultural context (and that of their informants, Lucretia and Samuel Partridge) as to Dickinson's actual personality. On a related front, it is worth noting here another celebrated spinster in Rebecca's family tree, though on a more distant branch. Just as Moses and Anna Dickinson began their family in the 1730s, another nest of Dickinsons was growing nearby. Nathan, born in Hatfield in 1712, eventually moved his family to a new settlement just to the east, where 112 years later his descendant, the poet Emily Dickinson, was born. She too would become a never-married woman whose perceived eccentricity attracted notice in her community, nineteenth-century Amherst, Massachusetts.

By the early twentieth century, both Dickinsons had been embraced by communities of single women, respected for their artistry and celebrated for their extraordinary personalities. In a presentation to the Pocumtuck Valley Memorial Association in the 1930s, "Spinsters of Yesteryear," Margaret Miller placed Rebecca Dickinson in a larger trajectory of the valley's never-married women. She asked her listeners to consider earlier generations of never-married women in order to contemplate "whether we are progressing intellectually as well as materially."[3] She shared some passages from Dickinson's diary, then turned to another Hatfield family, the Smiths. Joseph Smith had made a fortune in fattened cattle and land speculation. He and his wife had three sons and four daughters. None of the girls (and only one of the boys) ever married. In time, the family's wealth came to the youngest, "Sophy." Rich beyond imagination, in 1870 Sophia Smith used the tremendous resources at her disposal to establish one of the nation's first and most important institutions of higher education for women, Smith College.

Margaret Miller urged her audience to contemplate the difference that access to education made for unmarried women like Sophia Smith, Rebecca Dickinson, and herself.

As it happens, Sophia Smith also traced her roots back to Canada Waite, the infant captive. Sophia's grandfather Samuel and Rebecca's mother Anna were brother and sister. Born in 1796, Sophia Smith would certainly have known her distant relative, Rebecca Dickinson; she grew up near the Billings tavern and was nineteen years old when Rebecca died. What the younger woman made of her elder cousin and neighbor, a woman remembered in the village of Sophia's generation as an "oracle," we cannot know.

In the decades that followed Dickinson remained relevant to her community. In 1957 her bed hangings were included among the pieces of needlework displayed by Hatfield's Real Folks Society, a nineteenth-century organization within the Congregational church, initially inspired by Adeline Dutton Train Whitney's best-selling nineteenth-century novel celebrating conservative values and women as keepers of hearth and home. A quarter century later, as the nation celebrated its bicentennial in 1976, Margery Burnham Howe published *Deerfield Embroidery: Traditional Patterns from Colonial Massachusetts,* and again, Dickinson's striking needlework and moving story were front and center. By then the principle stewards of Rebecca Dickinson's memory had become two other never-married women, sisters Marion and Louisa Billings, born in 1880 and 1881 to Roswell and Carrie Graves Billings (who were descendants of Rebecca's nephew, Roswell Billings). Marion and Louisa had achieved the education Margaret Miller cherished. Both had attended Smith College (in the classes of 1901 and 1905, respectively). For some years Marion ran her family's tobacco business and taught school in Springfield and Hatfield, while Louisa became an instructor in physics at Smith College and taught in area public schools. The two women, who knew the Miller family and were young girls when Dickinson's diary surfaced, lived well into the twentieth century. Louisa died in 1976 and Marion followed in 1981—the last Billings to live in Hatfield. The curators of their own family history, they donated many artifacts to their town's historical society, helping preserve not just Rebecca's story, but many stories, in this important local archive. In

1996 Roswell and Richard Billings, having become the family keepers of Rebecca's diary, donated it to the library of the Pocumtuck Valley Memorial Association. And in 2003 Dickinson's extraordinary bed hangings became part of the collections of Deerfield's Memorial Hall Museum, a gift from Dickinson's descendant and namesake, Rebecca Billings. Today they sit alongside work of the Deerfield Society of Blue and White Needlework, helping to interpret for new generations of visitors the ways the handwork of the past illuminates vast changes in the lives of American women.

This book itself now joins that series of gestures by reestablishing Rebecca Dickinson's place in both community memory and American history. The accidental survival of Dickinson's extraordinary journal has allowed generations of readers to explore the revolution, and women's lives in those dramatic decades, in new ways, asking the pressing questions of their own time. Today Dickinson's goods have for the most part been scattered to the winds. The land she inherited from her father and gave to her nephews is part of the Conway State Forest, at the Hampshire and Franklin County line. The needlework lovingly bequeathed to her descendants is today preserved in local museums. Although Dickinson's home is long gone, Lucy Hubbard's tavern still stands, as does the house in which Dickinson died. The home of her longtime client Elizabeth Porter Phelps in time became a historic house museum, the Porter Phelps Huntington House, in Hadley, Massachusetts. One can walk those rooms and imagine the skilled gownmaker settling in to her work.

What otherwise remains she did not bequeath intentionally: her journal. Its fleeting moments of contentment form part of Dickinson's lesson for us, because they remind us how incomplete is the view that journals provide. Diaries are tricky things; we too easily mistake their immediacy for veracity. Dickinson's diary afforded her an opportunity to pose questions, test answers, explore possibilities, and articulate dissatisfactions that could not be shared elsewhere. It was a place to put truths, to be sure, but truths that were often partial, passing, ephemeral, contingent, and contradictory. It was no casual act when Dickinson stowed her journal under lock and key. As she phrased it, "God only knows my heart and has seen the secret enmity that is lodged there" (September 16, 1787). But now we, her readers, have seen that enmity, as well as her apprehension, embarrassment, terror, and resentfulness. But we have also glimpsed her contentedness and occasional pleasure. As the essayist Joseph Brodsky has written, "reaching us intact or in fragments," manuscripts like Dickinson's seem to speak across the ages. They "strike us of course with their durability and tempt us to assemble them, fragments especially, into a coherent whole, but they were not meant to reach us. They were, and still are, for themselves."[4]

Read for itself, Dickinson's text is a document of her most difficult moments, her most searching and conflicted hours. Through it we view her life, but only in part, and with distortions. But attending to those distortions is instructive, both for what they convey about singlehood and for what they suggest about journals as records of shifting, even competing, truths. Her journal, dolefully dolesome though it may be, is a tangle of apprehension and affirmation, of agency and acquiescence. It is on the one hand powerful evidence of the extraordinary pain experienced by a woman who deviated from convention. On the other hand, it is a record of extraordinary will and considerable pride. Above all, it is an artifact of independence.

PRIMARY SOURCES

this Day is the 22 of july 1787 here alone in this hous there has been a thunder Storm here this afternoon Some hard thunder and rain it is good to be where god's voice is to be heard there is no dread to me in that voice thunder never terrifies me but when it is very nigh and very loud the lords voice is in the City how many would fly away from this hous alone but it is good to be here the lord knows his Saints and gards the Place where they Dwell and if tha Should Perish in the Storm there Death would be Precias in his Sight there is no Storm nor no troble can sent my Soul from god there is no Sickness no Sorrow of no kind which will Seperate me from the love of god in Christ jesus no bar no bolts can bar the Soul from god for it is a Spark of heavenly fire which Came from god and will tend to the Senter as the fire flies toward the Sun So the Soul of the Spirit flys to god o my father make me to have more of thy one likeness Cure me of my Spot and blemishes and make me one with my father who is in heaven the Sabath is gon and the monday is gone tuesday is Come this Day

this is the 25 of july 1787 this Day makes one forty nine years of age the goodness of god has suffered me to live in his world it is god and god only to who i owe the length of my life there is malis Enuff round me to have taken it from me were the wicked Suffered to all them Selves but the god whose i am has kept me by his Power glory to the name of god for his Preserving mercy he has kept me from those Deadly Enimies who have Sought my life may my Soul never Stray from god but live within the [ark?] with god where Saten and his Emisesaries have no Power my Soul is affraid of Satan and the mallis of wicked men keep me o my father may not i be joined with the wicked i abhor there ways i would that god would Shelter me under the Shadow of his wing

the last night had a Sad Dreeme wich i hope will never Come to Pass me thought that i was in a Place where i Could not Escape it is a Sad thing to fall into the hands of the wicked may i never fall but live with god never Doubting his power to gard me by night and noon god has taken a fatherly Care of me for neer fifty years why Should i Doubt one who is of litel faith i am week in faith this Summer has given me a Sight of my Self i know that i am not my own the god who made me will Dispose of me in his own time and way there

is no way but to Submit to the will of god i know that it is best that god should govern the world and Dispose of me as he thinks best this forenoon Spent here alone in this hous mending my thin[gs] and have jest now recived an invitation to gow to Conway to St[ay] a Day or too i must Drop my Pen and leave it with god whethere [or] no i Shall take it up in this hous ever again

[th]is is the 2 Day of august how my time Spends i have been to Conway where i have had oppertunity of giving in my testimony for god but did it after a Poor manner there i See one of my old frinds whose eyes god had lately oppened how good the thoughts and words of a young Convert god of his great goodness make her more and more like her Divine lord and mastter who was meek and lowly of mind and heart may She grow in grace and be a Pattern of humilyty and bring great honnor to the Religion of jesus Christ She lost a beloved Sister betty bilings the wife of Elash bilings who Died better then a year agow how god orders the affairs of the world in order to bring about his own Purposses this mrs bilings has been no Seeker of god She was not used to religious Conversation in her fathers hous while She lived with her father Cornal williems here in this Place but She had the hapiness of marriing Squire bilings who was [a] good man and happe for her how the good Difuse blesings all arround where thei Dwell may my Soul Speak for god on all occations as oppertunity Presents and never fail to live up to the Rule of my Profesion so that i be no Stumble to those who are without

[my] Sheperd is the living lord now Shall my wants be well Supplyed Providense and holy word become my Safety and my guide Pastures where Salvation grows he makes me feed he makes me rest [th]ere living watters gently flows and all the food Divinely blest

this is Sunday august 5 Day 1787 this morning here alone in old hous there is the wisdom of god and the Power of god and the goodness of god to be Seen in all the things which Consern me in this life what Should i Doe was it not for this old hous it is a Safe Retreat from troble never o my Soul forget the kind Care of thy heavenly father in giving the[e] So many good things the use of this hous is a gift from god and may my Soul be truly thankfull for the gift it is good to find that god is a loading our lives with benefit how god has Preserved me this Summer when my foolish thoughts Surmised that i Should be very unhappy in this hous alone but that god whose tender Care is over all his works has made it a good habitation to me there is no Place in the whole world that i Can think in where i Could be So well accomadateed for Soul and body which makes me Cry this morning o the wisdom and the Power of god and the goodness of god which gives me life and health and Crowns my Dais with Content there is a great many family blesings which i know nothing of but the gifts of time alwa[ys] bring Sorrow along with them a numirous family and a great Estate bring a great Consern upon the minds of the owners more then a ballence for all the Comfort that tha bring god who knows them who would be the least in[jur]eed by them gives in wisdom to those few for after all the noise about the world there is but a few who gain the Riches of the earth a very few tha are many times a Curs and not a blesing Covet not there dainties tha are Danjerous Snares to Souls god has Provided better food for his Chosen ones tha are to feed on the Riches of his grace that deer bought Perchace the world was not bought at so deer a rate Consider o my Soul the Prise which was Paid for the Salvation of the Souls of men which was bought by the blood of the Son of god a wonderfull love that Died and Suffered for a Sinfull race of men a number of beings who will not look to god but through the glass of this world tha are born of the earth and there tha Dwell and there Cry is who will Shew us ena Earthly good there hope there Portien lies here tha Seek no better good but there is a number i hope who god Enlightens with the light of that grace and that glory which Springs from the throne of god those few who are the Chossen of god and are brought by a new birth into a neer relation to the father of there Spirits o the amazing thought that the love of god Should redeem Some few Sons and Daughters to himself and leave the world in wickedness be quiat o my Soul and tremble before that god who has made all things for himself Even the wicked which is reserved to the day of Evil this is the 12 of august a Satterday morning yesterday was att brother bilings there was mr Curzson Patte Church who boards there in the evining Came home to this hous alone i lited no Candel for the Darkness of my mind was far beyand~ the darkest Dungin there was no hope for me in the things of time jesse bilings was there which Put those Sad thoughts into my mind the Difference is not So great in our outtoward Condission as in the temper of our minds but my lot is of my own Chusing and of my own Contriving and how Could i help the matter it is ordered of god as well as Contrived by my Self the great all was lost and what is the great all of my Earthly Substence my mind which gazees after the great Prosperity of others this Day found my Self here alone in this hous tho the last night was undon by the Smallness of my faith ["this" erased] there is some thoughts which Comes in my mind by being here alone which gives me great trobel as the Conceit that no one Desires my Company that have out lived all my Connections with the world and it is tru that i have there is no hope for me in the things of time and the more need of Sending all my hopes to the heavenly world i do wonder att my Self that i Should be so Earthly minded and look after the things of the world as tho i Should be the better for any of them or think those anymore happy who have them

this morning awoke after a Strange Dream i thought that i was on a jorny with jesse bilings mare with one rein of my bridle broke my Self lost entangled among horses where i had to lead the Creture rather than have any Servis from her my Desire was to gow to meeting but was not able to find the way the first of my thoughts this morning was be still and know that i am god but the truth of those words have been Disputed by me a great many times this Day [erasure] So Early in the Day for it is not eight o Clock So great a mistry i be to my Self the few Days and months past have been quiat under the happy Shade of gods goverment and the last night did reble to make my Self unhappy the Prosperyty of the wicked and my own wicked heart with the Smallness of my faith have once more led me astray from god the eyes with which beheld my misries was the last evining Closed my Eyes was Set on the world to my Cost no peace where the world is Coveted a most wicked thought as tho god was not wise enought to Dispose of me without my help i am ashamed of my Self and wonder how i Could over look all the good things god has given me in a Covitious fit how i Can quarel with the goverment of god who has witheld nothing from me which would have been fore my good

EXCERPTS FROM FALL 1790

this Day 12 of Ceptember have been wandering from home have for some time been at a lois to know wether i had better goe a jorney or not how bewildered i am to Doe my Duti how to goe or Stay i know not will the kind Providence of god Direct me if god Shou[ld] give me health may the thanks be given to god and i Doe my Duti and go on my way rejoicing this holy Day have been musing and wondering whether i had better goe or Stay the lord Direct me at all times and in all things how to behave may my life and death be under the Spessial eye of heaven may my Soul rest all my cares with god looking and wishing that thy will may be Done on the Earth as in the world of Spirits and i be made willing in the Day of his Power god is my maker and my only Preserver how oft my Soul has tested of his love in his kind Protecttion by Day and by night if my Pen Should move with my breth it would be too Slow to Count the mercies as tha rise for tha every morning and fresh Every moment who Can tell the numbers time Cannot Count but Eternity a boundless never Ending Existence this soul of mine must love for Ever may my Soul be with god with Christ with the holy Spirit with the innumirable Company of angels and the Spirit of just men made perfect the Saints who are Crouned with Everlasting life may my unworthy thinking Part be found on the right hand of Christ in the day when he Shall make up his juels may the hiden life of the Christion be my daily walk may my soul bid Defience to the world and all the Powers of darkness and be a Cristion and a Saint in Deed and truth

the Sun is Sit and i am a going with my mother to See the widow of Captin Elisha ellis who has been Dead for Some time She is here a visiting his Children her home is west town where her Children Dwell time has made furrows in that face which was once beautifull She was maried twice liveed twenty years with each husband

this is the 14 of Ceptember yersterday was a Day to be noteed in this town for the great assembly of Peopel that was Convened on the training there was great works great heard Confusion a rigment of men with genereal Sheppard as there tha gathered in the Street and marched Down and up the Stre[et] tha went into the South medow and as many Spectaters as of th[en] three thousend at the least a great assembly but how few to the great Company whill arise at the last day or few Compared wi[th] the living who will live on the Earth when the last triumph Shall Sound i quit the Company with those wishes that god would own and bless them for thei appeared like the vally of Dead Souls that tha might fear god and walk before the lord in thruth & riteousne[ss] god of his tender love heard my Poor request wich was put up by me the last Sunday that no harm Should happen to them there was Saved from Death jeri ballard* who was Seven yers old when a hors tro[d] on his head the mercy was greater as he was of our family he is likely to be well Soon glory to god in the highest my Soul will Sing of mercy and the tender Care of angels

this is the 18 of Ceptember a thusday this week was buried the aged widow wells the oldest Person in town She was near Eighty Six years a long Space of time the widow miller is the [next] oldest this wwidow who is gone had the testimony of those who hear the lord She has been trained up in the School of affliction and greatly to her benifit her long late illness which has been ten years has been the tryal of her Patience i went to the grave after the funireal went to the hous of john allis there was mrs Partrige mrs Chapin the widow hurberd the widow allis Sister bilings Seven in all but wee Shall never more meet in this world my low State of health tells me that i must Die the Corps of my frinds and acquaintence give the Silient admonision that this body must Die and be had by the Silient grave to be lost to the living may my better Part rise to the new jerusilem to Praise and to Sing the wonders of gods love who has baught it and made as kings and Prist of the most high god

this holy Day have aded to my life which is 19 of Ceptember this Day was here mr newton of greenfield the Preacher he has gave us too good Sermons this afternoon he told us in a Comforting manner of the gospel hope my Soul was Edefied by the glory of god in the gospil hope or receiving the word of life as offered in the gospel of truth this day my Soul is very Sorifull my Sickness Stares me in the face but it will be well if i am Sick i Shall be better fited for my other trobles but be it as god appoints i would kiss the rod and bless the holy hand of god too troubles is better than one as it will Subdue this Stobouren heart of mine this Day have been greatly Pusled at the Prosperity of the Peopel in this world tha live in Pleashure and have more than heart Could wish no Sickness Comes nigh there habitations thei Swim in the Comforts of this life all that tha Doe Prospers in there hands there Children Dance at the Sound of the organ my Soul knows that this world is a vain Show Shut my eyes on those that have there good things here while i am full of Sores i have offended and broken gods holy law this Day have Cast away my hope Called the bible in question and have Strayed from god and all because i am a Sinner and am Sick and am a Stranger here in the world without hope without a home or a hous to be out of my head in i have this moment thoughts of those train of worthies who

* Dickinson's nephew, Jeremiah Ballard.

was Each and all worth a thousand of me tha was afflicted tormented Scorged whipt imprisened wandered in Caves and dens of the earth tha had here no Continuing City but Sought one to Come i Seek one here and have great greef beca[use] [the] world has Cast me of[f] i am ashamed of my Self of my Profess[ion] [an]d may justly Conclude that i am of the world only my Portion has [w]holly failed me as to this life and i am not in my Sins

lord im am thine but thou will Prope my faith my Patents and my love when men of Spite against me join thou art the Sword the hand is thine there hope there Potion lies below tiss all the hapiness thei know tiss all tha Seek thei take there Shares and leave the rest among there heirs this holy Day has aded to my life this holy Day god has given me there was here the Parents of mr lymen his brothe[r] and Sister mr lymen in the forenoon gave no the Saints Pilgrimage here in this world how the Saints was by there declareing that thei Sought a City whose makeer and bilder was god thei was Pilgrimas and Strangers here in this Evil world how my Soul felt the truth of the Subject how many times my Soul has Put on the Pilgrim and have Set out for the heavenly world with i mind Stedy fixed to Prossecute my jorney at all Eve[nts] how god has gave me Strength from time to time So that fifty too years have rolled over my head i am Poor as to the thing[s] in this life no hous no Children but Pilgrims want none i have the lot assined me by god the very best that Could have fell to me

this is the last Sunday in october this is the Saints Day tha have leave to worship god in his hous the wicked know nothing of those Choice blessings of the Saints it is there highest felisity to draw nigh to god it is as the lofty trumphet or the Soft musick of the ___il nothing was So Sweet to the Spalmmist it was Sweet as the honney on the honney Comb my Soul has tasted the Sweetness of the word to far exceed those who Divide the Spoil i have been feasted with the word in the hous of god but this Day am Detained by bodily indisposion i would this morning Commit my Soul to god to be excersised with that Sorrow that will best Cure me of that Deadly Distemper which is Called Sin i wish a fatal blow al that which is the Cause of my Sickness i have Prayed for my health but would beg of god to kill that sin which brings down the loss of my health this week back have been greatly Pusled to know whether i aught to Pray to god or why not Praise god in the time of Sickness my Soul knows that god is as good in the time of greatest Distress as in the time of the greatest Prosperity but one mercy i have gained at the hand of god to give thanks in the time of Sickness as in the Day of the finnest health and Sunshine this body of mine must Suffer tho the Soul is the active Part in Sining i have the week back been greaviously Pained but when it is gon where is it but the Soul or thinking Part will remember Some Sorrows of the mind which was twenti years Past is more fast on my mind then the Pain which i felt the week back i may with the Salmist Crye i am fearfully and wonderfully made this body and Soul must not Part till Death too loving frinds tha be but humble my mind o my father that this bodi of mine nay live here its appointed time Death is Comforttable to the Saint Compared with Distressing Pain my soul has rested on gods Promises and have no Cause to Doubt there is a rest for this bodi of mine in the grave i would wait gods will with the Patients but there is a rest for the Soul in the heavenly world a glorious rest for the Saint for exceeding all other injoyments Praise will be alwais in our mouths it is now very Dificult to Prais god aright the Soul will Sin this body of mine will be Sick i have Plead with god for health but Sickness is my Portien gods will must Stand and i would Sing of mercy for it is good to be sick it is good to be afflicted for thereby i have learned to keep thy Commands

on friday last the 28 of october 1790 was born to sister ballard a Daughter which her husband Called by the name of betsy the Sicth girl with one son which makes up her family god has in a wonderfull manner Caried her through many trobles may She gain the good of mercies and afflicttions this holy Day the 21 of november this Eleven months have been Sick but good when god gives Sickness Supremely good his kind hand Can make me thankfull for Sickness never was i truly gratefull for that mercy my Soul knows the justis and the loving kindness of god in the time of Sore Distress never was i more loth to be Sick then this fall god has heard my Poor reques[t] and has Set my feet in a longe rome i have but just tasted of Sickness and after a Poor manner have thanked god for it the great Duti of living to god is what my Soul longs for fit me o my father for the world of Spirits may i live to Speak the wonders of that grace which has Caried me through so many sick days and Painfull nights this afternoon mr lymen gave us to understand that the riteous are the Salt of the Earth my Soul has gained Strength by the Publick worship this day there is a fullness in Christ Surly god is the god of the Dissolute and those who are ready to Perist my Soul i wish to be humble under the mighty hand of god and not losse my troble but by the rebukes of thy Providence grow Stronger and Stronger and gain Clean hands and a Pure heart and find Christ my all in all

this year mr lymen has noted this year by the Death of thre great men Doctor frankling govenner bodin of this State who lately Died at Boston too was wise and good men the best name in the world is the name of a Saint this holy Sabath Detained by Sickn[ess] from the hous of god have in the week has been Sore Distressed with the Collick how every Day brought its trobles thanks be to the great god who has lent me life after Such distressing Pain this day awoke with a gratefull remembrence of gods mercies hit[h]erto the lord has helped us here will i Set up my E__esens the lord has been my Song in the time of great Darkness how my wicked heart has Strive with my maker i Cant be Sick i wont be Sick for there is none of my fellow beings to Shew me the least kind offis the last week was the 2 week in December a most Painfull week with me my mother near eighty as Stuped as Can be told a litel febel boy Charls and my bodi in Sore distress with the Collick no being to Come into See our Distress how it looks to feel our trobels ever by [l]ooking back on them but god has Caried me through the week back and thanks to that holy name

"ADDRESS TO THE LADIES," PUBLISHED IN THE NOVEMBER 16, 1767, *BOSTON POST-BOY & ADVERTISER*

Young ladies in town, and those that live round,
Let a friend at this season advise you :
Since money's so scarce, and times growing worse
Strange things may soon hap and surprize you:
First then, throw aside your high top knots of pride
Wear none but your own country linnen;
of Oeconomy boast, let your pride be the most
What, if homespun they say is not quite so gay
As brocades, yet be not in a passion,
For when once it is known this is much wore in town,
One and all will cry out, 'tis the fashion !
And as one, all agree that you'll not married be
To such as will wear London Fact'ry :
But at first sight refuse, tell 'em such you do chuse
As encourage our own Manufact'ry.
No more Ribbons wear, nor in rich dress appear,
Love your country much better than fine things,
Begin without passion, 'twill soon be the fashion

To grace your smooth locks with a twine string.
Throw aside your Bohea, and your Green Hyson Tea,
And all things with a new fashion duty;
Procure a good store of the choice Labradore,
For there'll soon be enough here to suit ye;
These do without fear and to all you'll appear
Fair, charming, true, lovely, and cleaver;
Tho' the times remain darkish, young men may be sparkish.
And love you much stronger than ever.

"TO A NEEDLE" (*AMERICAN MAGAZINE*, AUGUST 1769)

How! Cruel needle tell me how!
That hand like ivory or snow
Or these dear fingers smooth and white
Offended thus to raise thy spell
Of which such flagrant marks are found
In many a scratch and many a wound?
Henceforth her tender hand forbear
Her harmless fingers henceforth spare
Act, if thou canst, a nobler part
And urge thy point against her heart
That heart with which ev'n store compar'd
And crags and rocks is still more hard;
Strike subtle spear, and strike again!
There bent thy rage and wreck thy spleen
For coulds't thou there inflict a wound
The world with thy fame resound
That blood from thence thy point had dy'd
Which Cupid's keenest shaft defy'd

STUDY QUESTIONS

1. Primary source documents capture multiple perspectives on never-married women. Where do their authors seem to agree? In what ways do they disagree?

2. Rebecca Dickinson was a trained craftswoman, able to fabricate the fashionable clothing desired by her society. What were some of the features of craft skill as mastered by women like Dickinson? How does her artisanal work compare to other kinds of work women did in early America? How did her occupation influence her response to the American Revolution?

3. Boycotts are a familiar part of contemporary political life, but in the era of the American Revolution they were a new tool in the protestor's toolkit. Why and how were boycotts used by those eager to resist imperial policy? How did the writer of excerpt 2 seek to persuade women to participate? How are boycotts today the same, and how are they different?

4. Religious belief was the foundation of Dickinson's worldview, as it was for many of her neighbors. How did her faith shape Dickinson's understanding of her own life? How did it shape her interpretation of events in the public sphere?

5. The author suggests that Dickinson actually appreciated aspects of her life alone, even though she almost never said so in her diary. What evidence supports that argument? Is it convincing?

6. How do diaries compare to other kinds of sources historians rely on to write about the past? What are their strengths? What are their weaknesses?

7. To what degree do you think your own emotional and intellectual responses to Dickinson's story are products of contemporary assumptions about never-married women? Where do we see evidence of this eighteenth-century set of beliefs in our twenty-first-century world?

8. Collective memory—how communities remember and craft their own versions of history—is a theme the author emphasizes throughout the book. What are some examples here of collective memory being created or passed on? Can you think of examples of collective memory from any community to which you belong?

NOTES

PREFACE

1. Rebecca Dickinson's diary is owned by the Pocumtuck Valley Memorial Association (PVMA); its collections are housed at Memorial Libraries in Deerfield, Massachusetts. A typescript I prepared from the original is also on deposit there; all cites herein—the date or approximate date of the original entry, in parentheses after the quotation—refer to that source, and the diary is quoted with permission. Dickinson's spelling, grammar, and punctuation, as was typical in her day, vary greatly. The excerpts from the diary that are included at the back of this volume present these entries as they appear in the original, but in order to make her writings more comprehensible for today's readers, particularly college students for whom English is a second language, in the quoted passages in the chapters her spelling and grammar have been updated to reflect modern American usage. In the eighteenth century even the spelling of names could vary; for consistency's sake, I use the spelling "Rebecca" throughout, although her name is also spelled in various places Rebekah and Rebeca. Dickinson is also inconsistent about the date of her own birth, reporting it as July 25 in one instance and as July 13 in another. I have accepted the former.

2. Margaret Miller to George Sheldon, March 29, 1892, Margaret Miller Papers, Miller Family Papers, box I f. 6, PVMA, Memorial Libraries, Deerfield, Massachusetts.

3. See Margaret Miller, "An Old Maid's Diary," *New York Evening Post*, January 9, 1892. Partridge's reminiscences from ca. 1880 are published in Daniel White Wells and Reuban Field Wells, *History of Hatfield, Massachusetts* (Springfield, MA: F.C.H. Gibbons, 1910), 247–292; the quotation is on p. 256. He was born in 1806, so he was a small boy when Dickinson died. On "Aunt Bek," see Margaret Whiting, quoted in Margery Burnham Howe, *Deerfield Embroidery: Traditional Patterns from Colonial Massachusetts* (Charles Scribner's Sons, 1976), 62.

4. Mrs. Samuel [Lucretia] Partridge Recollections, as recorded in Margaret Miller notebook, 74–75, Margaret Miller Papers, PVMA; Lucretia was the wife of Samuel, whose own recollections, as dictated to Lucretia, are published in Wells and Wells, *History of Hatfield*.

5. Ibid.

INTRODUCTION

1. Amy M. Froide, *Never Married: Singlewomen in Early Modern England* (New York: Oxford University Press, 2005), 155.

2. Robert V. Wells, *Revolutions in Americans' Lives: A Demographic Perspective on the History of Americans, Their Families, and Their Society* (Westport, CT: Greenwood Press, 1982), 61.

CHAPTER 1

1. Timothy Dwight, *Travels in New England and New* York (1821), ed. Barbara Miller Solomon, 4 vols. (Cambridge: Belknap Press of Harvard University Press, 1969), 2:35.

2. Frederick Clifton Pierce, *Field Genealogy, Volume I* (Chicago: W. B. Conkey Co., 1901), 163.

3. Quoted in Frank Lambert, "The First Great Awakening: Whose Interpretive Fiction?" *New England Quarterly* 68, no. 4 (December 1995): 652; and Kevin Michael Sweeney, "River Gods and Related Minor Deities: The Williams Family and the Connecticut River Valley, 1637–1790" (PhD diss., Yale University, 1986), 260–261.

4. George Whitefield, *A Continuation of the Reverend Mr. Whitefield's Journal, from a Few Days after His Return to Georgia to His Arrival at Falmouth, on the 11th of March 1741. . . . The Seventh Journal* (printed by W. Strahan for R. Hett, and sold by T. Cooper, 1741), 45–46.

5. Franklin Bowditch Dexter, *Biographical Sketches of the Graduates of Yale College with Annuals of the College History* (New York: Henry Holt, 1903), 1:469. Also voting with Woodbridge was Hadley's Rev. Chester Williams.

6. Sylvester Judd manuscript, vol. 2:93, Forbes Library, Northampton, MA.

CHAPTER 2

1. Daniel White Wells and Reuben Wells, *A History of Hatfield, Massachusetts* (Springfield, MA: F. C. H. Gibbons, 1910), 141; and Lynne Bassett, "The Sober People of Hadley: Sumptuary Legislation and Clothing in Hadley Men's Probate Inventories, 1663–1731," in *Cultivating a Past: Essays on the History of Hadley, Massachusetts,* ed. Marla R. Miller (Amherst: University of Massachusetts Press, 2009), 191–210. Spelling and grammar in the quoted passage have been modernized.

2. Bassett, "The Sober People of Hadley: Sumptuary Legislation and Clothing in Hadley Men's Probate Inventories, 1663–1731," 202.

3. T. Waller, *A General Description of All Trades* (London: T. Waller, 1747).

4. *The Book of Trades* (London: Tabart and Co, 1807), 37.

CHAPTER 3

1. This account of the coming of the war relies heavily on Sweeney, "River Gods and Related Minor Deities"; see especially pp. 499–538.

2. *Book of Trades,* 34.

3. Elizabeth Porter Phelps memorandum book, August 14, 1768, as published in the *New England Historical and Genealogical Register* (January 1764), 22. All cites to this source note the date of Phelps's entry and the *NEHGR* issue and page, unless the passage is found in the unpublished segment of Phelps's diary, part of the Porter-Phelps-Huntington Family Papers owned by the Porter-Phelps-Huntington Foundation and housed in the Amherst College Library, cited as PPHFP. The spelling in Phelps's record has been modernized in this passage.

4. Ibid., November 11, 1770, *NEHGR* (April 1964): 111.

5. A firescreen attributed to Dickinson also survives in the collections of the Hatfield Historical Society. Dickinson's colorful screen is worked in flame stitch—straight, vertical stitches worked in brightly colored wool over three or four threads of canvas to create a variety of geometric patterns. Like her crewelwork, the firescreen also varies from other examples from the same period: typically worked more closely together, Dickinson's stylized pink and blue carnations float in isolation across a blue field.

6. Margery Burnham Howe, *Deerfield Embroidery: Traditional Patterns from Colonial Massachusetts* (New York: Charles Scribner's Sons, 1976), 62–87, esp. 67; in much of her discussion she is quoting Margaret Whiting.

7. Christie Jackson to author, January 26, 2011; my thanks to Christie for sharing her expertise on maritime imagery in needlework.

CHAPTER 4

1. Edmund S. Morgan and Helen M. Morgan, *The Stamp Act Crisis: Prologue to Revolution* (Chapel Hill: University of North Carolina Press, 1995), 109.

2. My thanks to Kevin Sweeney for sharing his insights on the nature of the revolution in western Massachusetts, a subject of his own research; this manuscript is informed by his extensive knowledge of and fresh perspective on these events.

3. As quoted and discussed in Gregory H. Nobles, *Divisions Throughout the Whole: Politics and Society in Hampshire County, Massachusetts 1740–1775* (Cambridge: Cambridge University Press, 1983), 157.

4. Patricia McCleary, *Elizabeth Murray: A Woman's Pursuit of Independence in Eighteenth-Century America* (Amherst: University of Massachusetts Press, 2000), 101, 133–135.

5. See Ms. S-418, "Hatfield, Mass, town proceedings," Massachusetts Historical Society, Boston, Massachusetts (hereafter MHS); and Richard D. Brown, "Massachusetts Convention of Towns, 1768," *The William and Mary Quarterly*, Third Series, 26, no. 1 (January 1969): 99, citing Hatfield General Records, 1741–1813, 191–193, Hatfield Town Hall.

6. Jonathan Judd Jr. diary, August 16, 1769, Forbes Library, Northampton, MA.

7. Both republished in James A. Henretta and Melvin Azawa, *Documents to Accompany America's History, Volume One: To 1877,* 7th ed. (Boston: Bedford/St. Martin's, 2011), 112–113.

8. As recorded in Wells and Wells, *History of Hatfield,* 182.

9. Ibid.

10. Amelia Miller and A. R. Riggs, eds., *Romance, Remedies, and Revolution: The Journal of Dr. Elihu Ashley* (Amherst, MA: Pocumtuck Valley Memorial Association in association with the University of Massachusetts Press, 2007), 58.

11. As quoted in Nobles, *Divisions,* 163. Spelling has been modernized in the quotation.

12. Elisha Billings letters, [July 1774?], Hatfield Town Papers, PVMA.

13. As quoted in Nobles, *Divisions,* 167.

14. Journal of Dr. Elihu Ashely, September 4, 1774, in Miller and Riggs, *Romance, Remedies and Revolution,* 114–115.

15. Seth Tribbs [September 15, 1774], Israel Williams Papers, MHS.

16. Ibid. It was Israel Williams Jr. who had failed to keep the fast; see Miller and Riggs, *Romance, Remedies and Revolution,* 116, n.365.

17. James Hunt [September 15, 1774], Israel Williams Papers, MHS.

18. Benjamin Read testimony, September 15, 1774, Israel Williams Papers, MHS. Spellings have been modernized in quotations from this source.

19. Ibid.

20. Ibid.

21. Ashley, August 25, 1774, in Miller and Riggs, *Romance, Remedies and Revolution,* 110.

22. Gregory Nobles poses this question in *Divisions,* 174.

23. William Read testimony, September 15, 1774, Israel Williams Papers, MHS; also quoted in Nobles, *Divisions,* 174.

CHAPTER 5

1. This and following quotations by Lyman are from Joseph Lyman, *A Sermon Preached at Hatfield December 15th, 1774, Being the Day Recommended by the Late Provincial Congress; to Be Observed as a Day of Thanksgiving* (Boston: Edes and Gill, 1775). Spelling in some instances has been modernized.

2. On the former, see Nobles, *Divisions,* 169, and Wells and Wells, *History of Hatfield,* 187; on the latter see Elihu Ashley, February 4, 1775, in Miller and Riggs, 166.

3. See Elizabeth Pendergast Carlisle, *Earthbound and Heavenbent Elizabeth Porter Phelps and Life at Forty Acres (1747–1817)* (New York: Scribner, 2007), 85.

4. Abby Maria Hemenway, *Vermont Historical* Gazetteer, *Volume V: The Towns of Windham County* (Brandon, VT: Carrie E.H. Page, 1891).

5. As quoted in Wells and Wells, *History of Hatfield,* 187.

6. Minutes of the Third Provincial Congress, July 5, 1775, as reproduced in *Province in Rebellion: A Documentary History of the Founding of the Commonwealth of Massachusetts, 1774–1775* (Cambridge: Harvard University Press, 1975), 2391.

7. Minutes of the Second Provincial Congress, May 1, 1775, as reproduced in *Province in Rebellion,* 1595.

8. As quoted in Nobles, *Divisions,* 177.

9. Ibid.

10. *General Records, 1741–1813,* 273, Hatfield Town Hall.

11. As quoted in Kevin Graffagnino, "'Vermonters Unmasked': Charles Phelps and the Patterns of Dissent in Revolutionary Vermont," *Vermont History* 57 (Summer 1989): 135.

12. Ephraim Holland Newton, *History of the Town of Marlborough* (Montpelier: Vermont Historical Society, 1930), 52.

CHAPTER 6

1. This discussion is based on *General Records, 1741–1813,* Hatfield Town Hall, 292; quotations are from this source as well.

2. Petition for freedom (manuscript copy) to the Massachusetts Council and the House of Representatives, January [13], 1777, http://www.masshist.org. Spelling has been modernized in this quotation.

3. Wells and Wells, *History of Hatfield,* 196–197.

4. My thanks to local historian Eric Weber for supplying this description of Dickinson's lot, which he has hiked.

5. Murray had been an inn holder since 1779. Julie Carroll and Patty Theberge, in "The Billings Family of Hatfield, MA" (unpublished typescript, Hatfield Historical Society, 1984), propose that Seth Murray's tavern was in the home of Silas and Miriam Billings. I was unable to locate the archival evidence on which this assertion is based; moreover, a diary entry from June 29, 1794, in which Dickinson expresses her great animosity toward Murray and describes what seems to be her one and only visit to the Murray home, suggests otherwise.

6. Will of Moses Dickinson, March 4, 1783, Hampshire County Registry of Probate Box 48, n. 13.

7. Wait built a house that still stands on Irene and Lucius's onetime land at the top of the hill. My thanks again to Eric Weber, who kindly supplied genealogical information on this family. Mr. Weber also supplied the information here on Wait.

8. Recounted in the *American Recorder,* published as *The American Recorder and the Charlestown Advertiser,* September 8, 1786.

9. Josiah Gilbert Holland, *History of Western Massachusetts* 1: 238 (Springfield, MA: Samuel Bowles and Company, 1855); Wells and Wells, *History of Hatfield*.

10. Sylvester Judd, as quoted in Leonard Richards, *Shays's Rebellion: The American Revolution's Final Battle* (Philadelphia: University of Pennsylvania Press, 2002), 8.

11. This army is sometimes referred to as a mercenary force, which misconstrues the events. Because the legislature was not in session and so could not vote an appropriation to mobilize militiamen, a group of Boston merchants provided the necessary bridge loan, which was subsequently repaid.

12. Harrison Williams, *The Life, Ancestors and Descendants of Robert Williams of Roxbury* (Washington, DC: W. F. Roberts Company, 1934), 136.

CHAPTER 7

1. This discussion is based on Michael E. Bell, *Food for the Dead: On the Trail of New England's Vampires* (New York: Carroll & Graf Publishers, 2001). My thanks to Kevin M. Sweeney for alerting me to this source. Though we might be surprised that recovery of this sort is even possible, the time it takes for a cadaver to become a skeleton varies widely; an adult corpse buried six feet deep without a coffin might take some five or ten years to decay, and the presence of a wooden or lead coffin does not necessarily accelerate or decelerate the process along predictable lines.

2. *A Sermon, Preached at the Execution of Abiel Converse, Who Was Executed at Northampton for the Murder of Her Infant Bastard Child, July 6th, 1788*. By Aaron Bascom, A.M., Pastor of the Church in Chester (Northampton, MA: Printed by William Butler, 1788). Spelling and grammar in the quotation have been modernized.

3. *Book of Trades: or, Library of the Useful Arts* (1807; reprinted, New York: Dover Publications, 1976), 34.

4. As quoted by Krishna Gorowara in "The Treatment of the Unmarried Woman in Comedy from 1584–1921" (PhD diss., Glasgow University, 1961), 322.

5. Excerpts from Sylvester Judd's interview with Catherine Parsons Graves (b. 1755), 1832, in Judd, "Northampton," 1:334, Sylvester Judd manuscript, Forbes Library, Northampton, MA.

6. "Samuel D. [and Lucretia A.] Partridge's Recollections," in Wells and Wells, *History of Hatfield*, 205, 256.

CHAPTER 8

1. For example, mid-July 1791, June 17, 1788, and mid-August 1791.

2. Elizabeth Porter Phelps memorandum book, August 3, 1806, Box 7 folder 3, PPHFP.

3. See Amy Froide's discussion in *Never Married: Singlewomen in Early Modern England* (Oxford: Oxford University Press, 2005), 154–181, esp. 157–158.

4. Cotton Mather's popular and often reprinted sermon *Ornaments for the Daughters of Zion* (Cambridge: S. Green, 1692), 74–75; and Mary Astell, *A Serious Proposal to the Ladies* (London: Richard Wilkin, 1697), 111–112. Spelling in the quotation has been modernized.

5. "The Heron: A Tale for Old Maids," *American Magazine* (November 1744).

6. William Hayley, *Philosophical, Historical and Moral Essay on Old Maids* (London: T. Cadell, 1786), 13–14.

7. *Collections of the Massachusetts Historical Society* (Boston, 1798; reprinted 1835), 183.

CHAPTER 9

1. Mather, *Ornaments,* 74.

CHAPTER 10

1. Wells and Wells, *History of Hatfield,* 209.

2. Kathryn Kish Sklar, "The Schooling of Girls and Changing Community Values in Massachusetts Towns, 1750–1820," *History of Education Quarterly* 33, no. 4 (Winter 1993): 519.

3. Ibid., 538.

4. Wells and Wells, *History of Hatfield,* 208.

5. Partridge reminiscences, in Wells and Wells, *History of Hatfield,* 249.

6. October 6, 1801, *Diary of Thomas Robbins, D. D., 1796–1854* 1: 152.

7. "List of Deaths, Hatfield," Hatfield Historical Society, and "Deaths," Dr. Lyman's book, 292.

8. Kathleen Barry, *Susan B. Anthony: A Biography of a Singular Feminist* (New York: New York University Press, 1988), 366.

CONCLUSION

1. Margaret Miller, "An Old Maid's Diary," *[New York] Evening Post,* January 9, 1892, 1.

2. "Margaret Miller," by Margaret C. Whiting, in the Margaret Miller papers, PVMA.

3. Margaret Miller, "Spinsters of Yesterday," in *History and Proceedings of the PVMA, 1930–38* (Deerfield, MA, 1950), 22.

4. Joseph Brodsky, "Homage to Marcus Aurelius" (1994), reprinted in *The Best American Essays, 1995,* ed. Jamaica Kincaid (New York: Houghton Mifflin Co., 1995), 5.

BIBLIOGRAPHIC ESSAY

Beginning in the late nineteenth century, several works have considered Rebecca Dickinson's life and times. Local antiquarian Margaret Miller published at least two accounts of Dickinson and her diary: "An Old Maid's Diary," *New York Evening Post,* January 9, 1892, 1; and "Spinsters of Yesterday," *History and Proceedings of the Pocumtuck Valley Memorial Association, 1930–38,* vol. 8 (Deerfield, MA: The Association, 1950), 23–31. Portions of Rebecca Dickinson's diary were also published by Daniel White Wells and Reuben Wells in *A History of Hatfield, Massachusetts* (Springfield, MA: F. C. H. Gibbons, 1910). Margery Burnham Howe discusses Dickinson's needlework in *Deerfield Embroidery: Traditional Patterns from Colonial Massachusetts* (New York: Charles Scribner's Sons, 1976). The most recent scholarship on Dickinson and the Deerfield Society of Blue and White Needlework is Suzanne L. Flynt, *Poetry to the Earth: The Arts and Crafts Movement in Deerfield* (Stockbridge, MA: Hard Press Editions, in association with Pocumtuck Valley Memorial Association, Deerfield, MA, and Hudson Hills Press, Easthampton, MA, 2012). My own article, "My Part Alone: The World of Rebecca Dickinson," appeared in the *New England Quarterly* 71, no. 3 (September 1998): 341–377.[*] In a subsequent book I examined Dickinson's work as a gownmaker; see *The Needle's Eye: Women and Work in the Age of Revolution* (Amherst: University of Massachusetts Press, 2006). Readers interested in digging deeper should consult these previously published works, more heavily footnoted than as revised here. A footnoted typescript of this book will also be placed on deposit at the Hatfield Historical Society.

Important primary sources, in addition to the diary itself, are "Dr. Lyman's Church Records," 1771–1867, Hatfield Town Hall; and the wills of Moses, Anna, Samuel, Rebecca, and Anna Dickinson, held in the Hampshire County Hall of Records, Northampton, Massachusetts, in box 48, nos. 10–11, 49–50, 37, and box 46, no. 13, respectively. Also essential is the memorandum book or diary of Dickinson's longtime client Elizabeth Porter Phelps, most of which was published sequentially in the *New England Historical and Genealogical Register* between January 1964 and October 1968 (the original is among the Porter-Phelps-Huntington Family Papers, housed at the Amherst College Library Archives & Special Collections). Phelps's biography sheds light on Dickinson's world as well; see Elizabeth Pendergast Carlisle, *Earthbound*

---

[*] That article was subsequently republished in Kriste Lindemeyer, ed., *Ordinary Women, Extraordinary Lives: Women in American History* (Lanham, MD: SR Books, 2000), and in Charles William Calhoun, *The Human Tradition in America from the Colonial Era Through Reconstruction* (Wilmington, DE: Scholarly Resources, 2002).

and Heavenbent: Elizabeth Porter Phelps and Life at Forty Acres (1747–1817) (New York: Scribner, 2007). Two additional local diaries that are indispensable to an understanding of revolutionary Hatfield are those of Elihu Ashley, housed at Memorial Libraries in Deerfield, Massachusetts and published in *Romance, Remedies, and Revolution: The Journal of Dr. Elihu Ashley,* ed. Amelia Miller and A. R. Riggs (Amherst: University of Massachusetts Press in association with PVMA, 2007); and the diary of Jonathan Judd Jr., housed at the Forbes Library in Northampton, Massachusetts. On Dickinson's would-be suitor Charles Phelps, see John Phelps, *Family Memoirs* (Brattleboro, VT: Selleck and Davis, 1886); and Kevin Graffagnino, "'Vermonters Unmasked': Charles Phelps and the Patterns of Dissent in Revolutionary Vermont," *Vermont History* 57 (Summer 1989): 133–159.

The standard history of Dickinson's Hatfield is Daniel White Wells and Reuben Field Wells, *History of Hatfield* (Springfield, MA: F. C. H. Gibbons, 1910). On Israel Williams, see Kevin Michael Sweeney, "River Gods and Related Minor Deities: The Williamses of New England, 1637–1790" (PhD diss., Yale University, 1986); see also his important articles "River Gods in the Making: The Williamses of Western Massachusetts," in *The Farm, Annual Proceedings of the Dublin Seminar for New England Folklife,* ed. Peter Benes (Boston: Boston University, 1988); *The Bay and the River: 1600–1900* (Boston: Boston University, 1982), 101–116; and "Mansion People: Kinship, Class, and Architecture in Western Massachusetts in the Mid Eighteenth Century" *Winterthur Portfolio* (Winter 1984): 231–255. Franklin Bowditch Dexter's *Biographical Sketches of the Graduates of Yale College with Annuals of the College History* (New York: Henry Holt and Co., 1903), 3:235–241, includes brief sketches and a list of Joseph Lyman's published sermons and pamphlets.

To date, the only extended consideration of never-married women in early America remains Lee Virginia Chambers-Schiller's monograph *Liberty, a Better Husband: Single Women in America: The Generations of 1780–1840* (New Haven, CT: Yale University Press, 1984). Chambers-Schiller's study subjects include Rebecca Dickinson, the earliest one. Her articles "Woman Is Born to Love: The Maiden Aunt as Maternal Figure in Ante-Bellum Literature," *Frontiers* 10 (1988): 34–43, and "Married to Each Other; Married to the Cause. Singlehood and Sibship in Antebellum Massachusetts," *Women's History Review* 17, no. 3: 341–357, join a small number of essays on never-married women in early America, which also include Zsuzsa Beren's "'The Best or None!' Spinsterhood in Nineteenth-Century New England," *Journal of Social History* 33, no. 4 (Summer 2000): 935–957, which carries the query into the antebellum era. Karin A. Wulf takes up the lives of a set of never-married women in "'My Dear Liberty': Quaker Spinsterhood and Female Autonomy in Eighteenth-Century Pennsylvania," in *Women & Freedom in Early America,* ed. Larry D. Eldridge (New York: New York University Press, 1997), 83–108; see also her larger work, *Not All Wives: Women of Colonial Philadelphia* (Ithaca, NY, and London: Cornell University Press, 2000). Martha Vicinus studied single women of Philadelphia at a later date in *Independent Women: Work and Community for Single Women, 1850–1920* (Chicago: University of Chicago Press, 1985); for the view from the south, see Christine Jacobson Carter, *Southern Single Blessedness: Unmarried Women in the Urban South, 1800–1865* (Urbana: University of Illinois Press, 2006). An important work on this subject in England is Amy M. Froide, *Never Married: Singlewomen in Early Modern England* (Oxford: Oxford University Press, 2005); see also Judith M. Bennett and Amy M. Froide, *Singlewomen in the European Past, 1250–1800* (Philadelphia: University of Pennsylvania Press, 1998) and the special issue "Winners or Losers? Single Women in History 1000–2000," *Women's History Review* 17, no. 3 (2008). An expansive treatment is found in *Women on Their Own: Interdisciplinary Perspectives on Being Single,* ed. Rudolph M. Bell and Virginia Yans (New Brunswick: Rutgers University Press, 2008).

A somewhat separate literature contemplates literary and print depictions of never-married women. Important work that informed this study includes Gwendolyn B. Needham, "New Light on Maids 'Leading Apes in Hell,'" *The Journal of American Folklore* 75, no. 296 (April–June 1962): 106–119; Mary Kelley, "A Woman Alone: Catharine Maria Sedgewick's Spinsterhood in Nineteenth-Century America," *New England Quarterly* 51 (1978): 209–225; Roslyn Belkin, "Rejects of the Marketplace: Old Maids in Charlotte Bronte's *Shirley*," *International Journal of Women's Studies* 4, no. 1 (1981): 51–66; Margaret J. M. Ezell, "'What Shall We Do with Our Old Maids?' Barbara Pym and the 'Woman Question,'" *International Journal of Women's Studies* (1984): 451–465; Micaela di Leonardo, "Warrior Virgins and Boston Marriages: Spinsterhood in History and Culture," *Feminist Issues* 5 (Fall 1985): 46–68; and more recently, Cindy McCreery, *The Satirical Gaze: Prints of Women in Late Eighteenth-Century England* (Oxford and New York: Oxford University Press, 2004).

On the legal context of marriage and singlehood, see Marylynn Salmon, *Women and the Law of Property in Early America* (Chapel Hill: University of North Carolina Press, 1986). Carolyn Heilbrun discusses the inability of women to construct figurative and literal narratives of their lives outside of available "plots" sanctioned by public discourse in *Writing a Woman's Life* (New York: Ballantine Books, 1988). Other scholarship that illuminates the lives of women both married and single includes Nancy F. Cott, "Divorce and the Changing Status of Women in Eighteenth-Century Massachusetts," *The William and Mary Quarterly*, Third Series, 33, no. 4 (October 1976): 586–614; and *The Bonds of Womanhood: "Woman's Sphere" in New England, 1780–1835*, 20th anniversary ed. with a new preface (New Haven, CT: Yale University Press, 2007). For an analysis of women's lives in an earlier era, see Laurel Thatcher Ulrich, *Good Wives: Image and Reality in the Lives of Women in Northern New England, 1650–1750* (New York: Vintage, 1991). Vivien Conger examines widows who did not remarry in *The Widows' Might: Widowhood and Gender in Early British America* (New York: New York University Press, 2009).

Several studies have examined the history of the family and early American sexuality. Good starting places include Susan Klepp, *Revolutionary Conceptions: Women, Fertility, and Family Limitation in America, 1760–1820* (Chapel Hill: University of North Carolina Press, 2009); Richard Godbeer, *Sexual Revolution in Early America* (Baltimore and London: Johns Hopkins University Press, 2002); and Ruth Bloch, *Gender and Morality in Anglo-American Culture, 1650–1800* (Berkeley: University of California Press, 2003). An essential article here is Cornelia Dayton, "Taking the Trade: Abortion and Gender Relations in an Eighteenth-Century New England Village," *The William and Mary Quarterly*, Third Series, 48, no. 1 (January 1991): 19–49 (see also http://history.uconn.edu/takingthetrade/about.php). On lesbians in England and early America, see Louise Crompton, "The Myth of Lesbian Impunity: Capital Laws from 1270 to 1791," *Journal of Homosexuality* 6 (Fall/Winter 1980/1981): 11–25; John D'Emilio and Estelle B. Freedman, *Intimate Matters: A History of Sexuality in America* (Chicago: University of Chicago, 1988; 3rd ed. 2012); and Godbeer, *Sexual Revolution* (cited above). For an entry into historical demography, see Robert V. Wells, *Revolutions in Americans' Lives: A Demographic Perspective on the History of Americans, Their Families, and Their Society* (Westport, Conn.: Greenwood Publishing Group, 1982).

On women and aging, the classic works are Terri Premo, *Winter Friends: Women Growing Old in the New Republic, 1785–1835* (Urbana: University of Illinois Press, 1990); David Hackett Fischer, *Growing Old in America* (New York: Oxford University Press, 1977); and Andrew Achenbaum, *Old Age in the New Land* (Baltimore, MD: Johns Hopkins University Press, 1978). Also helpful are Devoney Looser, *Women Writers and Old Age in Great Britain, 1750–1850* (Baltimore, MD: Johns Hopkins University Press, 2008); Thomas R. Cole, *The Journey of Life: A Cultural History of Aging in America* (Cambridge: Cambridge University Press, 1992);

and C. Dallett Hemphill, "Age Relations and the Social Order in Early New England: The Evidence from Manners," *Journal of Social History* 28, no. 2 (Winter 1994): 271–294.

There is a large literature on New England women in the American Revolution. Key works include Mary Beth Norton, *Liberty's Daughters: The Revolutionary Experience of American Women, 1750–1800* (Boston: Little, Brown, 1980); Alfred F. Young, "The Women of Boston: 'Persons of Consequence' in the Making of the American Revolution, 1765–1776," in *Women and Politics in the Age of the Democratic Revolutions,* ed. Harriet Applewhite and Darlene Levy (Ann Arbor: University of Michigan Press, 1990), 181–226; Barbara Clark Smith, "Food Rioters and the American Revolution," *The William and Mary Quarterly,* Third Series, 51, no. 1 (January 1994): 3–38; and Laurel Thatcher Ulrich, "'Daughters of Liberty': Religious Women in Revolutionary New England," in *Women in the Age of the American Revolution,* ed. Ronald Hoffman and Peter J. Albert (Charlottesville: University Press of Virginia, 1990), 211–243. Linda Kerber posited the term "Republican Mother" in *Women of the Republic: Intellect and Ideology in Revolutionary America* (Chapel Hill: University of North Carolina Press, 1980). See also Jacqueline Barbara Carr, *After the Siege: A Social History of Boston* (Boston: Northeastern University Press, 2005); and the excellent overviews offered by Joan R. Gunderson, *To Be Useful to the World: Women in Revolutionary America, 1740–1790* (New York: Twayne Publishers, 1996) and Carol Berkin, *Revolutionary Mothers: Women in the Struggle for America's Independence* (New York: Vintage, 2006). An important recent reevaluation of women's lives in the wake of the revolution is Rosemarie Zagarri, *Revolutionary Backlash: Women and Politics in the Early American Republic* (Philadelphia: University of Pennsylvania Press, 2007).

Biographies of other New England women who witnessed the American Revolution include Laurel Thatcher Ulrich, *A Midwife's Tale: The Life of Martha Ballard, Based on Her Diary, 1785–1812* (New York: Vintage Books, 1991); Rosemary Zaggari, *A Woman's Dilemma: Mercy Otis Warren and the American Revolution* (Wheeling, IL: Harlan Davidson, 1995); Patricia McCleary, *Elizabeth Murray: A Woman's Pursuit of Independence in Eighteenth-Century America* (Amherst: University of Massachusetts Press, 2000); Alfred F. Young, *Masquerade: The Life and Times of Deborah Sampson, Continental Soldier* (New York: Knopf, 2004), and Woody Holton, *Abigail Adams: A Life* (New York: Free Press, 2009). For the story of another craftswoman of the revolutionary era, see my own *Betsy Ross and the Making of America* (New York: Holt, 2010).

On the American Revolution more generally there is a vast literature, even if one narrows one's scope to work dedicated specifically to Massachusetts and/or New England. Points of entry most relevant to this story include Richard D. Brown, *Revolutionary Politics in Massachusetts: The Boston Committee of Correspondence and the Towns, 1772–1774* (New York: W. W. Norton & Co., 1970); Robert A. Gross, *The Minutemen and Their World* (New York: Hill and Wang, 1976); Gregory H. Nobles, *Divisions Throughout the Whole: Politics and Society in Hampshire County, Massachusetts, 1740–1775* (Cambridge: Cambridge University Press, 1983); Margaret Ellen Newel, *From Dependency to Independence: Economic Revolution in Colonial New England* (Ithaca: Cornell University Press, 1998); Alfred F. Young, *The Shoemaker and the Tea Party: Memory and the American Revolution* (Boston: Beacon Press, 1999); and Ray Raphael, *The First American Revolution: Before Lexington and Concord* (New York: New Press, 2002). See also Gary B. Nash, *The Unknown American Revolution: The Unruly Birth of Democracy and the Struggle to Create America* (New York: Viking Penguin, 2005). On Shays's Rebellion, see Leonard Richards, *Shays's Rebellion: The American Revolution's Final Battle* (Philadelphia: University of Pennsylvania Press, 2002). For an overview of state history in these decades, see Richard D. Brown and Jack Tager, *Massachusetts: A Concise History* (Amherst: University of Massachusetts Press, 2000).

DIARIES, LITERACY, AND EDUCATION

Several early and still valuable works on diaries, spiritual autobiographies, and meditational journals are Steven E. Kagle, *American Diary Literature, 1620–1799* (Boston: Twayne Publishers, 1979); Mary Moffatt and Charlotte Painter, *Revelations: Diaries of Women* (New York: Vintage Books, 1984); Margo Culley, *A Day at a Time: The Diary Literature of American Women from 1764 to the Present* (New York: Feminist Press of the City University of New York, 1985); and Suzanne L. Bunkers and Cynthia Huff, eds., *Inscribing the Daily: Critical Essays on Women's Diaries* (Amherst: University of Massachusetts Press, 1996), especially Judy Simons, "Invented Lives: Textuality and Power in Early Women's Diaries," 252–264. An important article (highly influential on my own early work on Rebecca Dickinson) is Barbara E. Lacey's "The World of Hannah Heaton: The Autobiography of an Eighteenth-Century Connecticut Farm Woman," *The William and Mary Quarterly*, Third Series, 45, no. 2 (April 1988): 280–304.

Among the earliest New England women's diaries known to survive is that of Mehetabel Chandler Coit (1673–1758), kept in 1714; see Michelle M. Coughlin, *One Colonial Woman's World: The Diary and Letters of Mehetabel Chandler Coit, 1673–1758* (Amherst: University of Massachusetts Press, 2012). Mary Beth Norton contemplates some misunderstood diary texts in "Getting to the Source: Hetty Shepard, Dorothy Dudley, and Other Fictional Colonial Women I Have Come to Know Altogether Too Well," *Journal of Women's History* 10, no. 3 (Autumn 1998): 141–154. Especially valuable on diaries and construction of the self in the era of Rebecca Dickinson is Barbara Taylor, "Separations of Soul: Solitude, Biography, History," *The American Historical Review* 114, no. 3 (June 2009): 640–651.

On women's literacy and access to education, the classic point of departure is Kenneth A. Lockridge, *Literacy in Colonial New England* (New York: W. W. Norton & Company, 1974). More recent work includes Gloria L. Main, "An Inquiry into When and Why Women Learned to Write in Colonial New England," *Journal of Social History* 24, no. 3 (Spring 1991): 579–589; Kathryn Kish Sklar, "The Schooling of Girls and Changing Community Values in Massachusetts Towns, 1750–1820," *History of Education Quarterly* 33, no. 4 (Winter 1993): 511–542 (special issue on the history of women and education); Joel Perlmann and Robert A. Margo, *Women's Work: American Schoolteachers, 1650–1920* (Chicago: University of Chicago Press, 2001); and E. Jennifer Monaghan, "Literacy Instruction and Gender in Colonial New England," *American Quarterly* 40, no. 1 (March 1988): 18–41 (special issue: Reading America), as well as her *Learning to Read and Write in Colonial America* (Amherst: University of Massachusetts Press, 2005). Most significant here is Mary Kelly's landmark study *Learning to Stand and Speak: Women, Education, and Public Life in America's Republic* (Chapel Hill: University of North Carolina Press, 2006).

WOMEN AND RELIGION

The religious context of Dickinson's life is informed by a wide range of scholarship. On the Reverend William Williams, see Philip Gura, "Sowing for the Harvest: William Williams and the Great Awakening," *Journal of Presbyterian History* 56 (Winter 1978): 326–341. There is a vast literature on the Great Awakening. On the phenomenon in Hatfield and Hampshire County, see Douglas L. Winiarski, "Jonathan Edwards, Enthusiast? Radical Revivalism and the Great Awakening in the Connecticut Valley," *Church History* 74, no. 4 (December 2005): 683–739; and George M. Marsden, *Jonathan Edwards: A Life* (New Haven, CT: Yale University Press, 2003). Though it is a long-standing concept in historical narratives, historian Jon Butler has suggested that the various religious revivals of the early eighteenth century cannot accurately be collapsed into a single event. For discussion of this question, see Jon Butler, *Awash in a Sea of Faith: Christianizing the American People* (Cambridge, MA: Harvard University Press, 1990); and Frank Lambert, "The First Great Awakening: Whose Interpretive Fiction?" *The New England Quarterly* 68, no. 4 (December 1995): 650–659.

On increasing numbers of women in the Congregational church, see Richard D. Shiels, "The Feminization of American Congregationalism," *American Quarterly* 33 (1981): 46–62. Helpful on the subject of conversion is Robert A. Rees, "Seeds of the Enlightenment: Public Testimony in the New England Congregational Churches, 1630–1750," *Early American Literature Newsletter* 3, no. 1 (Spring 1968): 22–29. An enlightening account of Hampshire County ministerial politics in this period is Gregory Nobles, *Divisions Throughout the Whole*, 36–74.

WOMAN AND WORK

Scholarship illuminating the eighteenth-century Connecticut Valley and New England economy includes Christopher Clark, *The Roots of Rural Capitalism: Western Massachusetts, 1780–1860* (Ithaca, NY: Cornell University Press, 1990); William N. Hosley, *The Great River: Art & Society of the Connecticut Valley, 1635–1820* (Hartford, CT: Wadsworth Atheneum, 1985); J. Ritchie Garrison, "Farm Dynamics and Regional Exchange: The Connecticut Valley Beef Trade, 1670–1850," *Agricultural History* 61, no. 3 (Summer 1987): 1–17.

To understand the "female economy," there is no better starting point than Laurel Ulrich's various publications, especially *Good Wives* and *A Midwife's Tale,* cited above, as well as Christopher Clark's *Roots of Rural Capitalism,* also cited above. Also important is Gloria Main, "Gender, Work, and Wages in Colonial New England," *The William and Mary Quarterly* 51 (January 1994). On Lucy Hubbard and other tavern-keeping women in particular, see Anne Lanning, "Women Tavern-Keepers in the Connecticut River Valley, 1750–1810," in *New England Celebrates* (Proceedings of the 2000 Dublin Seminar for New England Folklife) 25 (2002): 202–214; and David Conroy, *In Public Houses: Drink and the Revolution of Authority in Colonial Massachusetts* (Chapel Hill: University of North Carolina Press, 1995). On women in the clothing trades, see my own *The Needle's Eye* and "The Last Mantuamaker," *Early American Studies* 4, no. 2 (Fall 2006): 372–424. See also Karol K. Weaver, "Fashioning Freedom: Slave Seamstresses in the Atlantic World," *Journal of Women's History* 24, no. 1 (Spring 2012): 44–59; Amy Louise Erickson. "Eleanor Mosley and Other Milliners in the City of London Companies 1700–1750," *History Workshop Journal* 71.1 (2011): 147–172; and Jacqueline Barbara Carr, "Marketing Gentility: Boston's Businesswomen, 1780–1830," *The New England Quarterly* 82, no. 1 (March 2009): 25–55. On housework more generally, see Jane C. Nylander, *Our Own Snug Fireside: Images of the New England Home, 1760–1860* (New Haven, CT: Yale University Press, 1994). The broader context of women in the commercial economy is illuminated by Cornelia Hughes Dayton, *Women Before the Bar: Gender, Law and Society in Connecticut, 1639–1789* (Chapel Hill: University of North Carolina Press, 1995).

On the lives of enslaved and free black women and men in New England in this period, good points of entry include Elise Lemire, *Black Walden: Slavery and Its Aftermath in Concord, Massachusetts* (Philadelphia: University of Pennsylvania Press, 2009); C. S. Manegold, *Ten Hills Farm: The Forgotten History of Slavery in the North* (Princeton: Princeton University Press, 2010); Joanne Pope Melish, *Disowning Slavery: Gradual Emancipation and "Race" in New England, 1780–1860* (Ithaca, NY: Cornell University Press, 1998); Catherine Adams and Elizabeth H. Pleck, *Love of Freedom: Black Women in Colonial and Revolutionary New England* (New York: Oxford University Press, 2009); and John Wood Sweet, *Bodies Politic: Negotiating Race in the American North, 1730–1830* (Philadelphia: University of Pennsylvania Press, 2003).

There is a lively literature on consumption and fashion in the years Dickinson witnessed. The best sources for entering those discussions include Kate Haulman, *The Politics of Fashion in Eighteenth-Century America* (Chapel Hill: University of North Carolina Press, 2011); Richard Bushman, *The Refinement of America: Persons, Houses, Cities* (New York: Alfred A. Knopf, 1992); John Brewer and Roy Porter, eds., *Consumption and the World of Goods* (New York: Routledge, 1993); Cary Carson, Ronald Hoffman, and Peter J. Albert, eds., *Of Consuming Interests: The Style of Life in the Eighteenth Century* (Charlottesville: University Press of Virginia, 1994); and Amanda Vickery and John Styles, eds., *Gender, Taste and Material Culture in Britain and North America, 1700–1830* (New Haven, CT: Yale University Press, 2006). On the role of goods and consumption in the coming of the revolution and women's participation in the marketplace, see T. H. Breen, *The Marketplace of Revolution: How Consumer Politics Shaped American Independence* (New York: Oxford University Press, 2004); and Ellen Hartigan O'Connor, *The Ties That Buy: Women and Commerce in Revolutionary America* (Philadelphia: University of Pennsylvania Press, 2009); as well as Michael Zakim, "Sartorial Ideologies: From Homespun to Ready-Made," *The American Historical Review* 106, no. 5 (December 2001): 1553–1586; Linzy Brekke Aloise's essay "To Make a Figure: Clothing and the Politics of Male Identity in Early National America," in *Gender, Taste and Material Culture* (cited above); and Mary O'Dowd, "Politics, Patriotism, and Women in Ireland, Britain and Colonial America, c. 1700–1780," *Journal of Women's History* 22, no. 4 (Winter 2010): 15–38.

For a good introduction to eighteenth-century clothing construction in England, see Janet Arnold, *Patterns of Fashion: Englishwomen's Dresses and Their Construction, c. 1660–1860* (New York: Drama Book Specialists, 1972); and Nora Waugh, *The Cut of Women's Clothes, 1600–1800* (New York: Theatre Arts Books, 1969), and also *The Cut of Men's Clothes, 1600–1800* (New York: Theatre Arts Books, 1969). For the American side of the Atlantic, see Linda Baumgarten, *Eighteenth-Century Clothing at Williamsburg* (Williamsburg: The Colonial Williamsburg Foundation, 1986); and Meredith Wright, *Put on Thy Beautiful Garments: Rural New England Clothing, 1783–1800* (Montpelier, VT: The Clothes Press, 1990). Also valuable are Claudia Kidwell, *Cutting a Fashionable Fit: Dressmaker's Drafting Systems in the United States* (Washington, DC: Smithsonian Institution Press, 1979); and "Riches, Rags and In-Between," *Historic Preservation* 4 (1976). The geometrical challenge of dressmaking is described in Christopher Zeeman, "Mathematics Applied to Dressmaking," *Costume* 28 (1994): 97–102. My understanding of how craft skill operates has been deeply influenced by the scholarship of Edward S. Cooke, especially *Making Furniture in Preindustrial America: The Social Economy of Newtown and Woodbury, Connecticut* (Baltimore, MD: Johns Hopkins University Press, 1996). On the dressmaking trade in the nineteenth century, see Wendy Gamber, *The Female Economy: The Millinery and Dressmaking Trades, 1860–1930* (Champaign: University of Illinois Press, 1997). The discussion of fashion information networks here is informed by Richard D. Brown, *Knowledge Is Power: The Diffusion of Information in Early America, 1700–1865* (Champaign: University of Illinois Press, 1997). On sumptuary law and clothing in Hatfield's parent town of Hadley, see Lynne Bassett, "The Sober People of Hadley: Sumptuary Legislation and Clothing in Hadley Men's Probate Inventories, 1663–1731," in *Cultivating a Past: Essays on the History of Hadley, Massachusetts*, ed. Marla R. Miller (Amherst: University of Massachusetts Press, 2009).

To explore the making and meanings of ornamental needlework in the eighteenth century, consult museum catalogs like Susan Schoelwer, *Connecticut Needlework: Women, Art, and Family, 1740–1840* (Hartford: Connecticut Historical Society; Middletown, CT: Distributed by Wesleyan University Press, 2010), as well as Jane Nylander's article on needlework in Hosley, *The Great River* (cited above). Two classic works on bed hangings are Ann Pollard Rowe, "Crewel Embroidered Bed Hangings in Old and New England," *Boston Museum Bulletin* 71, nos. 365/366 (1973): 102–164; and Abbott Lowell Cummings, ed., *Bed Hangings: A Treatise on Fabrics and Styles in the Curtaining of Beds, 1650–1850* (Boston: Society for the Preservation of New England Antiquities, 1961). In terms of Dickinson's own distinctive head cloth, one of the only discussions of maritime imagery in needlework is Christie Jackson, "Unfurling the Katurah Reeve Bedcover: A Story of Candlewicking, Maritime Culture, and One Family's Legacy" (unpublished manuscript, Winterthur Program in American Material Culture, 2007).

Lastly, two major statements that review the broad outlines of women's history as it presently stands are Terri L. Snyder, "Refiguring Women in Early American History," *The William and Mary Quarterly* 69, no. 3 (July 2012): 421–450; and Cornelia H. Dayton and Lisa Levenstein, "The Big Tent of U.S. Women's and Gender History: A State of the Field," *Journal of American History* 99 (2012): 793–817.

INDEX